IMAGES
of America

Marian Coffin Gardens at Gibraltar

ON THE COVER: The pool is one of Gibraltar's most iconic spots. Now a self-sustaining bog, complete with koi fish and a bullfrog, the pool was conceived of as being a much more formal space. It was one of the earliest parts of the garden to actually be constructed, having been built in 1916, and like the rest of Gibraltar no expense was spared: an invoice sites the pool as costing $10,689.75, an equivalent of nearly $250,000 in 2020. Swimmers could enter the pool via a staircase at either short end and would be shaded in their swim by a mature maple (*Acer*) tree, which Coffin was cognizant of designing around. Following their swim, they could dry off and change in the pool house, accessible via a small staircase and visible in the background of this image. (Preservation Delaware, Inc.)

IMAGES of America

MARIAN COFFIN GARDENS AT GIBRALTAR

Erin Fogarty and Jules Bruck, PhD

ARCADIA PUBLISHING

ISBN 978-1-4671-0754-9

Published by Arcadia Publishing
Charleston, South Carolina

Printed in the United States of America

Library of Congress Control Number: 2021948112

For all general information, please contact Arcadia Publishing:
Telephone 843-853-2070
Fax 843-853-0044
E-mail sales@arcadiapublishing.com
For customer service and orders:
Toll-Free 1-888-313-2665

Visit us on the Internet at www.arcadiapublishing.com

This work is dedicated to the memory of Marian Coffin and to all those who, like her, overcame difficult obstacles to create an important legacy.

Contents

Acknowledgments

The authors would like to express their gratitude to the organizations and individuals who helped us locate and allowed us to borrow the materials included in this publication. This project has been a labor of love, and we are thankful for the opportunity. We are especially appreciative of Joan Sharp, who, from the beginning, supported our endeavor and provided us with important documents, including original Marian Cruger Coffin plans and blueprints for the gardens at Gibraltar. This project allowed us to connect with individuals who have contributed to the garden over time, including Iris Gestram, who kindly provided original photographs, and Rodney Robinson, who shared important stories relative to the 1999 garden renovation.

Additionally, we are incredibly appreciative of the cooperation of the archival staff at the Winterthur Museum, Garden and Library; the Smithsonian Archive of American Gardens; and the Hagley Museum, who helped us access materials despite pandemic roadblocks.

Thanks to the Board of Directors of Preservation Delaware, Inc., (PDI), including Pres. Michael H. McGrath, American Institute of Certified Planners (AICP); officers Barbara Warnell, Bryan Hudson, CPA, Jeremy Rothwell, Michael J. Emmons Jr., and James Wolfe; members Dennis Coker, Jay Cooperson, Michael Falstad, Wade Catts, Cheryl Renée Gooch, PhD, Leila Hamroun, Terri Lottmann, John Mateyko, Dr. Abdullah R. Muhammad, Dan Parsons, Alexandra Tarantino, Greg Shelton, and Bradley Skelcher, as well as executive director Jay W. McCutcheon, for providing us support and encouragement as well as stories notes, photographs, slides, pamphlets, and other documents.

This publication would not have been possible without Mary Ellen Wilson, former PDI board member, who helped lay the groundwork for the project, and the constant support of our families, including Jules's husband, Tony Middlebrooks, and Erin's parents, Susan and Greg, and sister, Gracie.

INTRODUCTION

Marian Coffin's life did not turn out the way anyone in her life might have planned. Born in 1876 in the fashionable village of Briarcliff, New York, to Julian Rose and Alice Church Coffin, it was anticipated that she would live a similar life to her parents—inherit money, marry up, and live a quiet life in Westchester County. However, upon her father's untimely death in 1883, she and her mother were plunged into genteel poverty, with a social standing that kept them from taking up the few jobs available to women at this time. Without money to maintain their home in what is now the Upper West Side, Coffin and her mother quickly moved upstate, where her mother and grandparents raised her in Geneva.

There, Coffin developed a lifelong love of art and the outdoors. She honed her skills in watercolor on the shores of Seneca Lake and began to learn of the burgeoning field of landscape architecture from her uncle Benjamin Church, an engineer at Olmsted and Vaux, who played a key role in the construction of Central Park. While Marian Coffin was not formally educated in her youth—her mother's financial position precluded attendance at a boarding school and Coffin's own frequent bouts of childhood illness often got in the way of her at-home education by governesses—her time in Geneva provided her with a form of education that, arguably, would prove more important, and certainly more influential, in the direction her life would take.

Knowing the importance of social capital in the early life of a young woman, Coffin's grandparents ensured that, although low in funds, she had enough to take part in fashionable balls, parties, and charity engagements. While Coffin never married—the fate expected of her and the role these parties were meant to play—following her completion of Massachusetts Institute of Technology's architecture program, these connections proved incredibly valuable. It was there she met and befriended the future heirs and heiresses for whom she later designed—Frederick Vanderbilt, Marjorie Merriweather Post, and Henry Francis duPont among them. The friendship with duPont was one of the most important of her life. Over the nearly 60 years, the two vacationed together, visited frequently, and sent letters and gifts back and forth. Moreover, Henry Francis duPont employed Coffin multiple times himself, while also securing commissions for her from many family members, including his distant cousin and her husband, Isabella duPont Sharp and Hugh Rodney Sharp.

The Sharps were a young family when they purchased a simple and outdated (by their standards) house—in 1916, it still lacked running water and any sort of heating—on a hill overlooking the city of Wilmington. Sharp had fallen in love with the house, which was occupied by the two unmarried daughters of the founder of his family's church, when seeing it while driving home from his job as the personal secretary to Pierre S. duPont, the future founder of Longwood Gardens.

The house was on the edge of the city, a location not quite fitting with the sprawling estates of Isabella's duPont cousins in what is now known as "Chateau Country" outside of Greenville, Delaware, but also not quite a city house. Instead, it was a "Country Place," an estate on the smaller side, defined as usually less than 10 acres, that mirrored the grand estates of Europe and the most fashionable design styles while remaining accessible to the city. The style built upon the work of pioneering architects like Frederick Law Olmsted, Andrew Jackson Downing, and Beatrix Farrand, all of whom Marian Coffin used as influences in her work, as well as the Beaux-Arts classicism, in which Coffin was trained.

In a way, Wilmington, Delaware, was the perfect place for the Country Place movement to flourish. Estates built in that style appealed to a very specific type of person: those who had the money for an elaborate, professionally designed estate and the continuing income to employ staff to maintain it, while still needing to commute to a typical job. The DuPont Chemical Corporation caused a flood of executives into Wilmington, and many of them came from backgrounds of privilege, including from the duPont family itself, who would have been accustomed to estate life. It is this, and the relatively compact city surrounded by farmland and rolling hills, which fostered many country places in the area within a relatively short period.

Indeed, it was because of the DuPont Corporation that Hugh Rodney Sharp, known as Rodney, who grew up downstate, moved to Wilmington in the first place, and because of his wife's ties to the duPont family that they purchased the house they chose. In the years following their property purchase, the couple expanded the house to three times its original size. Eventually, they would commission Marian Coffin not once but twice to design a landscape to complement the house. Over five years, Coffin created a series of garden rooms that masterfully navigated the steep incline from the house to street level and a formal garden that remained livable for the Sharps and their four children. Every part of Gibraltar tells a story—the strong axis speaks to Coffin's Beaux-Arts training; the wild plantings to her admiration of garden designer Gertrude Jekyll; and the statues and teahouse are tangible reminders of the Sharp family's many trips abroad to Italy.

However, it was a story that was almost never told. Neglect and abandonment of these country Places burgeoned after the Great Depression. Maintenance expenses were overbearing, and as the original owners passed away, the homes were inherited by family members who did not share their parents' love of gardens. Gibraltar is no different. In a way, it is a wonder that the estate survived when comparable nearby properties—St. Amour, the H. Fletcher Brown Mansion—were lost to development pressures. This survival is attributed to the work of dedicated local activists, who are the main reason the gardens of the estate remain and are now free and open to the public.

One

ABOUT MARIAN COFFIN

Born into the East Coast upper class, Marian Cruger Coffin (September 16, 1876–February 2, 1957) would have been expected to enter into marriage with an equally esteemed man. And yet, as a result of her father's early death and her mother's resulting lack of money, she decided to pursue a career instead. In her youth, she loved art and the outdoors. She looked up to her uncle, an engineer, who had helped with the design of Central Park in New York City. His influence led her to enroll in the Massachusetts Institute of Technology's (MIT) landscape gardening program. Unable to find work upon completion of her studies in 1904, she set up a design practice. In a parallel of what her life was expected to become, she became sought to design gardens for the upper-class groups with whom she engaged socially, becoming one of America's earliest and most successful female landscape architects. The hardscapes she designed were all characteristic of the Neoclassical, Beaux-Arts style she learned at MIT. The garden rooms were separated and included strong axial connections that created a formal and balanced structure. In addition, she included symbolic garden elements, such as mythological statuary pieces. Against the hardscape's rigid formal lines, she skillfully added plants to soften, energize, and delight. Influenced by the horticultural colorist Gertrude Jekyll, Coffin learned to expertly mix plant cultivars in both pale and vibrant complementary color schemes that were somewhat wild yet restrained. In many ways, Coffin's designs reflect a time when design and society were at a crossroads, one that required a balance that she learned to navigate well. Although she designed intricate, sprawling plans for some of the most famous families of her time, she is best known for her small-scale, urban designs on less than three or four acres.

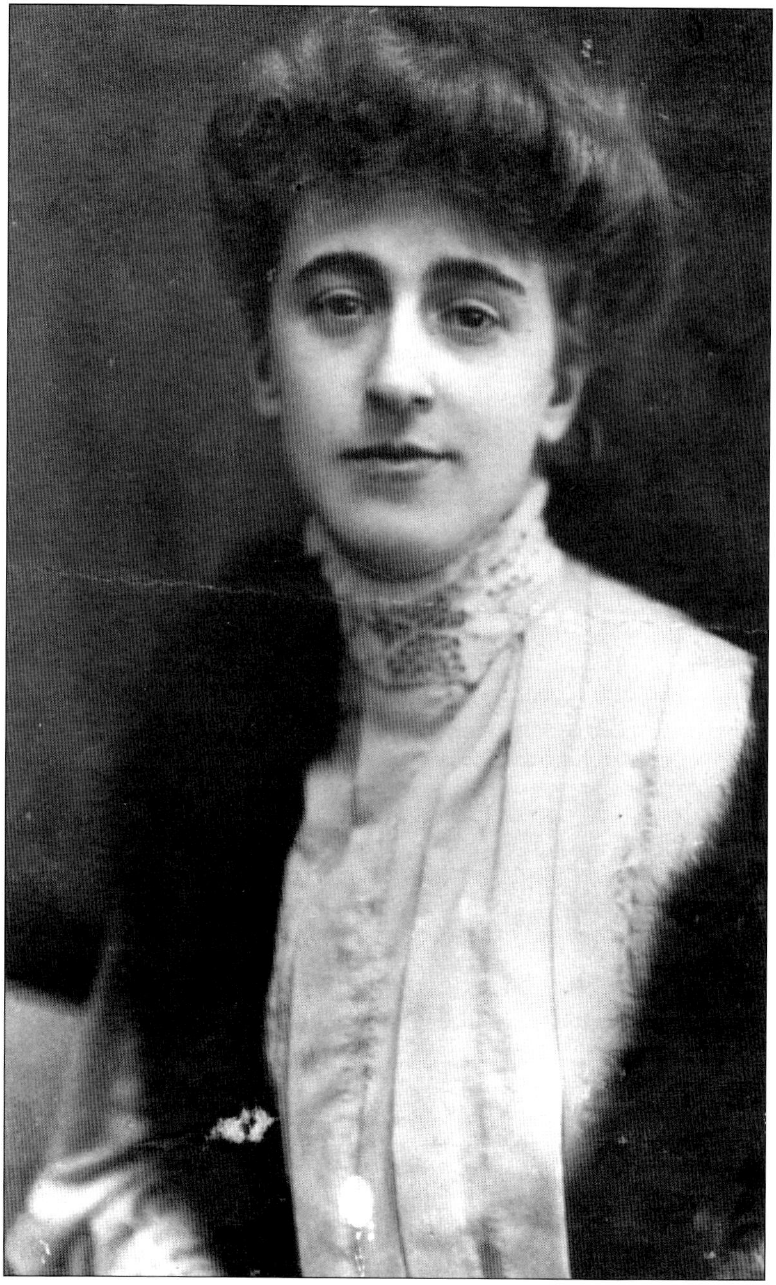

Coffin was born in 1876 to an upper-class family in Westchester County, New York, a descendant of early New England settlers, and is a distant cousin of artist John Trumbull. Faced with poverty after her husband's death when Coffin was seven, her mother, Alice Church Coffin, brought her upstate to live with her brother John Barker Church, an engineer working for Olmsted and Vaux during the design of Central Park. There, she fell in love with the nature that surrounded her. Despite her mother's precarious financial position, Coffin was introduced to the East Coast society circuit once she came of age, as was traditional for women of her hereditary social status. Society would be her first introduction to future clients, including the Fricks, Vanderbilts, and Winterthur's Henry Francis (H.F.) duPont. (Winterthur.)

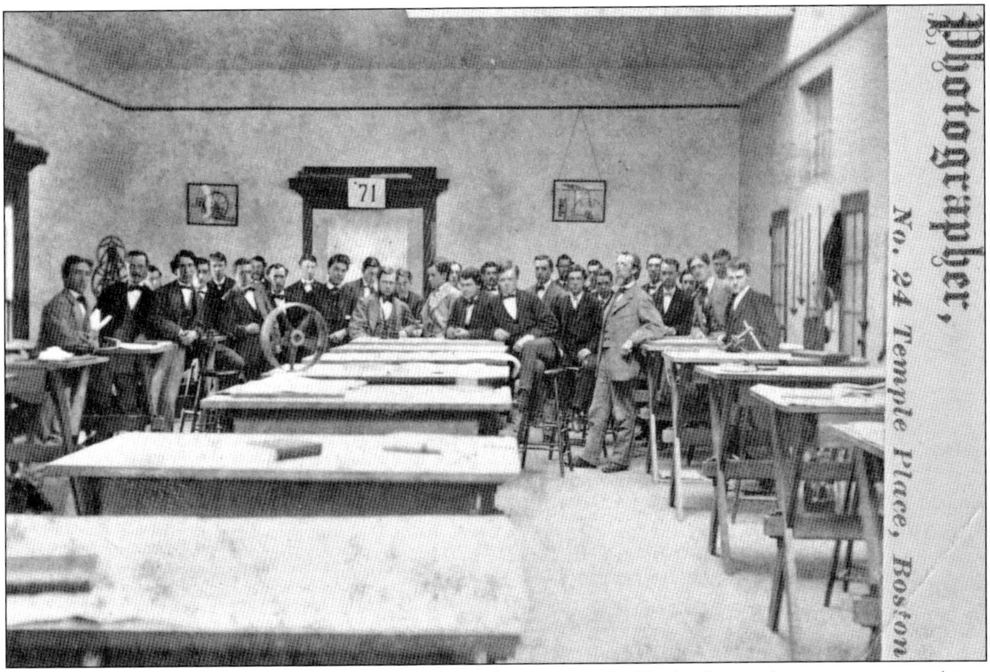

As a woman from an elite family in the early 20th century, Coffin had two choices upon reaching maturity: marry a man of equal status who would support her and her mother or take a job. She chose the latter in a move that a colleague would later call "almost suicide and distinctly matrimonial suicide." Encouraged by the success of landscape architect Beatrix Farrand, her uncle's work, and her childhood love of art, Coffin decided to enroll in MIT's new "landscape gardening" program held in Rodgers Hall, shown below. Having never attended a formal school, and lacking any education in math, she was not accepted. Unperturbed, she was privately tutored for a year before being admitted conditionally. As a woman, she was allowed to attend classes but could not receive a degree. Educated in the Beaux-Arts theory in labs just like the one above, her program emphasized classical elements such as fountains and statuary situated within simple, modern planting beds, and pathways. (Above, Boston Public Library; below, Library of Congress.)

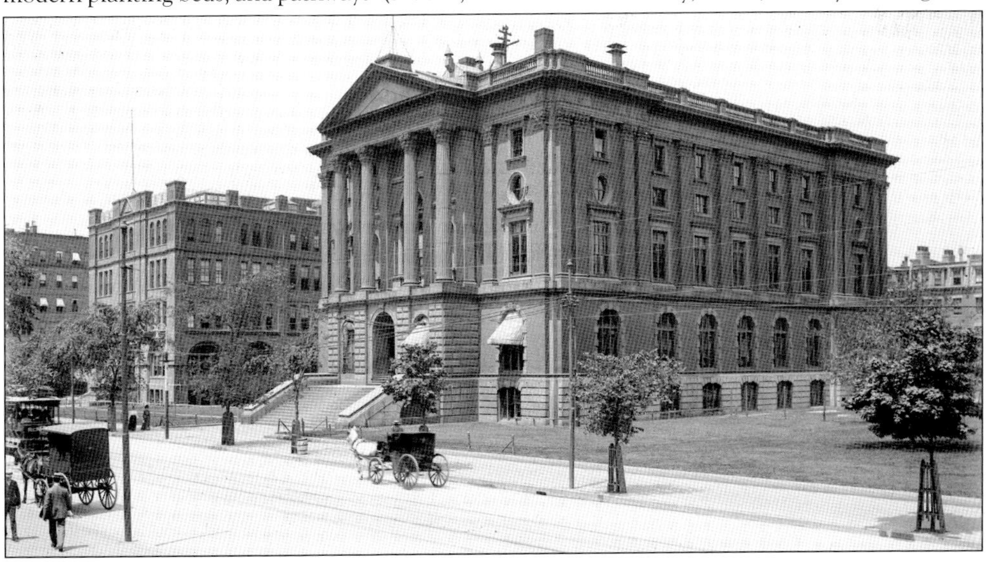

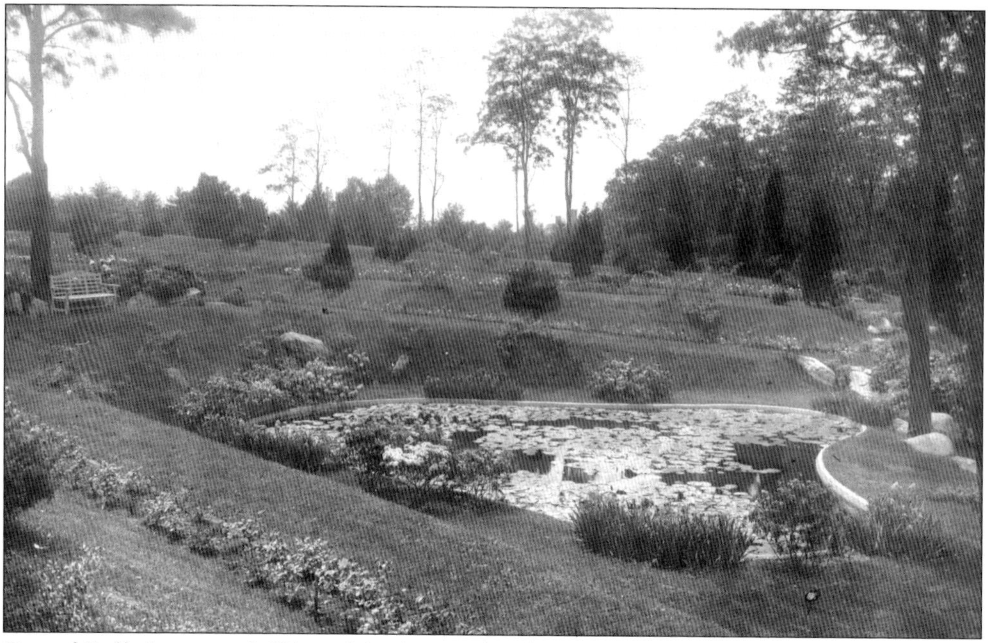

One of Coffin's peers at MIT was Martha Brookes (later Hutcheson.) Brookes was also admitted to MIT on a conditional basis one year before Coffin with an intention to improve the grounds of hospitals near her home in Vermont. Unlike Coffin, however, Brookes did not complete the program; she dropped out after two years due to the lack of horticultural emphasis in the curriculum. Still, she would become a successful landscape architect, designing many spaces similar to Coffin's works, including the grounds of Bennington College and, as seen here, the Welwyn estate in Glen Cove, New York. Unlike Coffin, Brookes would marry after her education and spend her later years educating young women (called "farmerettes") in agriculture. (Both, Smithsonian Archive of American Gardens.)

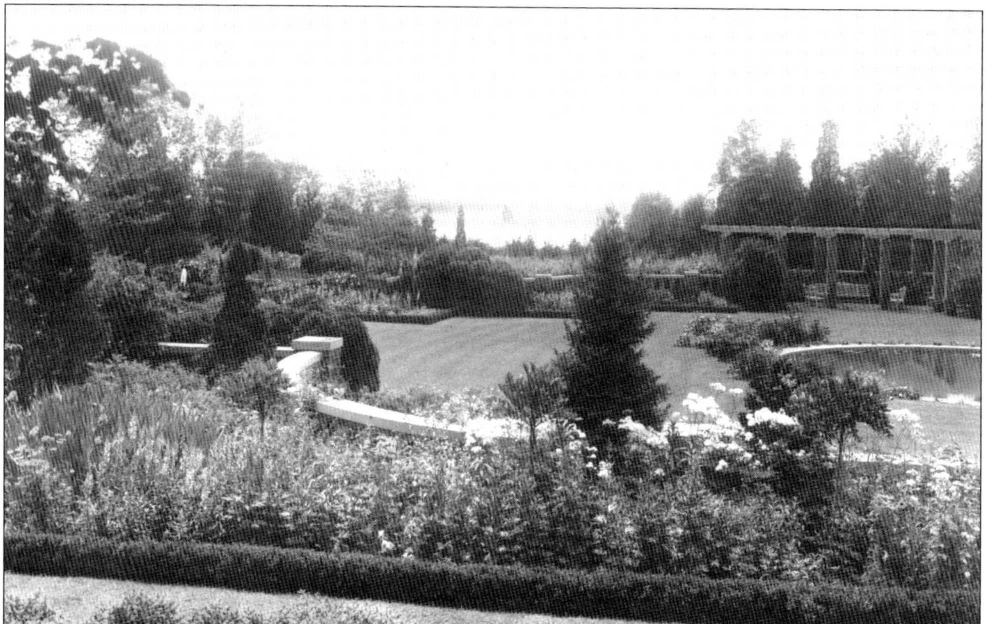

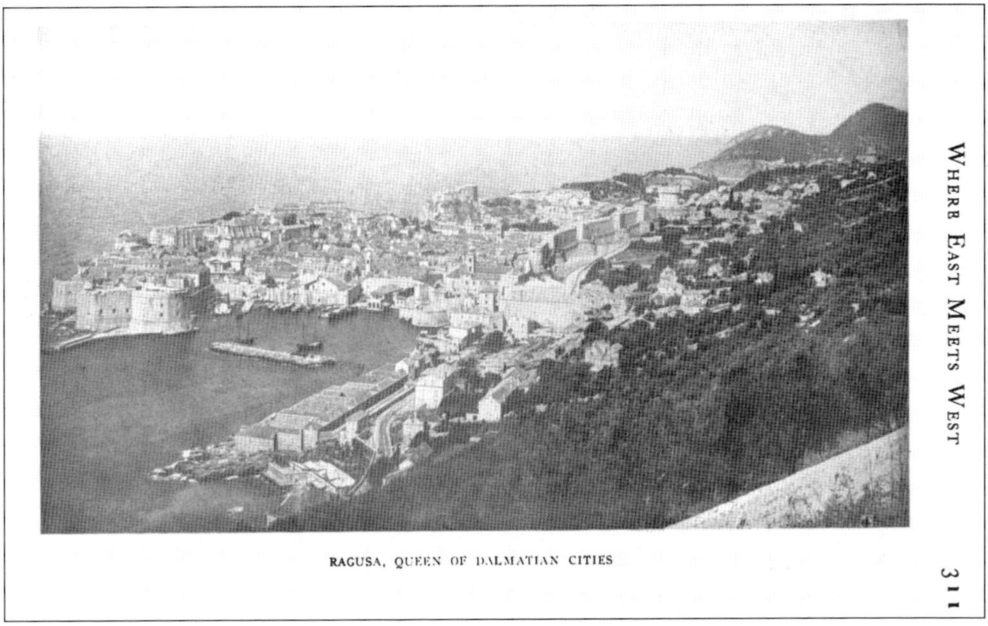

Following her completion of studies at MIT, Marian Coffin, along with her mother and friend Henry Francis duPont, set out upon the "Grand Tour" compulsory for her social class. While the trip included the traditional stops in Italy, France, and England—where she met her longtime hero Beatrix Farrand—Coffin also went off the beaten path into Montenegro, Bosnia, and Dalmatia (now Croatia). This experience was Coffin's first brush with fame as her photographs from the trip, along with a written article, were published in the May 1908 issue of *National Geographic*. In this work, Coffin explored not only the physical geography of the region but also the traditional costumes and bazaar culture of the countries. (Both, *National Geographic*.)

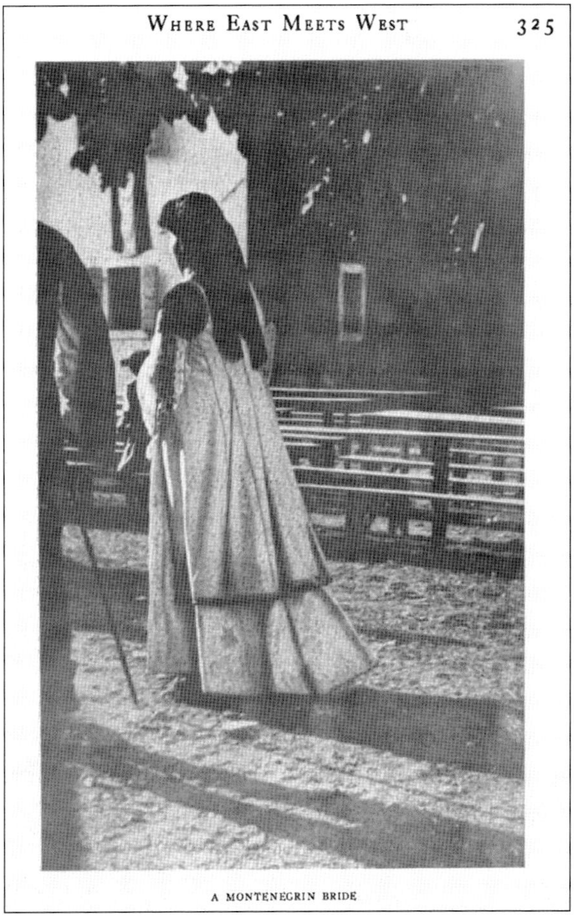

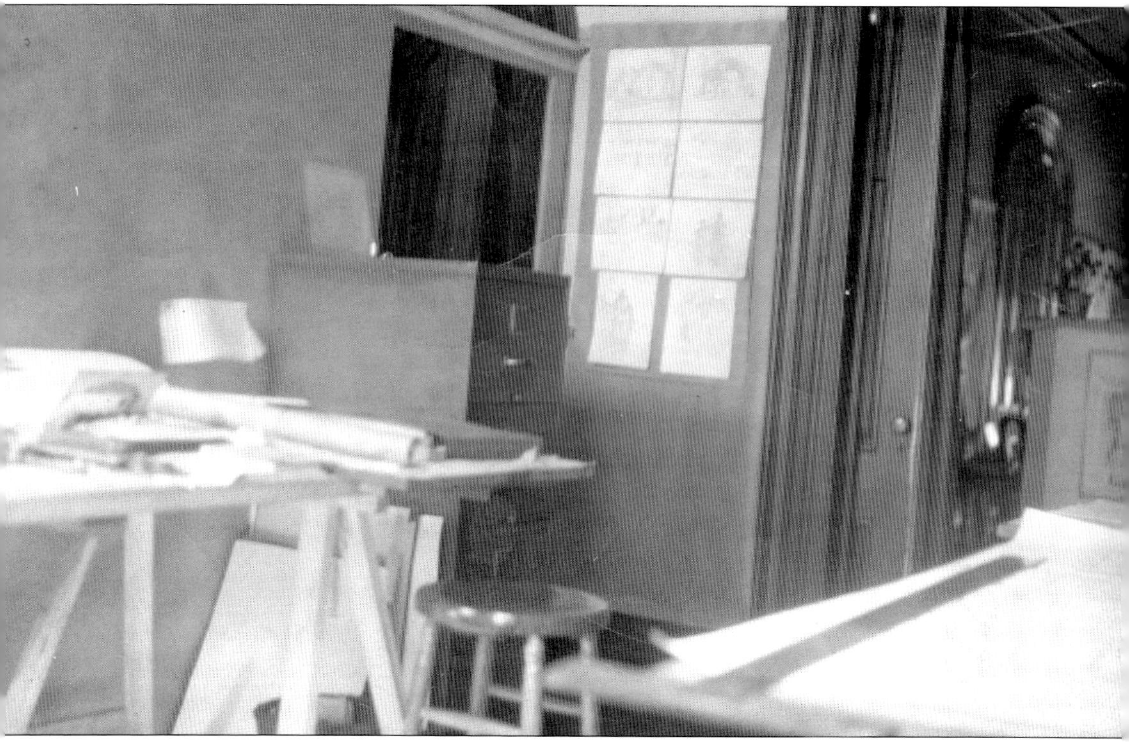

On her European trip, she met figures such as novelists Edith Wharton and Henry James and early landscape designer Gertrude Jekyll, whose work strongly inspired Coffin's designs. However, upon returning to the States, more roadblocks faced Coffin. According to Coffin, despite her education, no architecture firms "would employ [her] because of strong prejudice against women in the profession." Instead, she decided to found a private practice. Unable to afford both an apartment and an office, she lived and worked in a three-room apartment in the National Arts Club at 15 Gramercy Park in New York. One of the first social clubs to allow women to be members from the outset, Coffin was in good company with other trailblazing members, including sculptor Anna Hyatt Huntington and portraitist Cecilia Beaux. Coffin kept her office at the National Arts Club for more than 10 years, gradually hiring mostly women design staff until moving her practice uptown to Lexington Avenue in 1918. (Winterthur.)

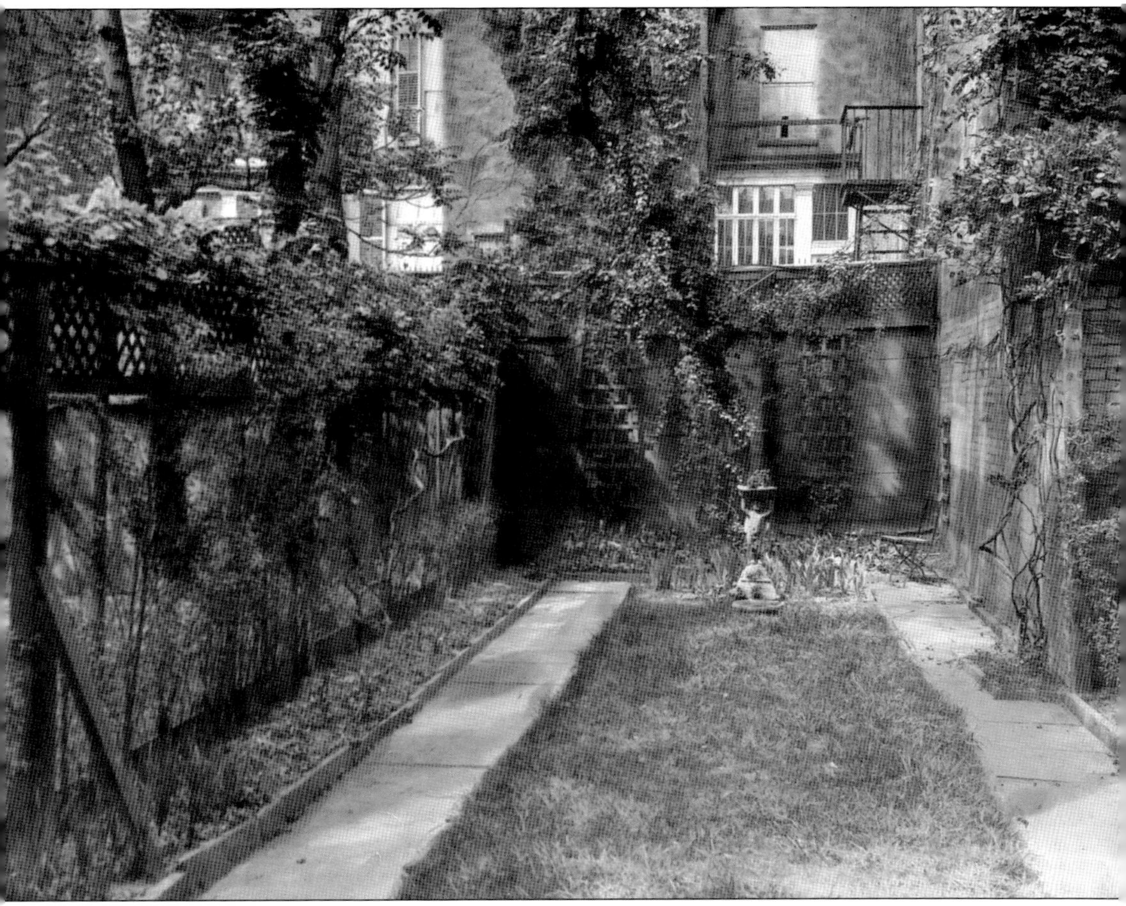

This design, completed for a woman named Vivian Spencer, was likely Coffin's smallest work. While no date can be confirmed for the design, Coffin's comments in interviews about beginning her work with very small spaces, and images showing the garden as fully matured by 1915, seem to indicate that it was one of her earliest. The garden was situated on a narrow lot behind a townhome on West Twelfth Street in Lower Manhattan and was relatively simple in design. A birdbath was the main focal point of the lawn axis—if it can even be called that—with beds bordering the lawn and laid stone paths going all the way around. Unlike Coffin's later commissions, which often featured bulbs and flowers that succeeded each other over three seasons, this design seemed to focus only on spring. Plantings were dominated by tulips, daffodils, and lilacs, with a privet (*Ligustrum sp.*) hedge providing some year-round color and structure. (Library of Congress.)

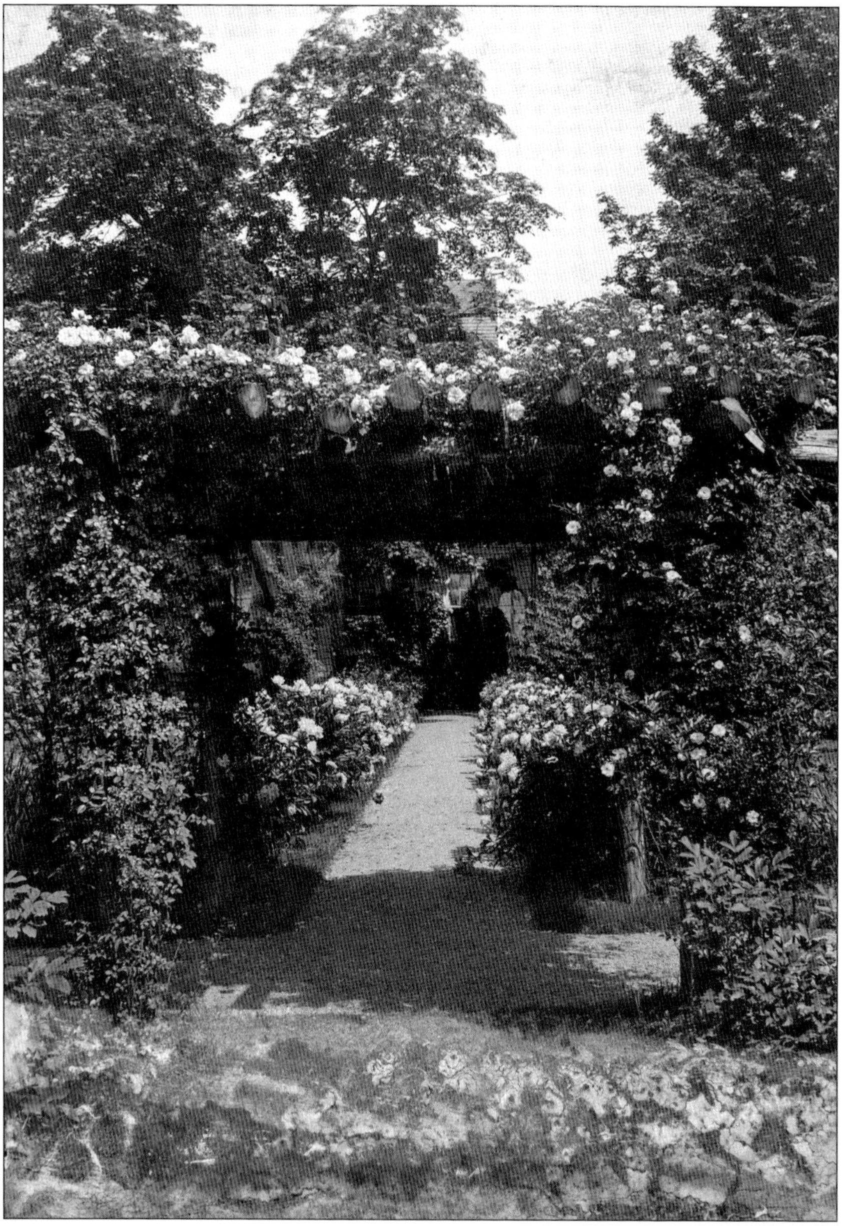

This garden, which Coffin designed in 1906 for the Sprague family, was her first commissioned work. Located in a Long Island suburb, the garden was relatively small and located in a new subdivision. Exhibiting hallmarks of Coffin's Beaux-Arts training, including straight pathways and a progression from formal to informal as one moved away from the house, the garden also shows signs of what would become Coffin's trademark style. The transition from formal to informal was gradual, and variety was achieved not through naturally occurring features but through a variety of differently sized trees and shrubs. She stuck to color schemes, but instead of sharply delineated plant masses, drifts of flowers bled into each other, showing her inspiration from Gertrude Jekyll, whom she recently met. Coffin's commissions would be similar for most of her career, albeit scaled-up versions, as she continued to design gardens in residential areas surrounding newly constructed homes. (Winterthur.)

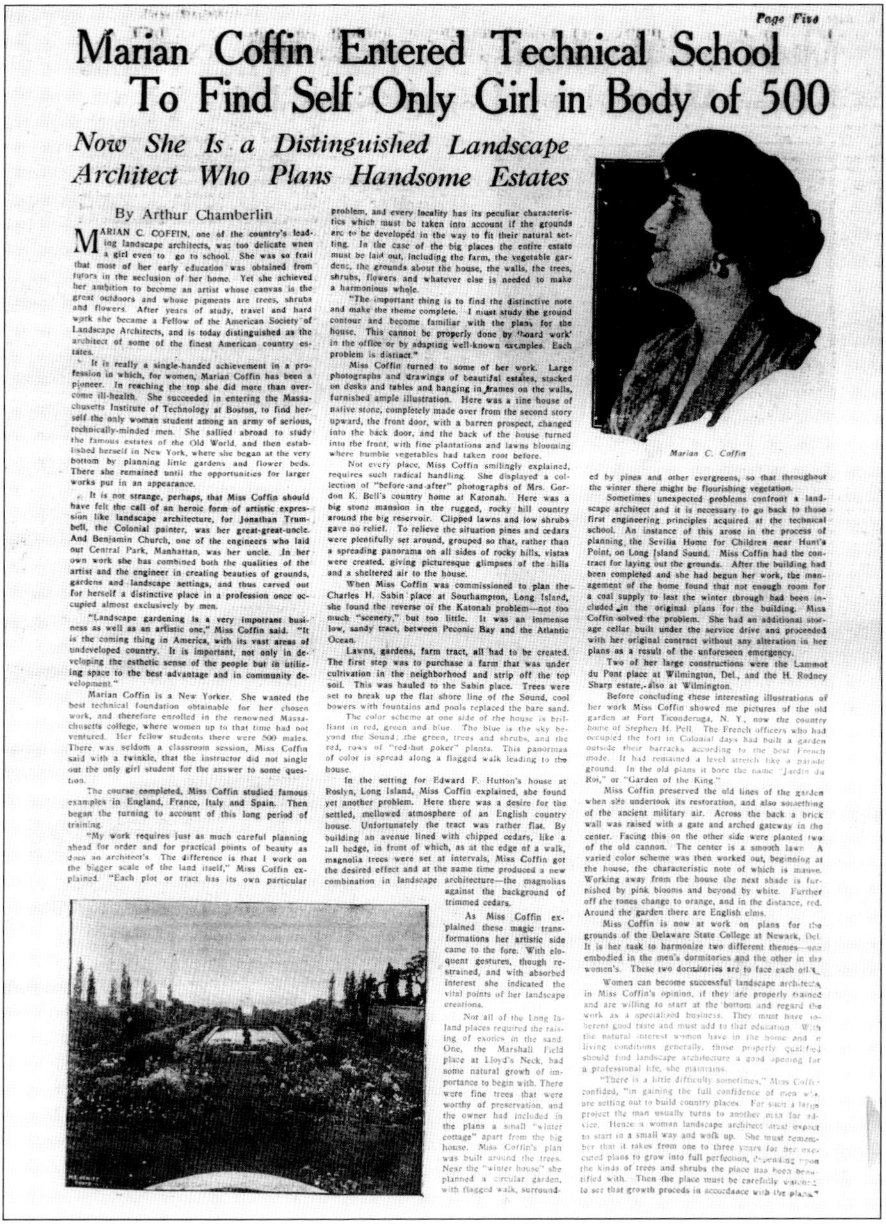

Page Five

Marian Coffin Entered Technical School To Find Self Only Girl in Body of 500

Now She Is a Distinguished Landscape Architect Who Plans Handsome Estates

By Arthur Chamberlin

MARIAN C. COFFIN, one of the country's leading landscape architects, was too delicate when a girl even to go to school. She was so frail that most of her early education was obtained from tutors in the seclusion of her home. Yet she achieved her ambition to become an artist whose canvas is the great outdoors and whose pigments are trees, shrubs and flowers. After years of study, travel and hard work she became a Fellow of the American Society of Landscape Architects, and is today distinguished as the architect of some of the finest American country estates.

It is really a single-handed achievement in a profession in which, for women, Marian Coffin has been a pioneer. In reaching the top she did more than overcome ill-health. She succeeded in entering the Massachusetts Institute of Technology at Boston, to find herself the only woman student among an army of serious, technically-minded men. She sallied abroad to study the famous estates of the Old World, and then established herself in New York, where she began at the very bottom by planning little gardens and flower beds. There she remained until the opportunities for larger works put in an appearance.

It is not strange, perhaps, that Miss Coffin should have felt the call of an heroic form of artistic expression like landscape architecture, for Jonathan Trumbell, the Colonial painter, was her great-great-uncle. And Benjamin Church, one of the engineers who laid out Central Park, Manhattan, was her uncle. In her own work she has combined both the qualities of the artist and the engineer in creating beauties of grounds, gardens and landscape settings, and thus carved out for herself a distinctive place in a profession once occupied almost exclusively by men.

"Landscape gardening is a very impotrant business as well as an artistic one," Miss Coffin said. "It is the coming thing in America, with its vast areas of undeveloped country. It is important, not only in developing the esthetic sense of the people but in utilizing space to the best advantage and in community development."

Marian Coffin is a New Yorker. She wanted the best technical foundation obtainable for her chosen work, and therefore enrolled in the renowned Massachusetts college, where women up to that time had not ventured. Her fellow students there were 500 males. There was seldom a classroom session, Miss Coffin said with a twinkle, that the instructor did not single out the only girl student for the answer to some question.

The course completed, Miss Coffin studied famous examples in England, France, Italy and Spain. Then began the turning to account of this long period of training.

"My work requires just as much careful planning ahead for order and for practical points of beauty as does an architect's. The difference is that I work on the bigger scale of the land itself," Miss Coffin explained. "Each plot or tract has its own particular problem, and every locality has its peculiar characteristics which must be taken into account if the grounds are to be developed in the way to fit their natural setting. In the case of the big places the entire estate must be laid out, including the farm, the vegetable gardens, the grounds about the house, the walls, the trees, shrubs, flowers and whatever else is needed to make a harmonious whole.

"The important thing is to find the distinctive note and make the theme complete. I must study the ground contour and become familiar with the plans for the house. This cannot be properly done by 'board work' in the office or by adapting well-known examples. Each problem is distinct."

Miss Coffin turned to some of her work. Large photographs and drawings of beautiful estates, stacked on desks and tables and hanging in frames on the walls, furnished ample illustration. Here was a fine house of native stone, completely made over from the second story upward, the front door, with a barren prospect, changed into the back door, and the back of the house turned into the front, with fine plantations and lawns blooming where humble vegetables had taken root before.

Not every place, Miss Coffin smilingly explained, requires such radical handling. She displayed a collection of "before-and-after" photographs of Mrs. Gordon K. Bell's country home at Katonah. Here was a big stone mansion in the rugged, rocky hill country around the big reservoir. Clipped lawns and low shrubs gave no relief. To relieve the situation pines and cedars were plentifully set around, grouped so that, rather than a spreading panorama on all sides of rocky hills, vistas were created, giving picturesque glimpses of the hills and a sheltered air to the house.

When Miss Coffin was commissioned to plan the Charles H. Sabin place at Southampton, Long Island, she found the reverse of the Katonah problem—not too much "scenery," but too little. It was an immense low, sandy tract, between Peconic Bay and the Atlantic Ocean.

Lawns, gardens, farm tract, all had to be created. The first step was to purchase a farm that was under cultivation in the neighborhood and strip off the top soil. This was hauled to the Sabin place. Trees were set to break up the flat shore line of the Sound, cool bowers with fountains and pools replaced the bare sand.

The color scheme at one side of the house is brilliant in red, green and blue. The blue is the sky beyond the Sound; the green, trees and shrubs, and the red, rows of "red-hot poker" plants. This panormaa of color is spread along a flagged walk leading to the house.

In the setting for Edward F. Hutton's house at Roslyn, Long Island, Miss Coffin explained, she found yet another problem. Here there was a desire for the settled, mellowed atmosphere of an English country house. Unfortunately the tract was rather flat. By building an avenue lined with chipped cedars, like a tall hedge, in front of which, as at the edge of a walk, magnolia trees were set at intervals, Miss Coffin got the desired effect and at the same time produced a new combination in landscape architecture—the magnolias against the background of trimmed cedars.

As Miss Coffin explained these magic transformations her artistic side came to the fore. With eloquent gestures, though restrained, and with absorbed interest she indicated the vital points of her landscape creations.

Not all of the Long Island places required the raising of exotics in the sand. One, the Marshall Field place at Lloyd's Neck, had some natural growth of importance to begin with. There were fine trees that were worthy of preservation, and the owner had included in the plans a small "winter cottage" apart from the big house. Miss Coffin's plan was built around the trees. Near the "winter house" she planned a circular garden, with flagged walk, surrounded by pines and other evergreens, so that throughout the winter there might be flourishing vegetation.

Marian C. Coffin

Sometimes unexpected problems confront a landscape architect and it is necessary to go back to those first engineering principles acquired at the technical school. An instance of this arose in the process of planning the Sevilia Home for Children near Hunt's Point, on Long Island Sound. Miss Coffin had the contract for laying out the grounds. After the building had been completed and she had begun her work, the management of the home found that not enough room for a coal supply to last the winter through had been included in the original plans for the building. Miss Coffin solved the problem. She had an additional storage cellar built under the service drive and proceeded with her original contract without any alteration in her plans as a result of the unforeseen emergency.

Two of her large constructions were the Lammot du Pont place at Wilmington, Del., and the H. Rodney Sharp estate, also at Wilmington.

Before concluding these interesting illustrations of her work Miss Coffin showed me pictures of the old garden at Fort Ticonderoga, N. Y., now the country home of Stephen H. Pell. The French officers who had occupied the fort in Colonial days had built a garden outside their barracks according to the best French mode. It had remained a level stretch like a parade ground. In the old plans it bore the name "Jardin du Roi," or "Garden of the King."

Miss Coffin preserved the old lines of the garden when she undertook its restoration, and also something of the ancient military air. Across the back a brick wall was raised with a gate and arched gateway in the center. Facing this on the other side were planted two of the old cannon. The center is a smooth lawn. A varied color scheme was then worked out, beginning at the house, the characteristic note of which is mauve. Working away from the house the next shade is furnished by pink blooms and beyond by white. Further off the tones change to orange, and in the distance, red. Around the garden there are English elms.

Miss Coffin is now at work on plans for the grounds of the Delaware State College at Newark, Del. It is her task to harmonize two different themes—one embodied in the men's dormitories and the other in the women's. These two dormitories are to face each other.

Women can become successful landscape architects in Miss Coffin's opinion, if they are properly trained and are willing to start at the bottom and regard the work as a specialized business. They must have inherent good taste and must add to that education. With the natural interest women have in the home and in living conditions generally, those properly qualified should find landscape architecture a good opening for a professional life, she maintains.

"There is a little difficulty sometimes," Miss Coffin confided, "in gaining the full confidence of men who are setting out to build country places. For such a large project the man usually turns to another man for advice. Hence a woman landscape architect must expect to start in a small way and work up. She must remember that it takes from one to three years for her executed plans to grow into full perfection, depending upon the kinds of trees and shrubs the place has been beautified with. Then the place must be carefully watched to see that growth proceds in accordance with the plans."

Marian Coffin caused somewhat of a stir as she became more active within the design trade. Prior to World War I, it was very uncommon for women to occupy roles within skilled careers, and even more so for someone with a background and pedigree like Coffin's. This article, published by the *Brooklyn Daily Eagle* in 1925, makes sure to highlight her relation to 18th-century artist Benjamin Trumbull and the well-known Schuyler family. Coffin's early career, although assisted by this novelty, was far from easy, as in her words "there [was] a difficulty . . . in gaining the full confidence of men who set out to build country places. For such a large project the man usually turns to another man for advice." However, after working up from very small commissions, her inherent skill and eye for design soon shone through, with her being praised as not just one of the most prominent female architects, but "the architect of some of the finest American country estates." (Creative Commons.)

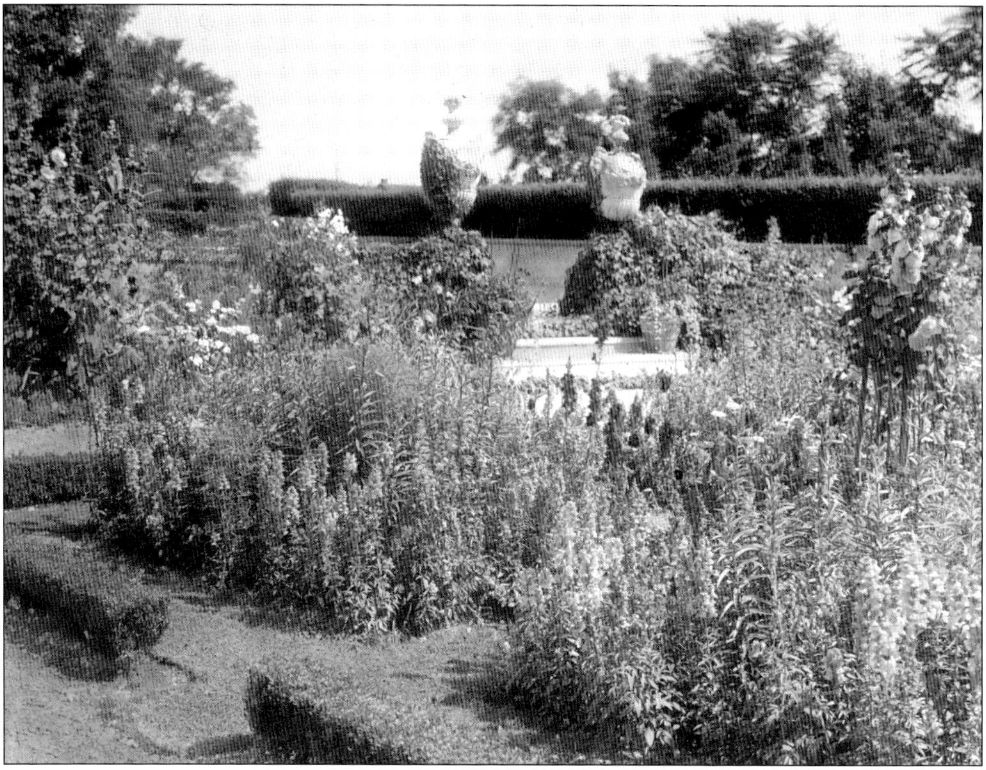

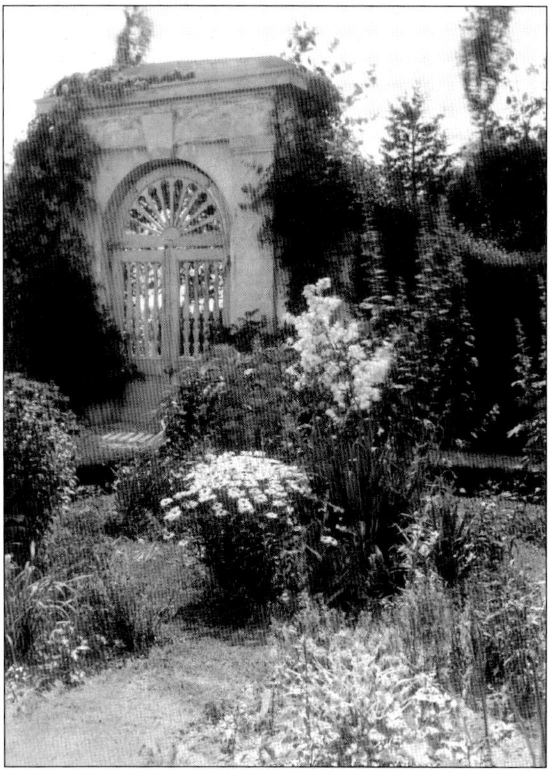

Coffin's first major residential commission, beginning in 1910, was at Southampton's incredibly ornate Villa Mille Fiori. The home conformed to Beaux-Arts sensibilities, having been designed in an Italianate style modeled after the Villa Medici in Rome. Coffin's design lived up to the estate's name, which translated to "House of Thousand Flowers" or "House of Wildflowers." While the design is no longer extant, having been demolished in the 1960s, surviving images and blueprints show an axially symmetrical garden with a grand lawn leading from the house's loggia to a formal parterre, with naturalistic flowers spilling out of beds and over architectural follies and statuary. While more strictly neoclassical than Coffin's later works, this design still shows hints of what her unique style would become. (Both, Library of Congress.)

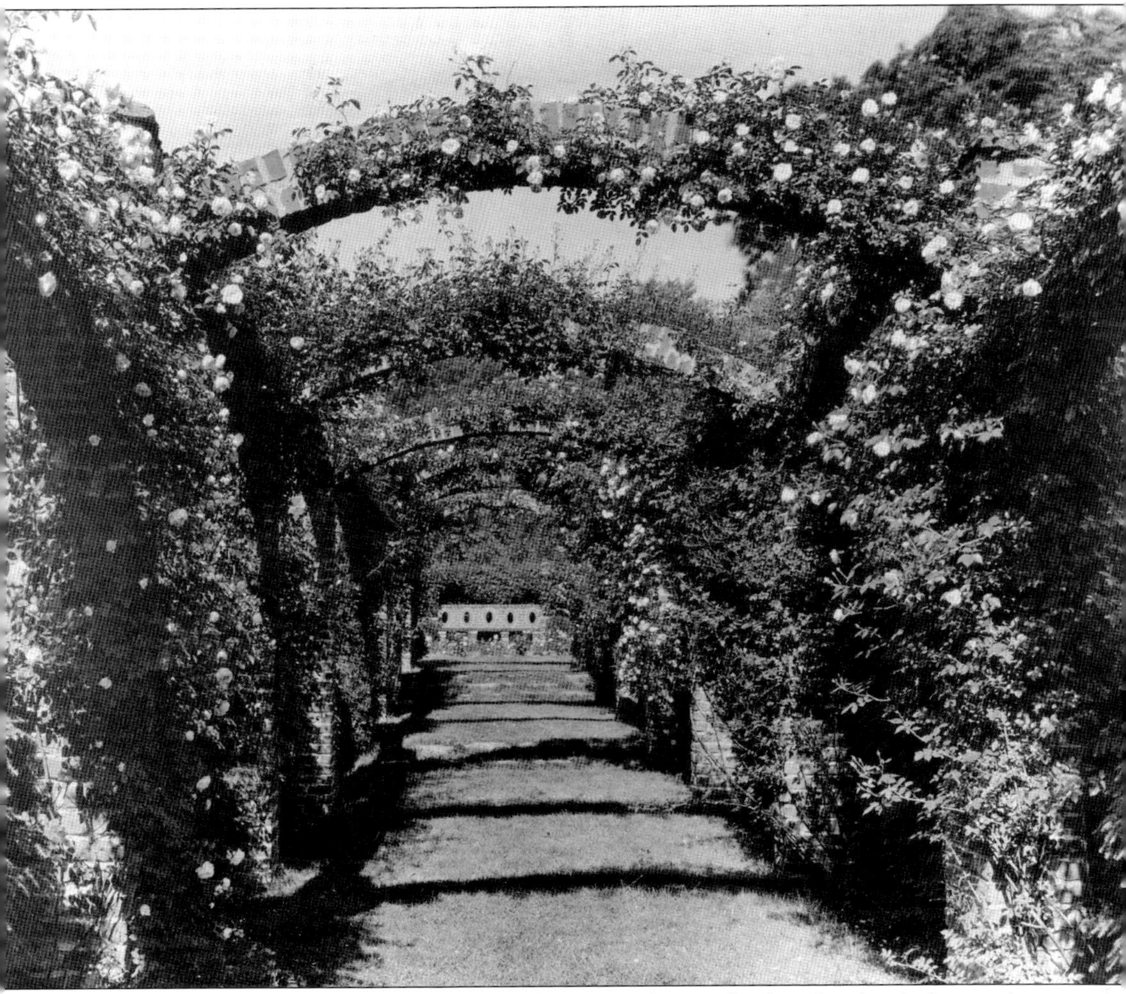

Slowly, Coffin began getting commissions from the society elites with whom her family frequently socialized, and in these gardens, she began to experiment with form and design. In 1920, she was commissioned by cereal heiress Marjorie Merriweather Post and her husband, Edward Francis Hutton, to design the landscape for their home in Wheatley Hills, New York. Their gardens constituted a series of "rooms," which carefully balanced the Tudor formality of the house with playful elements mirroring the house, which included structural posts carved in the shape of English terriers. The garden included a woodland clearing of topiaries and these modern geometric beds. Coffin also included a brick rose arbor, which doubled as a formal walkway. The landscape is still accessible as the Post Campus of Long Island University. (Winterthur.)

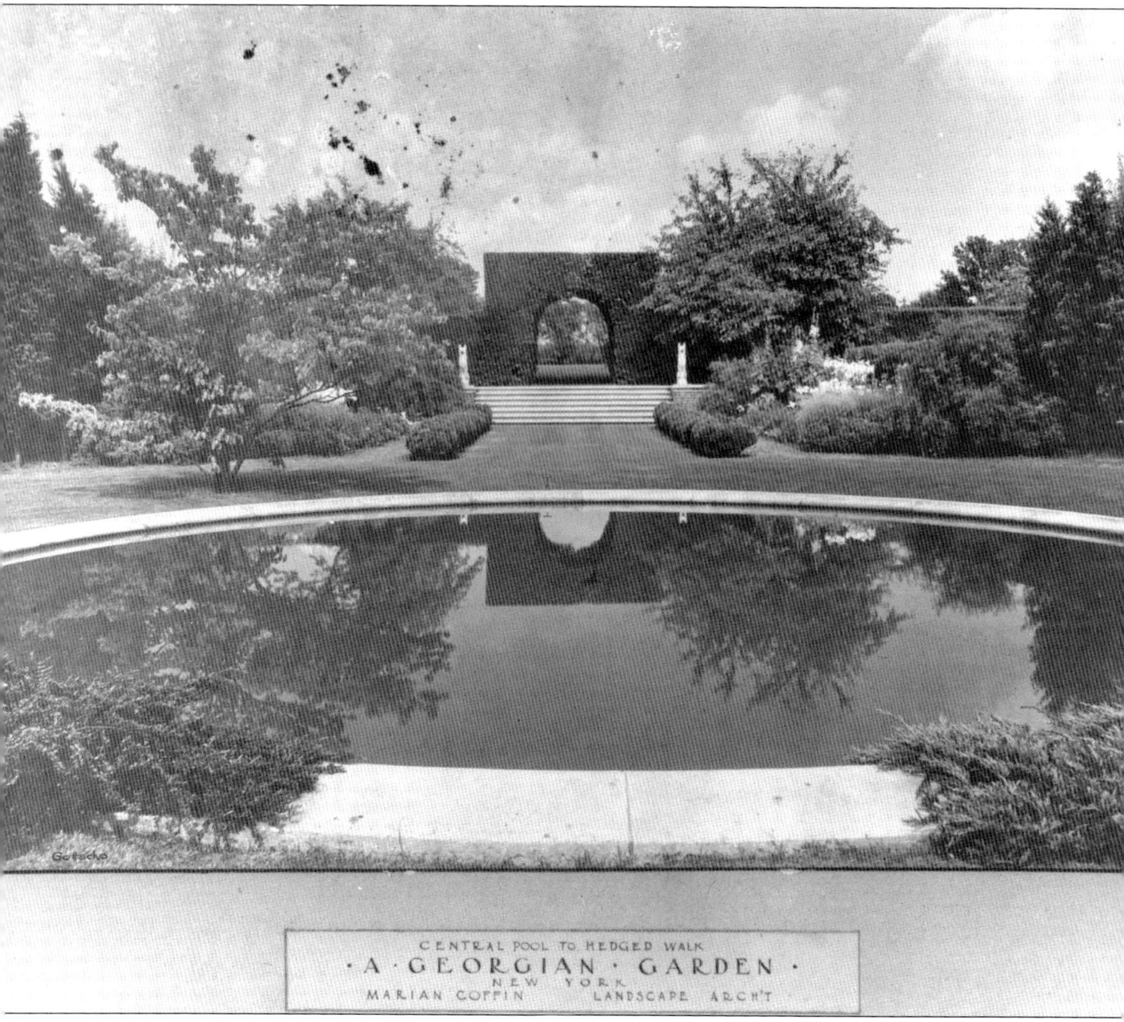

Coffin also designed Clayton, the Long Island estate of Childs Frick, heir to a Pittsburgh steel fortune. This design was more classically designed but remained experimental in the development of her design style. A major element of Clayton's landscape was this large pool, which she accented with a privet hedge that she had trained as a Roman arch. She surrounded the pool with flower borders in a gradient from pale pinks to reds to blues to yellows. The garden also included scrolled beds and parterres, large fountains, and long strolling allées. Today, the landscape functions as a sculpture garden for the Nassau County Museum of Art, which occupies the former mansion. (Winterthur.)

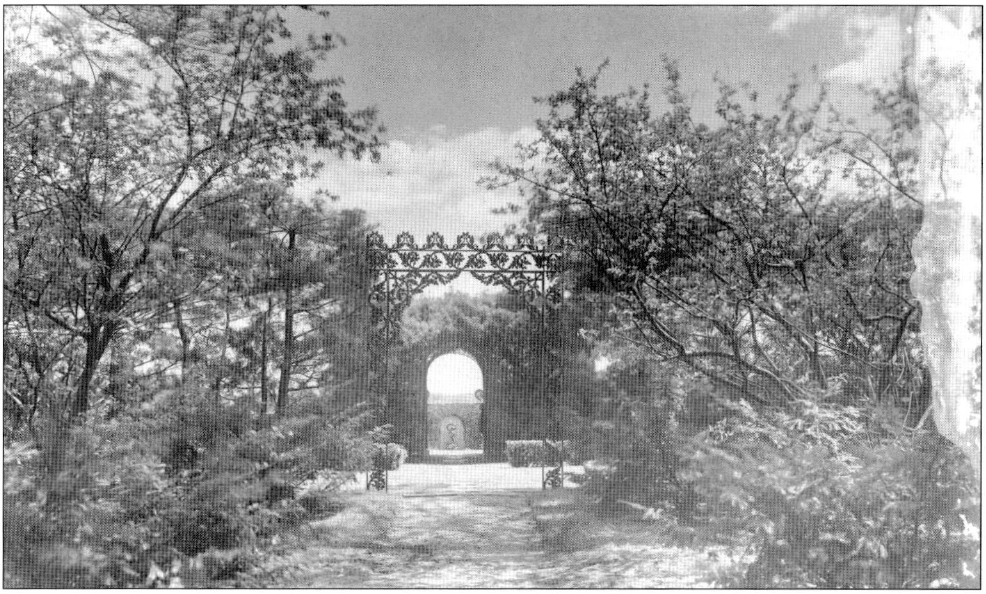

Part of Coffin's unique design practice involved frequent visits to commissioned properties to assess their construction progress. However, it was only at the Oaks, in Bridgeport, Connecticut, that she returned to one property to complete commissions for two different owners. Coffin's first commission at the site, completed sometime before 1917, was a formal walled garden completed for Jonathan Godfrey, which bears a striking resemblance to designs she would later complete at Winterthur and Fort Ticonderoga. In her book *The Livable House, Its Garden* (1917), Ruth Dean praised the design's restraint, its wide paths, and swaths of lawn, saying that it "would seem smaller and less reposeful if the same spaces were covered all over with flower beds." The estate is no longer extant, falling into ruins before being razed in 1990 to accommodate a new housing development. (Above, Winterthur; below, Smithsonian.)

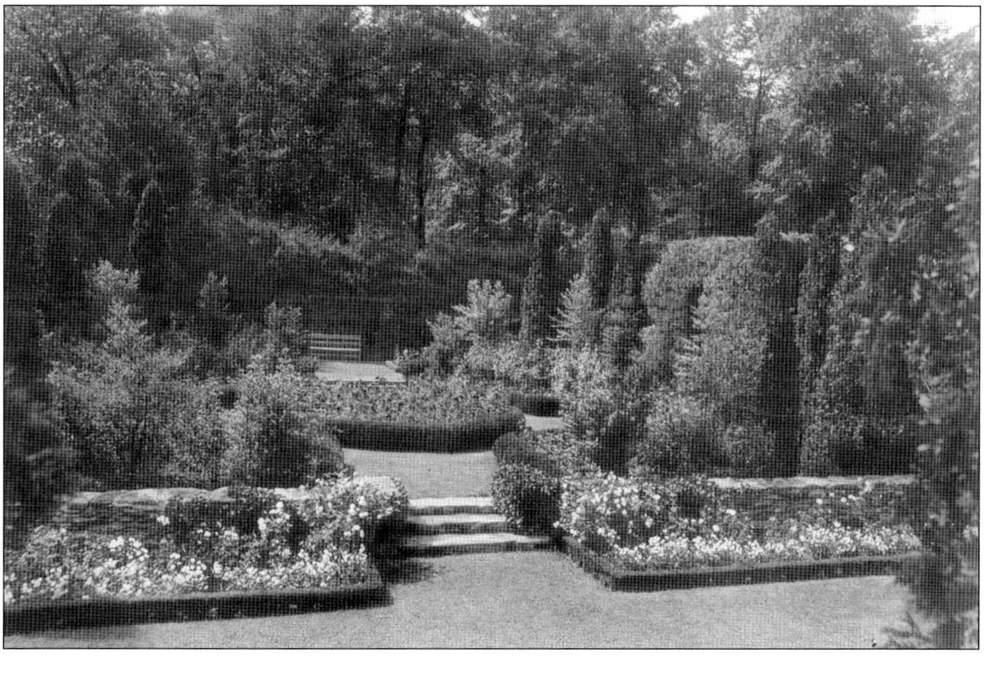

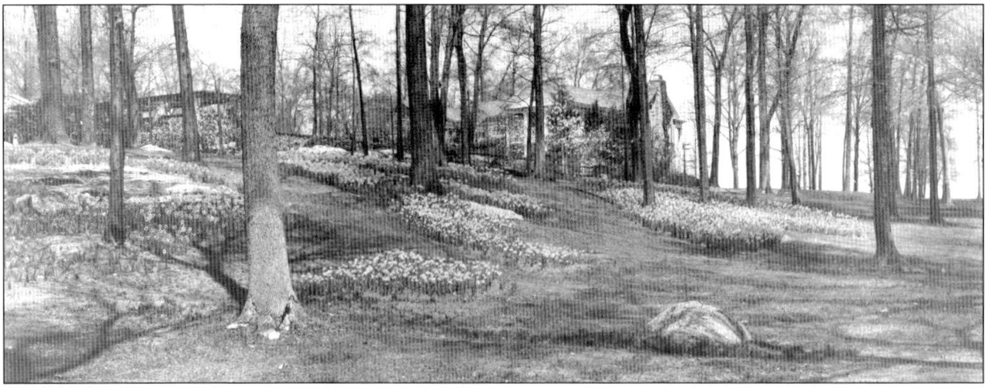

Coffin's second design at the Oaks, commissioned by Edgar Bassick in 1927, was in a new design style for her. This garden was much more naturalistic than any of her previous works, centering around the exposure of a large rock ledge. She designed a series of trickling waterfalls and placed a coordinating path of granite steps. She cleared out some of the extant trees to increase light levels and planted long drifts of daffodils and crocuses in a design that paralleled the March Bank her old friend H.F. duPont was working on at Winterthur. In this image, the house is just barely glimpsed through the copses of trees. The winding path was a masterful design choice to increase the feeling of space. Following its completion, the Bassick design won Coffin the Gold Medal of Honor from the Architectural League of New York in 1930. (Above, Winterthur; below, Smithsonian.)

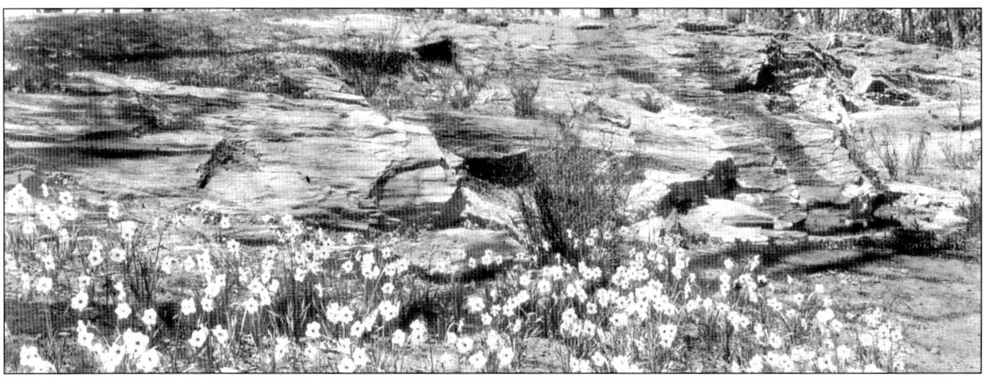

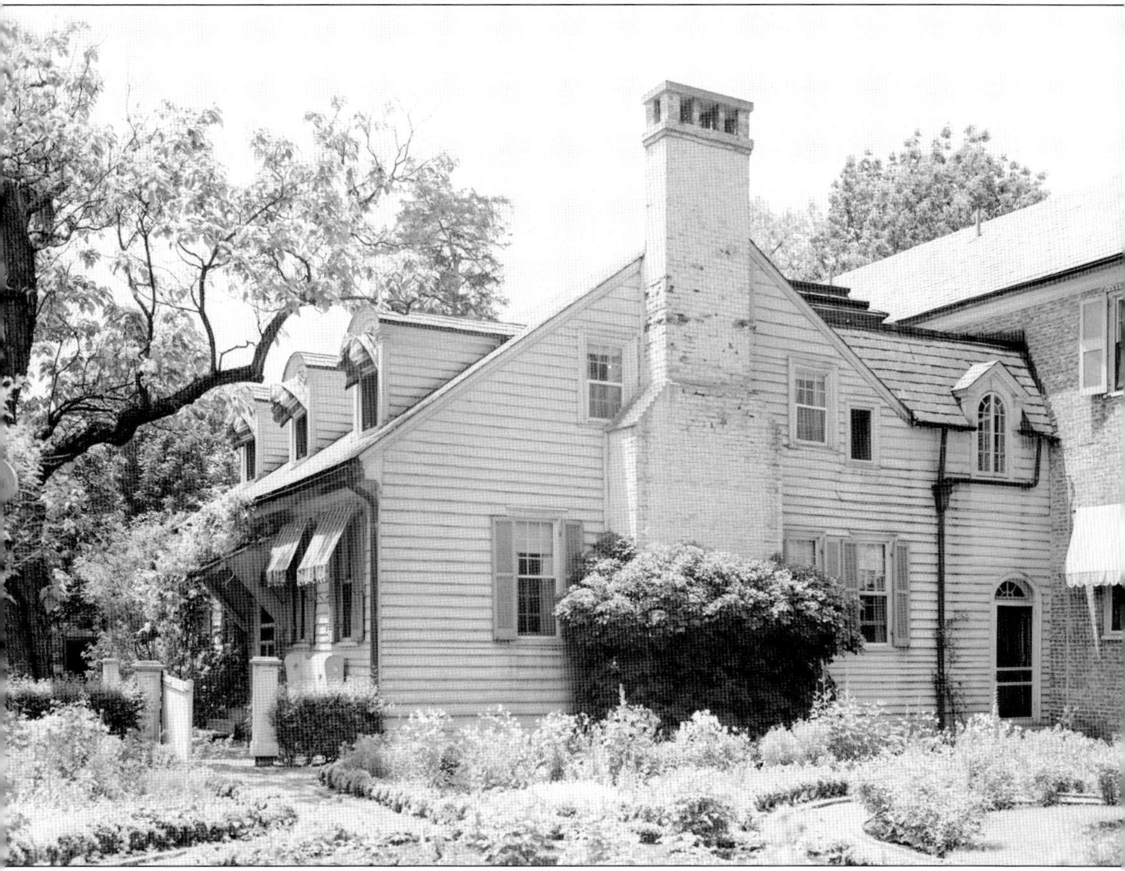

Even early in her career, Coffin began to show her capacity for adjusting her design style to suit its context. She believed that a garden should be seen as an extension of the house, both aesthetically and as living space. While Coffin completed most of her commissions at new-construction sites in the same Beaux-Arts style in which she was trained, occasionally, she would have to deviate from her norm for an extant home. Such was the case when, in 1910, she was commissioned by William Marshall Bullitt to design a landscape at his ancestral home in Louisville, Kentucky, which was built in 1791. While the farther reaches of the design mirror the Beaux-Arts style—a strong axis leads from the home to a birdbath and tennis court—the area nearer to the house is instead designed as a Colonial Revival knot garden, with three adjoining circles bordered by boxwoods and filled with herbaceous perennials. Coffin would later complete similar designs at the Daughters of the American Revolution (DAR) headquarters in Philadelphia and at the Corbit-Sharp House in Odessa, Delaware. (Library of Congress.)

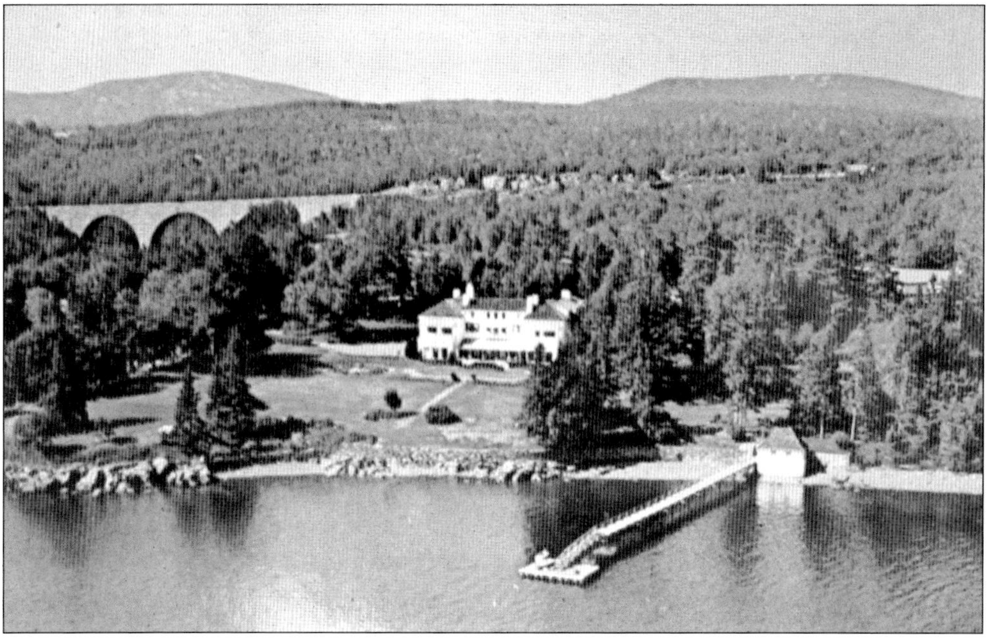

Marian Coffin's northernmost commission was for Frederick Vanderbilt, at his summer home in Bar Harbor, Maine. Its landscape was similar to many of her other Country Place commissions—geometric hedges surrounding beds of naturalistic plants, with sloping forested lawns. Paths were either grass or flagstone. These images show Sonogee when it was used briefly as a museum in the 1970s, prior to being turned into a nursing home, with all but the first floor demolished. Despite attempts to expand her work into deep New England and out into the Chicago area, Coffin's practice never expanded farther west than Ohio, and for the most part it remained clustered in the Mid-Atlantic and Northeast. (Both, Erin Fogarty.)

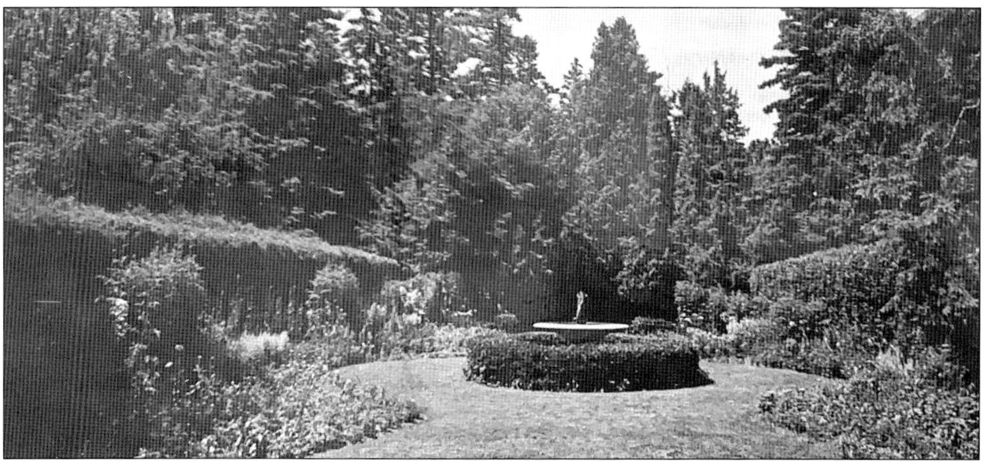

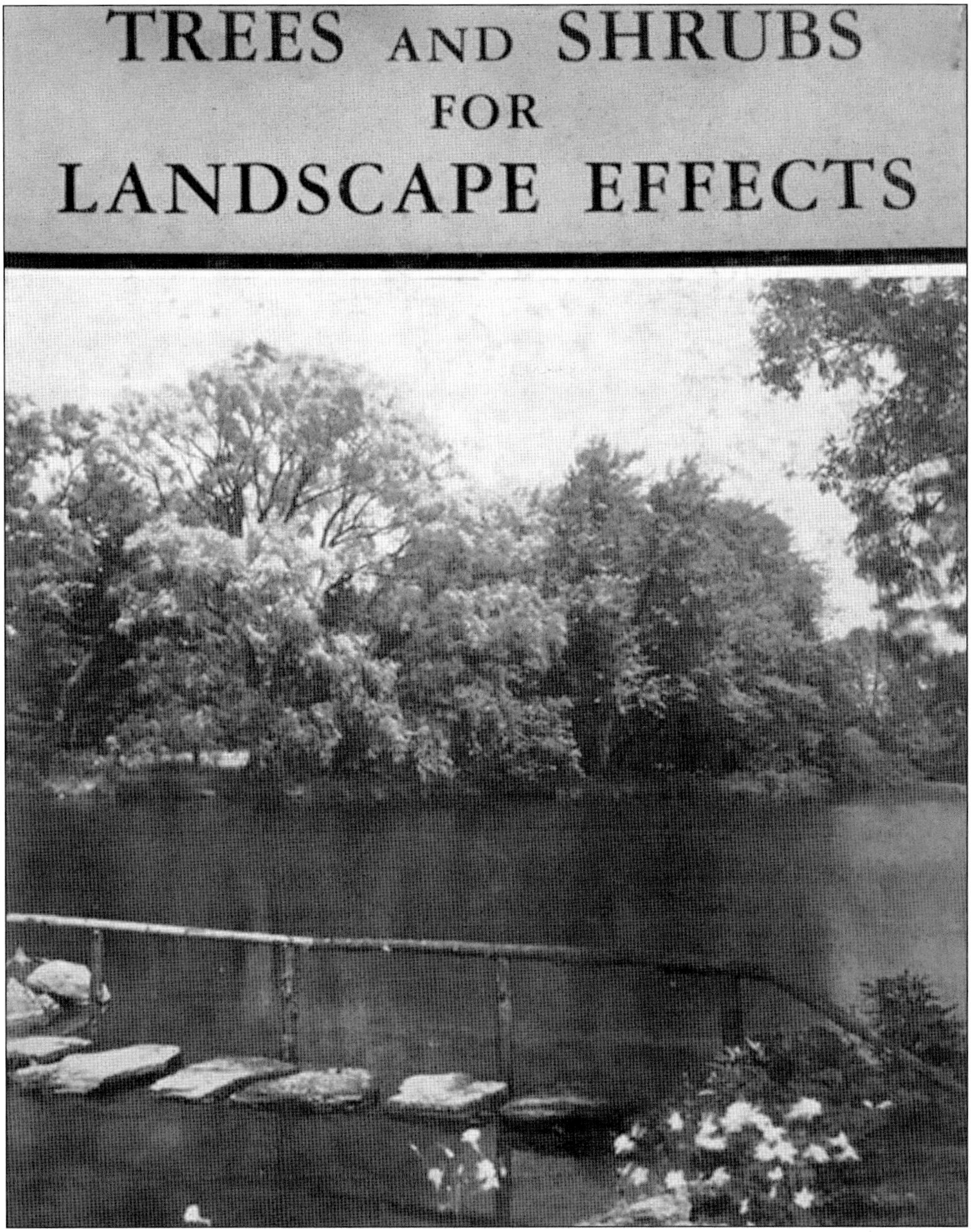

The Country Place Era, and resulting lifestyle, inspired many of Coffin's early commissions. This era came to a screeching halt after the 1929 stock market crash, and it disappeared nearly entirely after World War II, after which only the wealthiest of persons could afford large city estates and manors with formal gardens. Around the same time, Coffin became ill, and rather than spending large amounts of time visiting her commissions, she had to slow down her physical activity. To occupy her time and gain an income during this period, Coffin turned to writing. She published a number of journal and magazine articles and began working on a monograph. Her book *Trees and Shrubs for Landscape Effects* was published by Charles Scrivener and Sons in January 1940. She also began work on a second book, *The Seeing Eye*, but never finished it. The manuscript is now lost. (Erin Fogarty.)

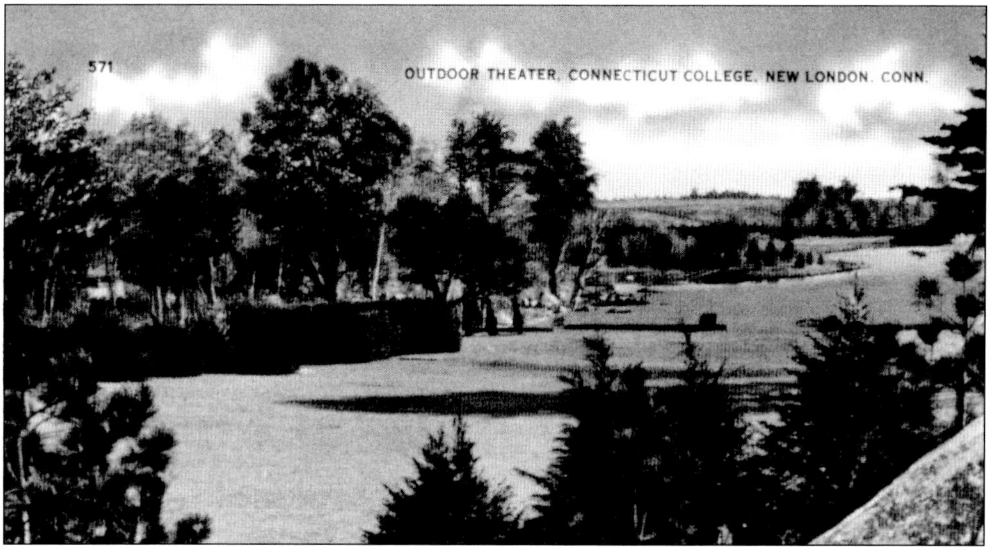

Education and career success for women was a lifelong passion for Marian Coffin. At her practice, she chiefly employed women as design associates and administrators and often rented out rooms at her New Haven home to women attending local universities. She also completed a number of commissions for educational institutions that served women, including, as seen below, the Foxcroft School in Virginia, a boarding school for young girls, and the institution shown above that is now Connecticut College, which operated as an all-women's school from 1909 to 1969. Both designs are rather naturalistic, featuring lawns interrupted by copses of trees, with sporadic beds of flowering plants closer to buildings. (Above, Erin Fogarty; below, Library of Congress.)

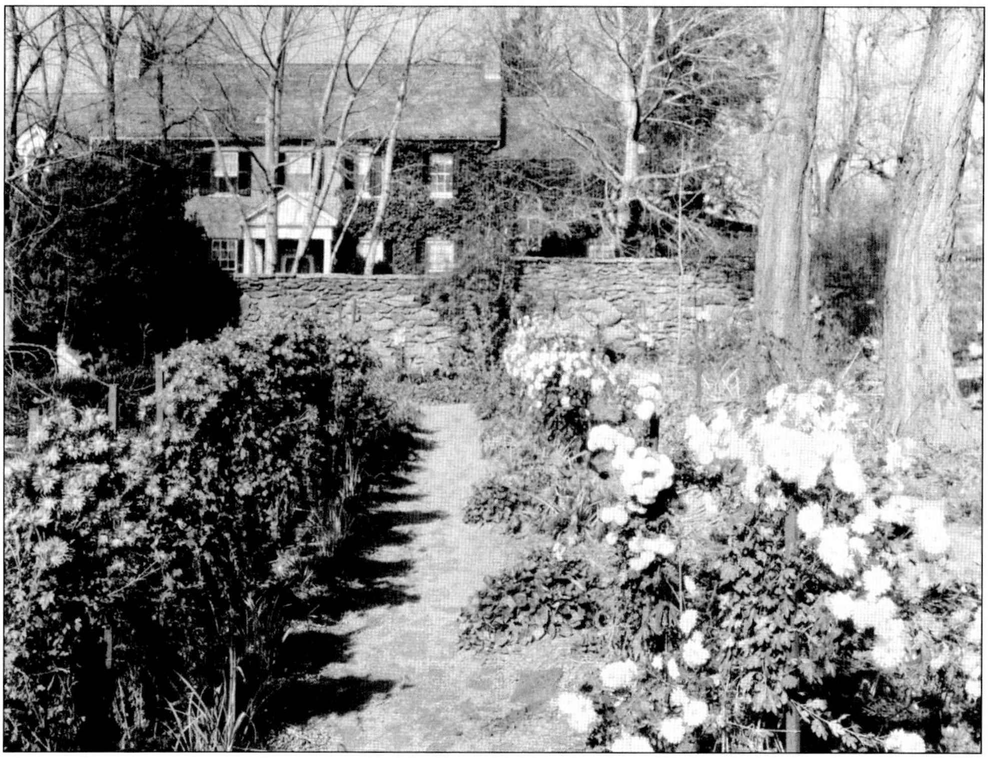

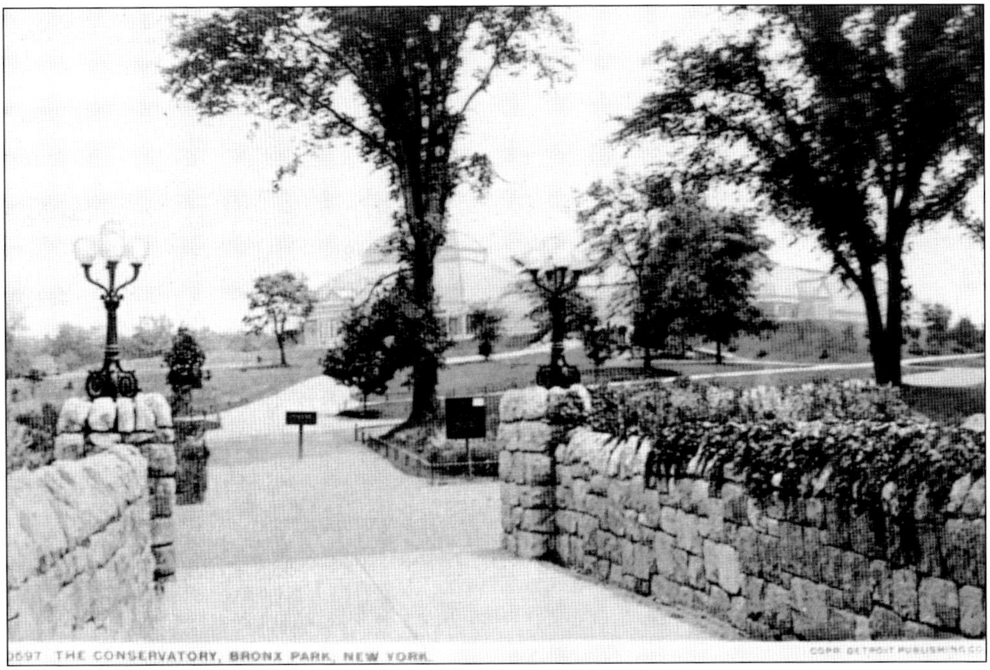

In addition to writing and publishing, Coffin began to see an increase in institutional commissions following the Great Depression. These designs ranged from small, such as a courtyard for a yacht club in Rhode Island, to very large, as in the case of the New York Botanical Gardens (NYGB), as seen here. In 1948, Henry Francis duPont, a longtime friend of Coffin's and the president of NYBG's board, hired her to consult on designs for the public landscape. In the following two years, Coffin completed revisions to their Beatrix Farrand–designed rose garden and designed the Montgomery Conifer Collection. She also designed the gardens' lilac collection, but her designs were not executed until the 21st century. (Both, Erin Fogarty.)

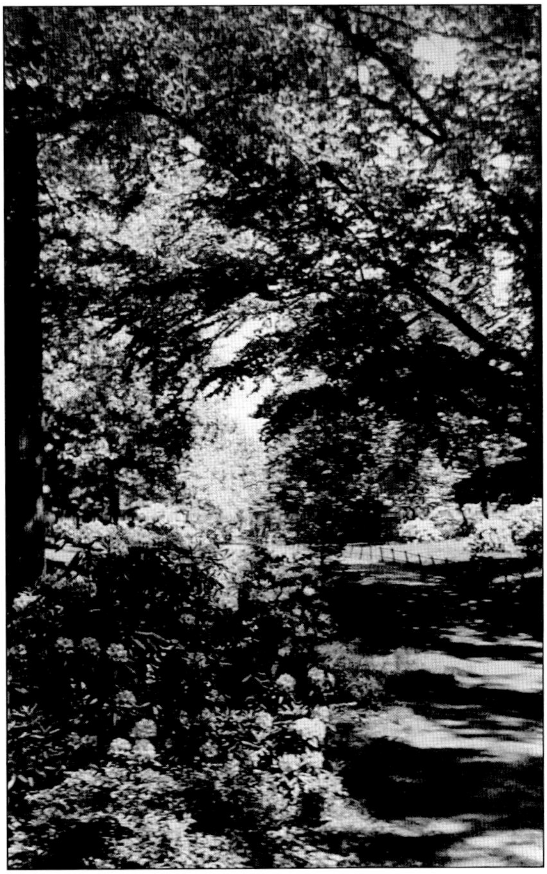

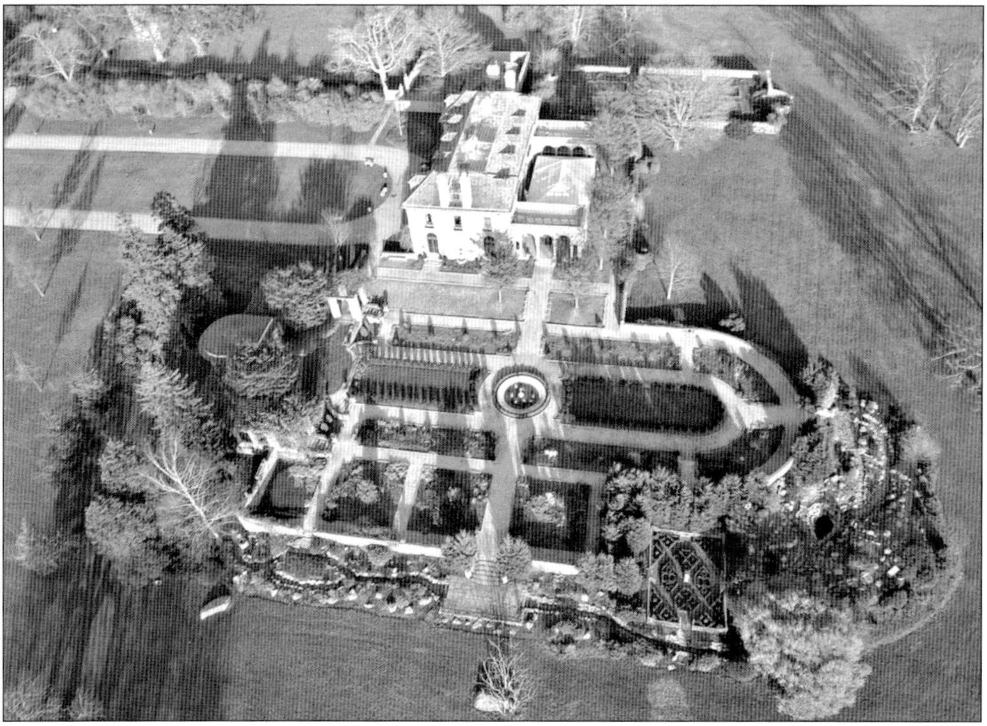

New York Botanical Gardens was not the only place where Marian Coffin revisited a design done by Beatrix Farrand; she did the same at Eolia, the Waterford, Connecticut, home of Standard Oil heir Edward Harkness. Following Farrand's 1929 retirement, Coffin was hired by the Harkness family to "refresh" the extant design, mostly through changes in plantings. While Italianate Neoclassical in form, the garden also featured Near East and Moroccan influences. The garden was meant to be walked through, as well as viewed from a loggia attached to the house, as seen below. The landscape is still extant, and is now part of Harkness Memorial State Park. (Above, Creative Commons; below, Getty Images.)

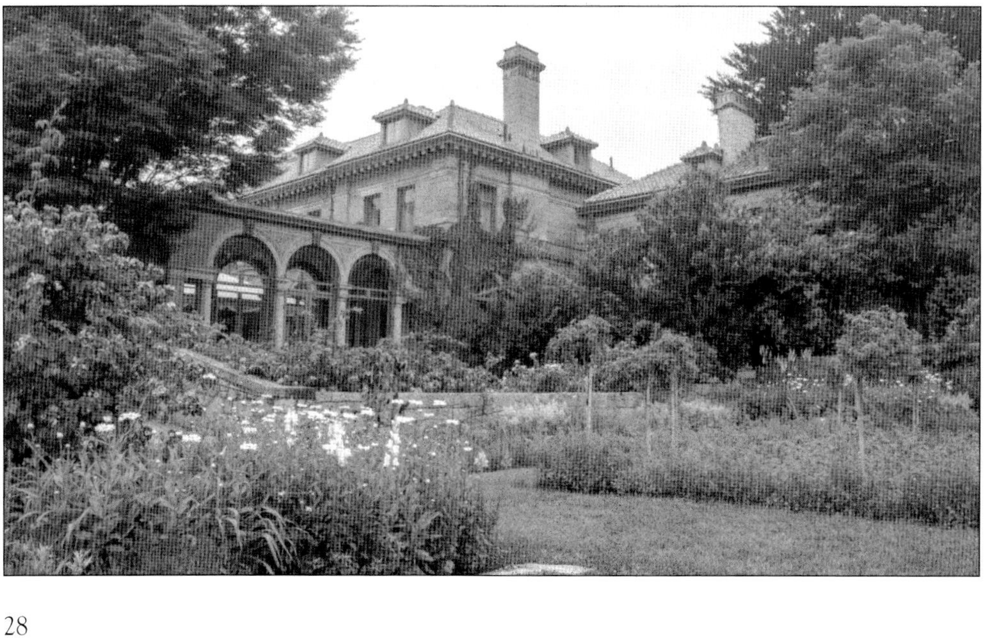

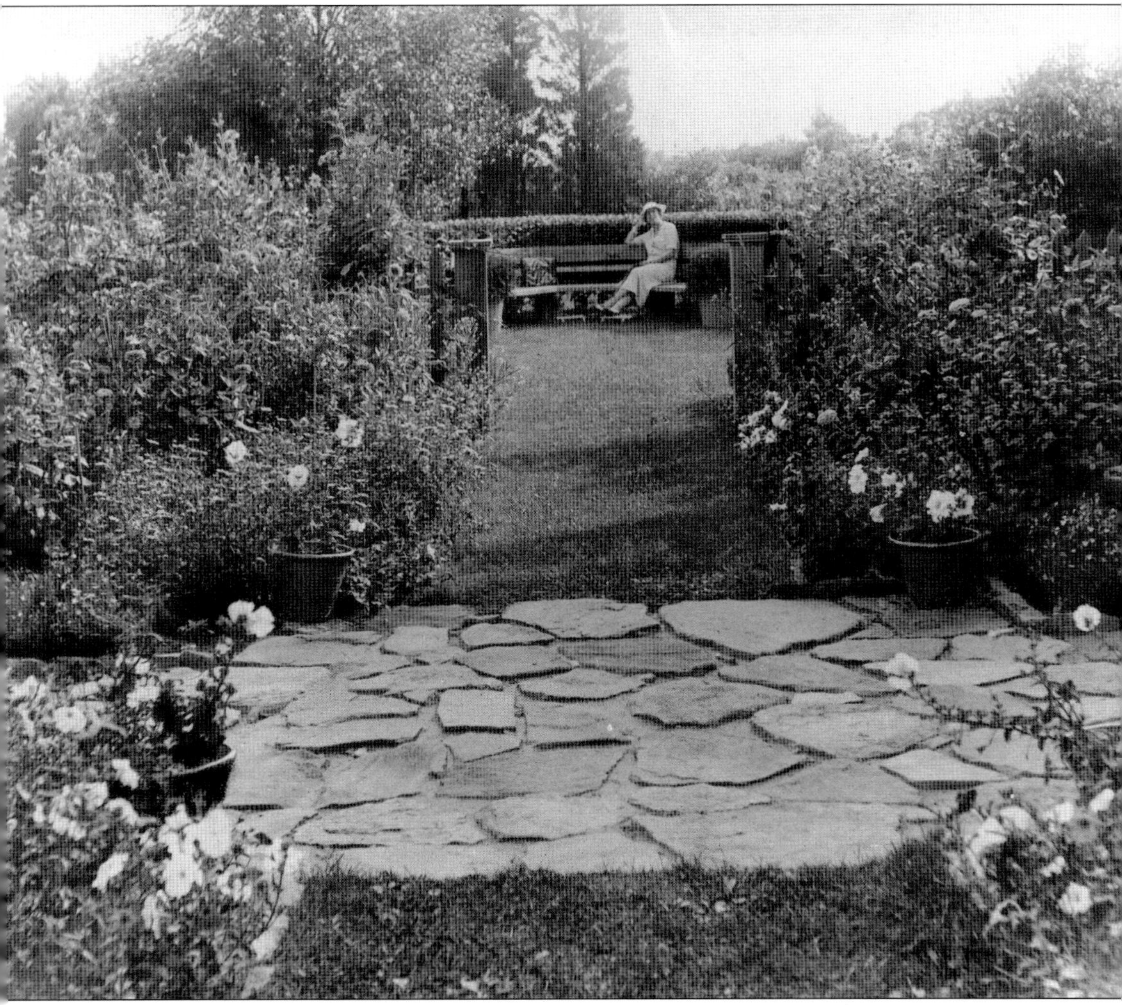

Of all the gardens Coffin designed, her longest-lasting project was likely her own home in Watch Hill, Rhode Island, called Wendover. Coffin bought the shingle foursquare summer home in 1921. She described it as "bleak grey . . . and standing four-square to the winds of heaven on a bare hill." She quickly set to work digging out the hill to construct an 80-foot grass terrace, which she bordered with deep, long flower beds. In front of the house, she built a quartered garden that mirrored the house's interior design. While she laid out her landscape initially when she purchased the house, she continuously worked on it until her death. She relished time at Wendover, and even as she became more well-known and moved her practice out of the city, many of her letters describe how she wished to extend her summers there as long as possible to delay leaving. Here, she is seated in her newly created garden in about 1921. (Winterthur.)

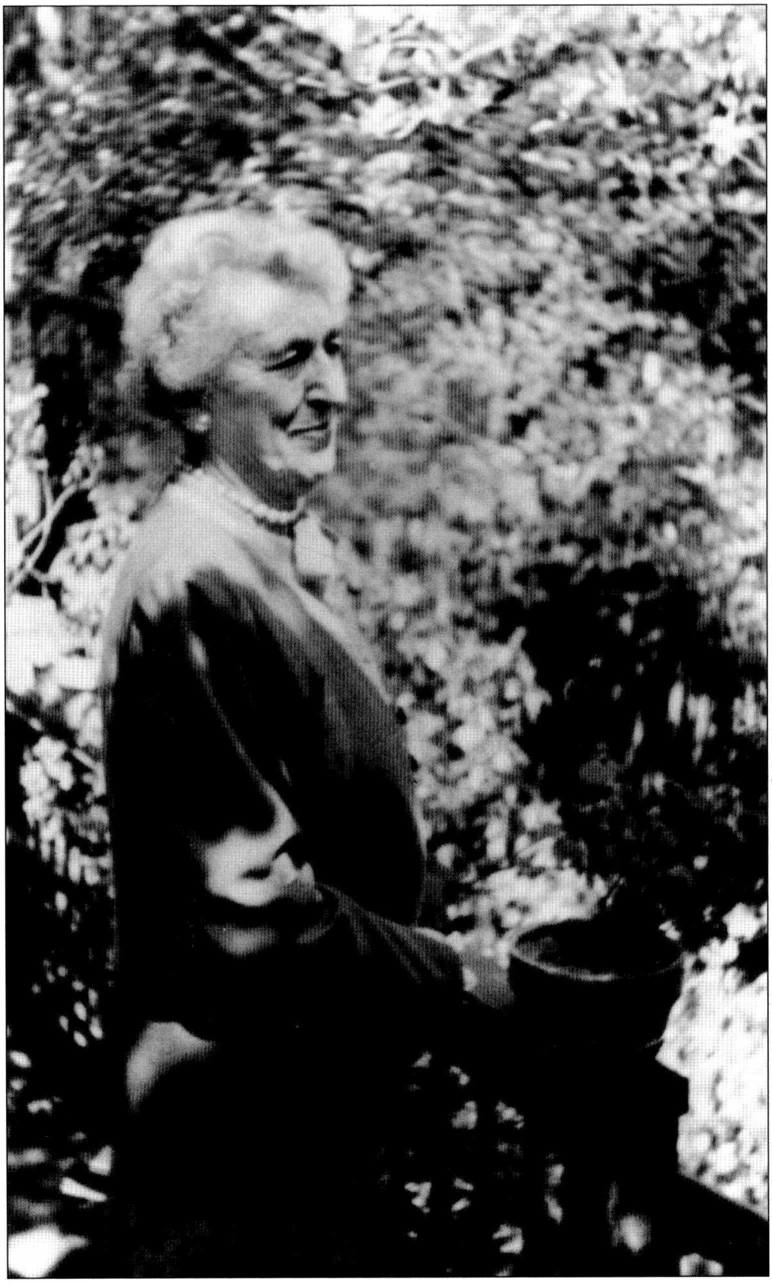

Marian Cruger Coffin passed away in 1957 at her home in New Haven, Connecticut, where she relocated her practice after leaving New York. Because of a number of health problems that plagued her in her later years, many of her later commissions revolved around that city. She often worked for Yale professors, but she made a point to come back to Delaware, with additions to her gardens at Winterthur and Christ Church among her final projects. While Coffin's life was far from normal for the time—she never married, or even had any known romantic partners, an oddity for her time—she lived a full and successful life. Not only did she have many commissions in her own practice, but many of her mostly female design assistants also went on to be successful designers on their own. (Winterthur.)

Two

Gibraltar and Its Inhabitants

In the mid-1840s, John Rodney Brincklé, a cotton merchant, built a three-story Italianate house out of locally quarried blue granite just outside the city of Wilmington, Delaware. He decided to name his estate Gibraltar after the city in Spain, as the home was situated on a large rock outcropping. The estate at this time was spread over 71 acres, which comprised not only the house and formal gardens but also laundry yards, kitchen gardens, small farm plots, and housing for tenants and household staff. Rodney Brincklé, a bachelor, later inherited the estate. He then sold the house to his brother Samuel, a reverend who later founded Christ Church Parish and who occupied the home for three-quarters of a century. In 1909, Samuel Brincklé's two unmarried daughters, Susan and Elizabeth, sold the home and just over six adjoining acres to Hugh Rodney Sharp and his new wife, Isabella Mathieu duPont Sharp. The couple had married less than a year earlier and felt the house, although deteriorated and lacking plumbing, was a perfect future home. Sharp worked in the city as a DuPont executive, and Isabella's mother's estate, St. Amour, was less than a mile away. They enlarged the house for the first time in 1915, nearly doubling its size via a three-story addition made of stone from the same quarry as the original house. This would have been at about the same time that they commissioned Coffin to design the gardens. They also completed a second addition in 1927. The Sharps lived at Gibraltar for 60 years, during which time they raised three children and entertained many guests.

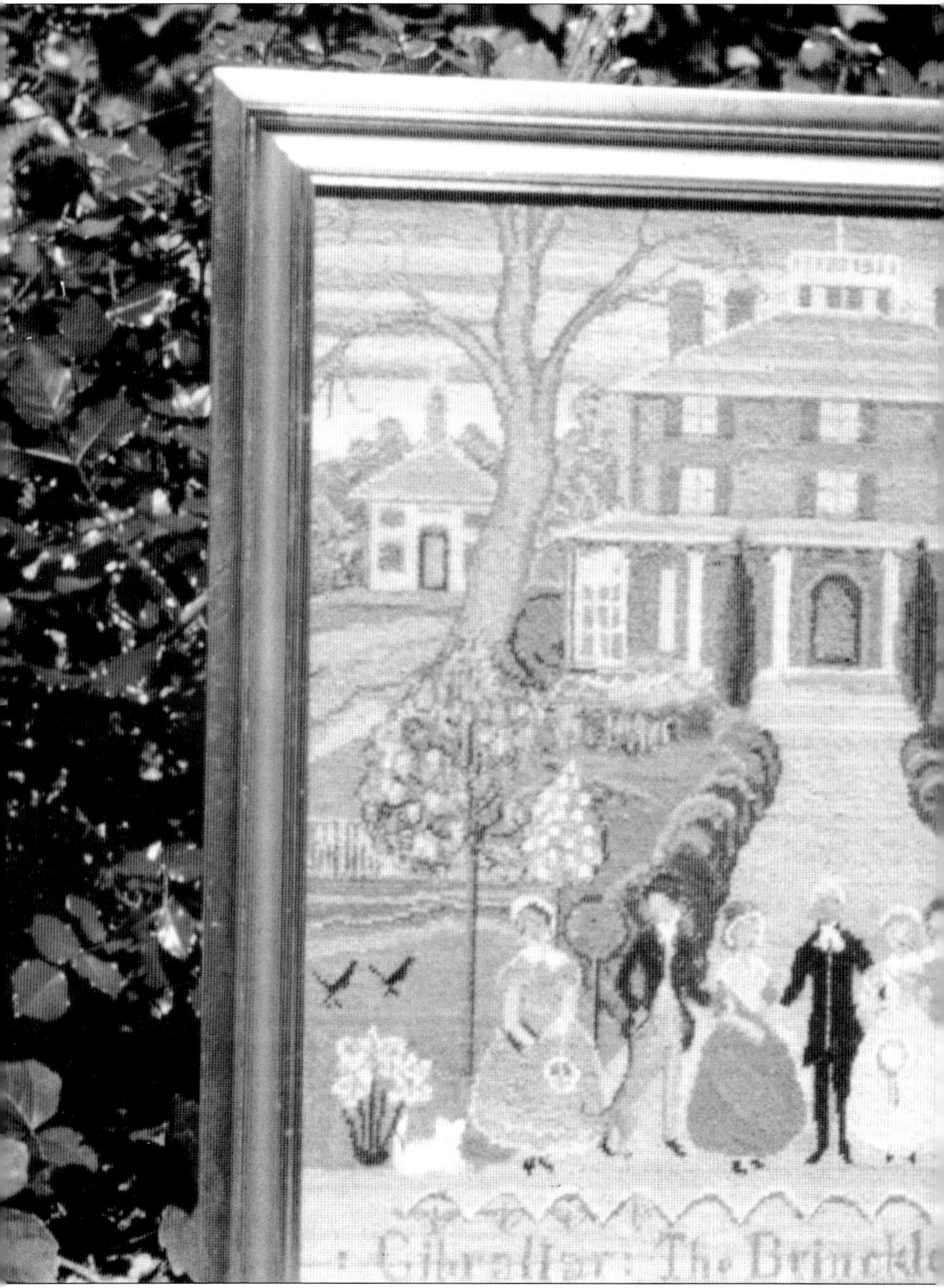
Gibraltar: The Brinckle

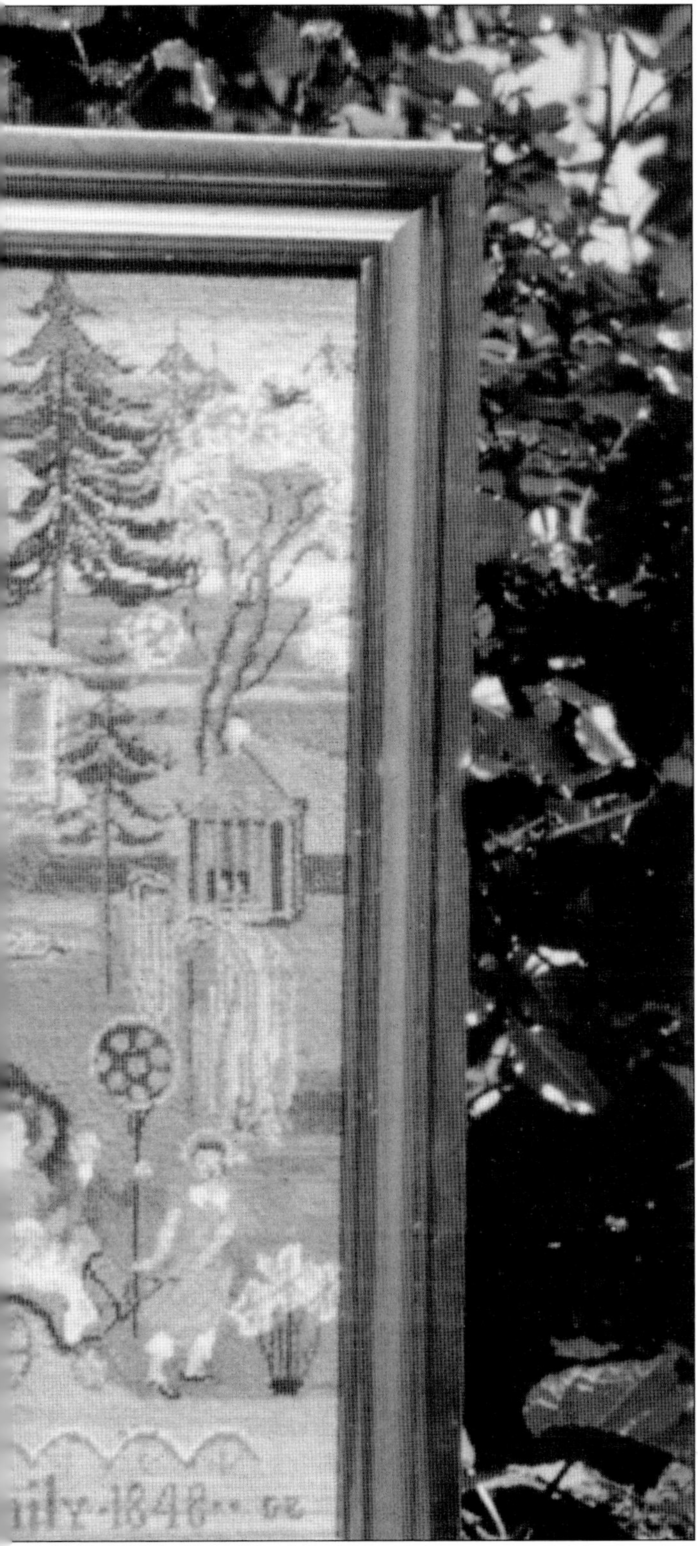

A photograph of an embroidery sampler, this piece is a remarkable representation of Gibraltar's Brincklé-era landscape and the family who resided there. While the piece is dated as 1848, the ages of the children place it to about 1843. Centered in the foreground is the owner, Samuel, holding the hand of his wife, Julia. To their right appear to be daughters Elizabeth and Susan. Further right are sons Samuel, John, and, in the carriage, an infant, William. Next to them is Margaret. On the far left is likely Samuel's brother John, the original builder of the house, and eldest daughter, Anna. The piece seems to corroborate accounts describing significant water features in the landscape, as seen to the family's left, as well as hint at two undocumented summerhouse structures. (Winterthur.)

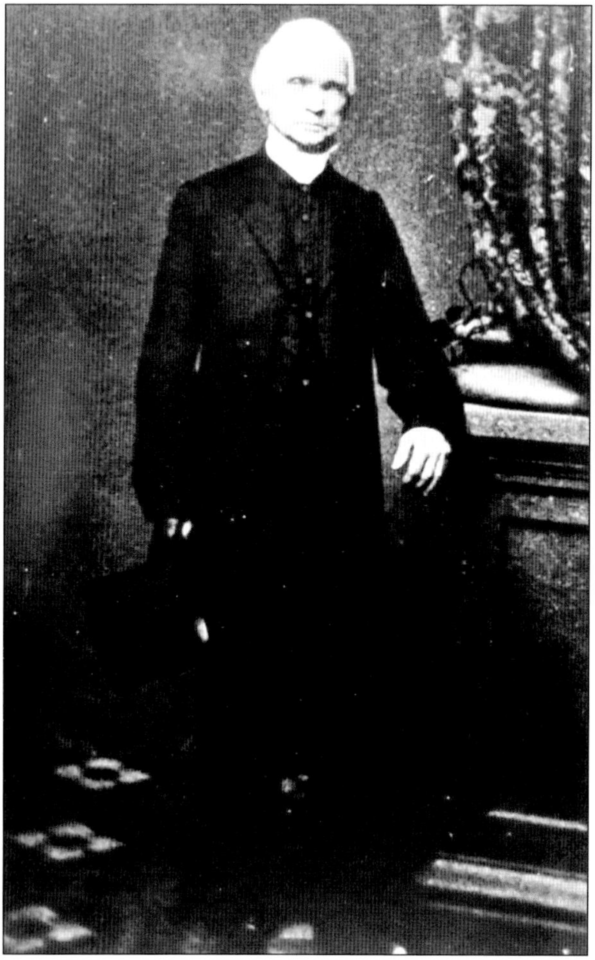

Samuel Brincklé, whose family was the first to inhabit Gibraltar, became the first pastor to lead Christ Church, the religious institution most closely related to the DuPont Corporation. Brincklé and the family decided to found the church as an offshoot of an already existing Sunday school for factory employees as a way to make religion more accessible to those who were not educated in Latin, the de facto religious language of the day. It was a huge success. At the church's first meeting in its newly constructed building, there were 100 people over capacity in attendance. Brincklé remained as the rector of the church until his death in 1863. (Left, PDI; below, Delaware Public Archives.)

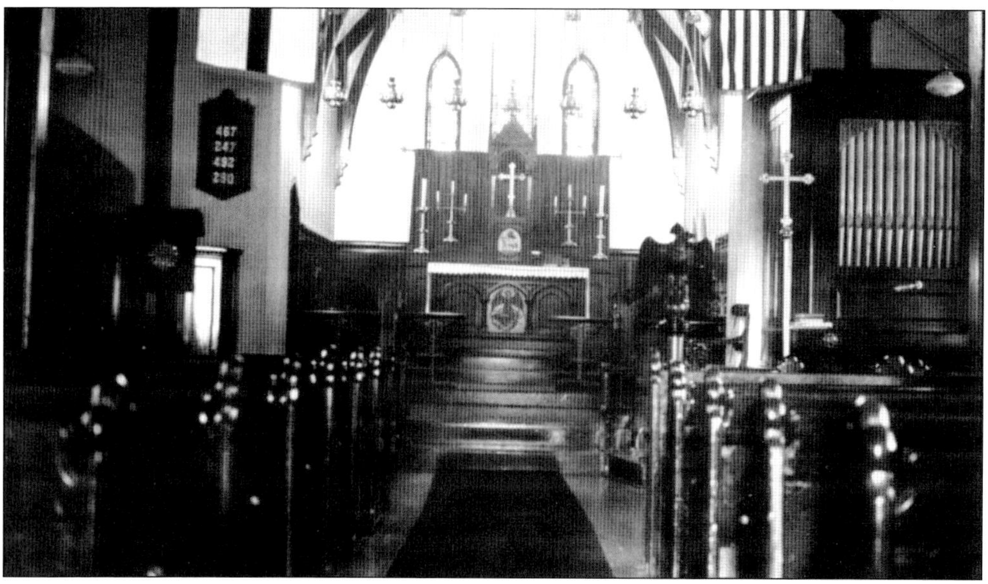

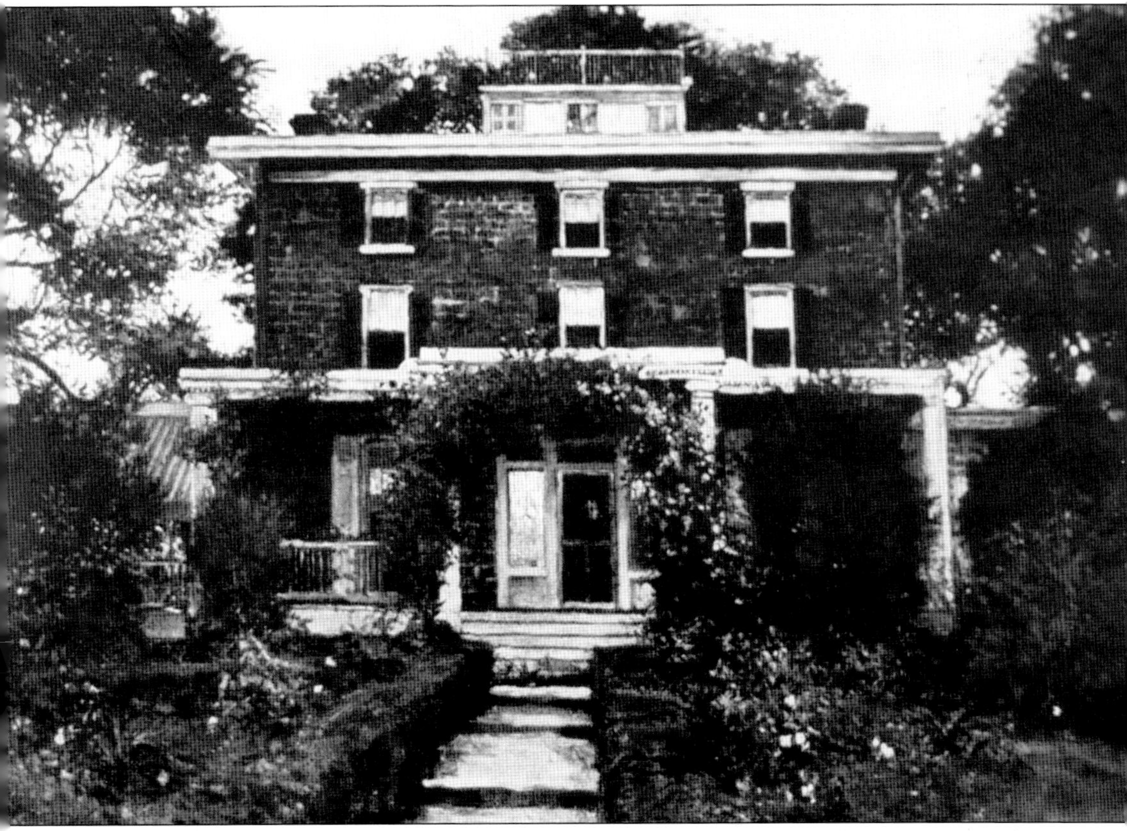

This image, a copy of a painting by Stanley Arthurs, shows Gibraltar around 1911, just after the Sharps purchased the property. Arthurs, a student of Howard Pyle, was often commissioned to paint duPont family homes. Although by this time the Sharps had purchased the estate, they had not yet commissioned the garden, and as such, it is the best visual for the Brincklé-era gardens. Julia Brincklé, a granddaughter of Samuel Brincklé, described her family's home as having a conservatory on one side, a kitchen on the other, with boxwood-hedged gardens leading to a pond for carp just under the overlook. A grotto was approximately at the future site of the grand staircase. The gardens surrounding the house were in the naturalistic style popular at the time, with flowering cherry trees (*Prunus sp.*), magnolias, ferns, and peonies. Little of this garden survives except, perhaps, the naturalistic area on the north side of the property. The location of this painting is unknown and is likely in a private collection. (PDI.)

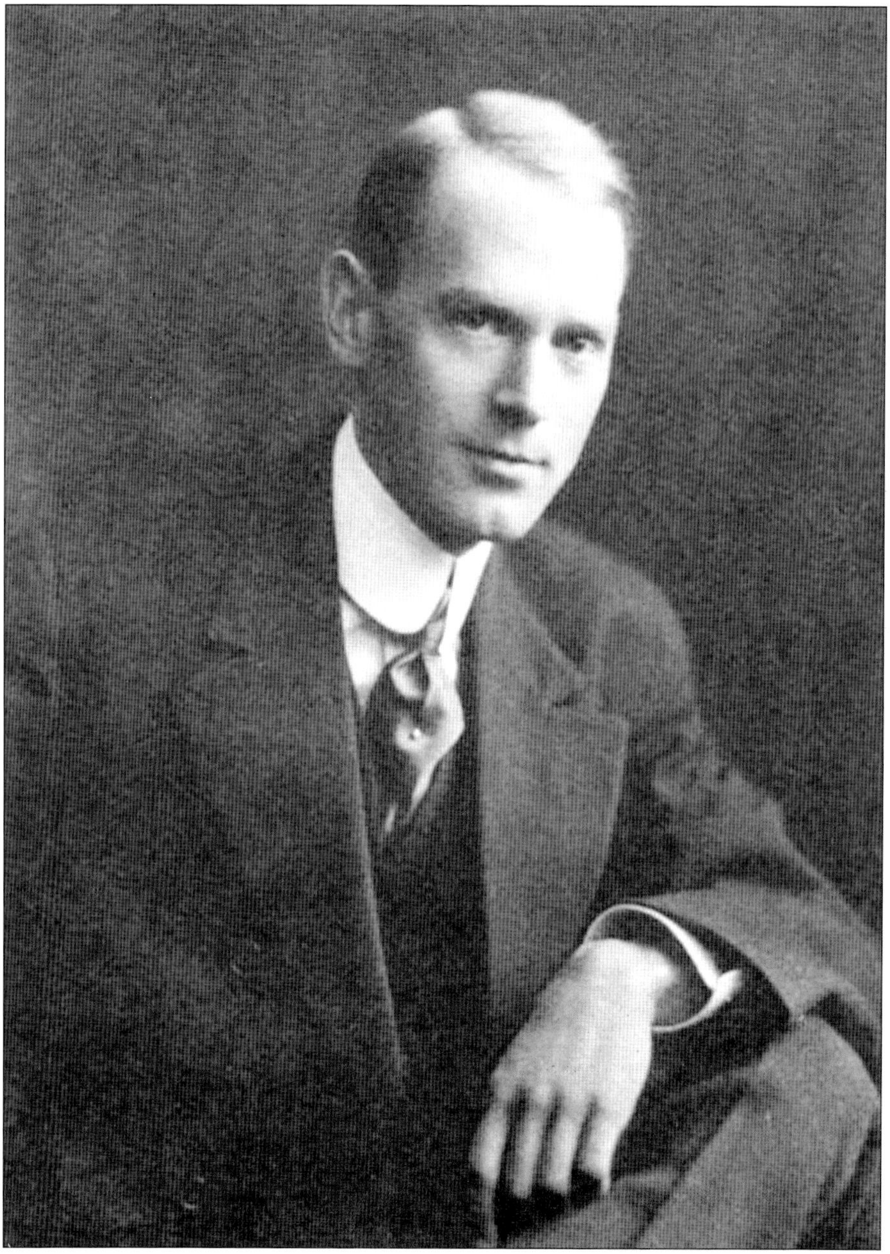

Hugh Rodney Sharp was born the youngest of four children near Seaford, Delaware, on July 30, 1880, to Eli and Sallie Brown Sharp. Compared to his situation later in life, Sharp had a relatively modest, but still privileged, upbringing. While Sharp was born on a family farm outside of Seaford, his family moved to Lewes when he was very young. In Lewes, Eli was the collector of the port, in charge of collecting import tax at the bustling docks. There, Sharp was educated in a small private school before continuing on to Delaware College, now the University of Delaware. It appears he did not take school entirely seriously, saying in an oral history that he "didn't work much [while at college], I'm afraid." After graduation, he returned to southern Delaware for several years to teach, before becoming the private secretary to Pierre S. duPont, through whom he likely met his wife. (Hagley.)

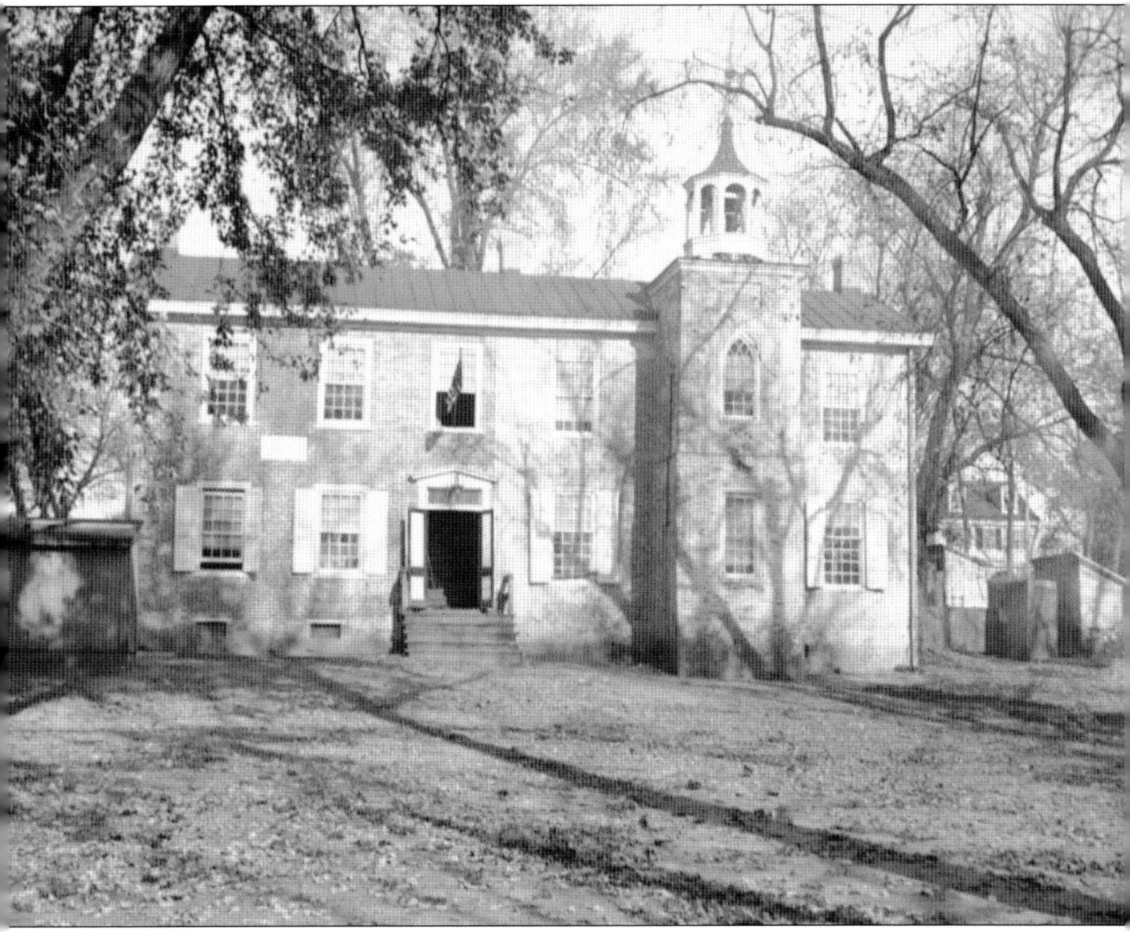

Around 1904, prior to working for the DuPont Corporation, Sharp spent two years as what he called the "principal teacher," supervising a staff of three at this building in Odessa, Delaware. At the time, the town and its school were experiencing a period of hardship due to a slump in shipping, which was the area's main industry. It was not until more than 10 years later that Odessa would receive its first electric light. While Sharp stated in an oral history taken later in his life that he did not set out to become a teacher, he "really had a good time" while at the school. Following this experience, Sharp continued a lifelong affection for the small village. In the 30 years preceding his death, he single-handedly financed the restoration of at least 15 buildings within the town. Odessa is also where Sharp developed an appreciation for Colonial architecture, which features prominently in his later work with the University of Delaware. (Delaware Public Archives.)

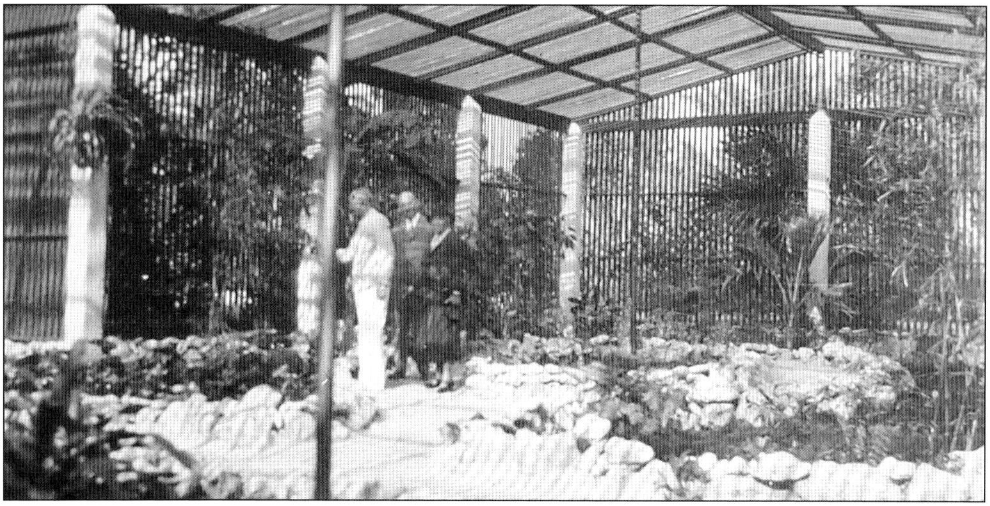

What Sharp loved even more than his gardens were his greenhouses, which he had at Gibraltar and at his winter house in Florida—where he is seen above with P.S. duPont. The blueprint of Sharp's greenhouse complex at Gibraltar is pictured below. The greenhouse was located above the garages and primarily featured flowers, which could be used in bouquets in the house. The original design shows that Sharp planned on roses and carnations, among others. He held his hothouse plants in such high esteem that, at his funeral, his casket was covered with ivy he grew in his own greenhouse. (Above, Hagley; below, Sharp family.)

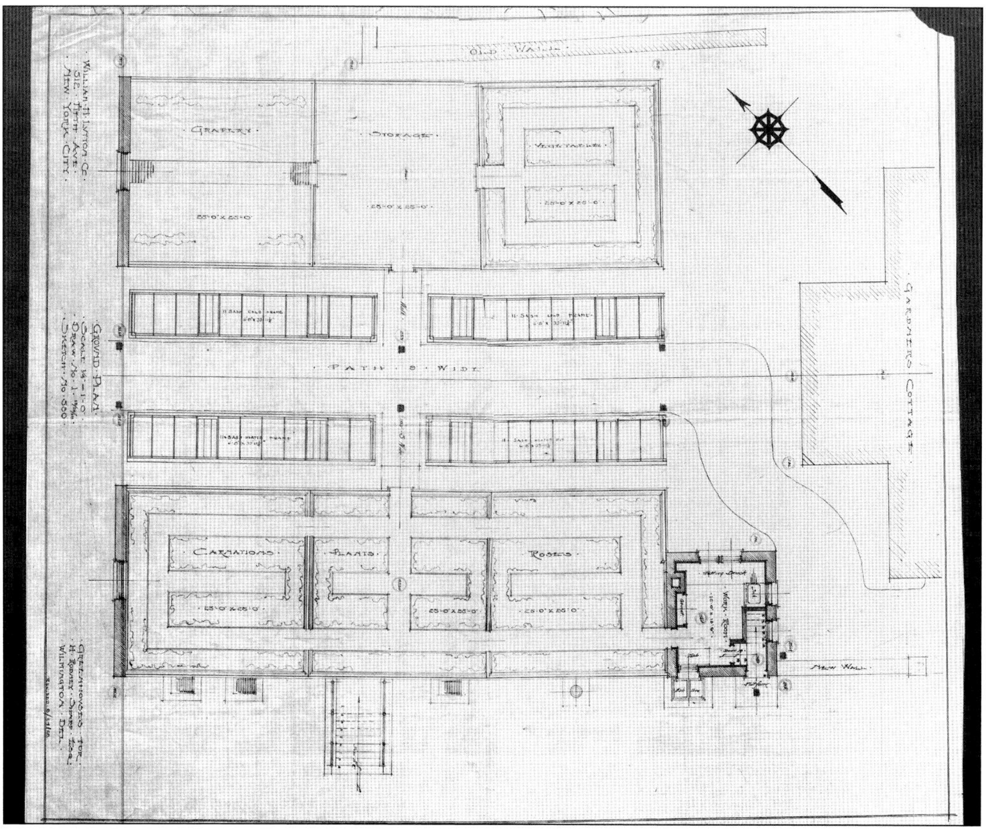

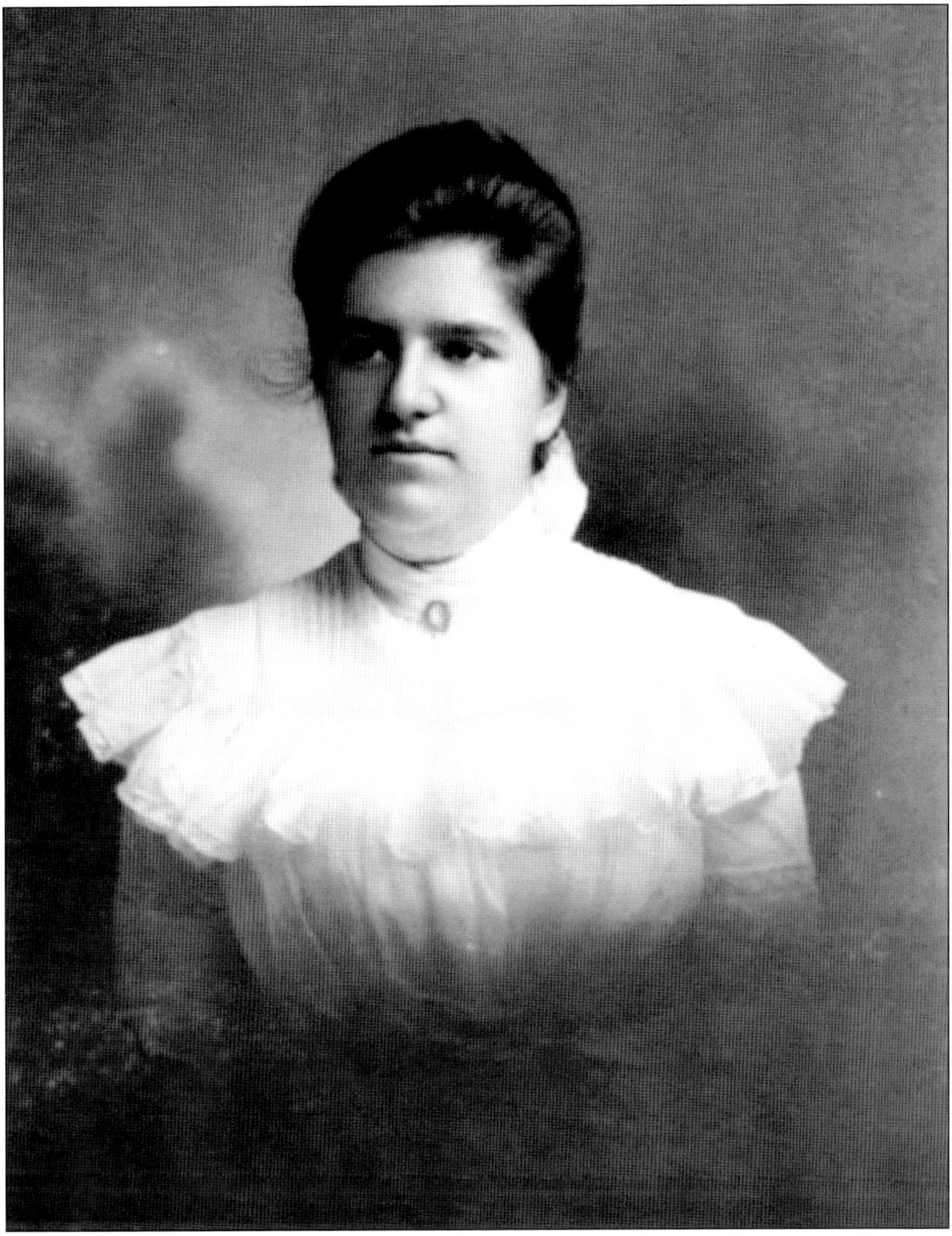

Isabella Mathieu duPont was born in Philadelphia in May 1883, the second-youngest of Lammot duPont and Mary Belin's 11 children. Although being born into the wealthy and influential duPont family afforded her certain privileges, unlike many of her cousins, Isabella was raised outside the cluster of family estates on the Brandywine. Instead, she spent her early years living at the now demolished Powelton House in Philadelphia while her father founded a dynamite manufacture. Sadly, Lammot duPont died in a factory explosion less than a year after his daughter's birth, and in 1892, the family moved closer to his family, settling at the St. Amour estate near Gibraltar. Little is known about Isabella's life at St. Amour, but photographs show an idyllic adolescence in which the family dog, Blot, features prominently. (Hagley.)

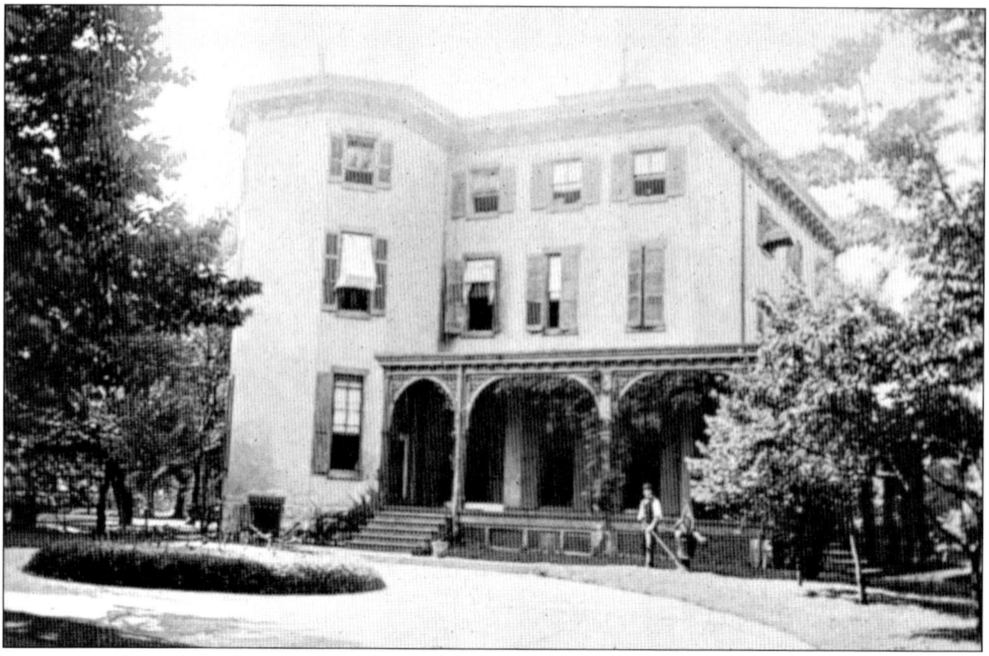

Isabella duPont Sharp grew up in this house on the corner of Thirty-fifth and Powelton Avenue in Philadelphia. While the area is now densely developed into townhomes and apartments and the home no longer stands, at the time she and her family lived there, it was an upper-class suburb dominated by newly built twin homes and large estates. Photographic evidence shows a bucolic childhood for Isabella and her siblings, including hammocks in the wooded yard, sleigh rides in the winter, and rabbits as pets. Here, Isabella can be seen with her younger sister, Margaretta, taking their dolls for a walk in matching stickwork carriages. (Both, Hagley.)

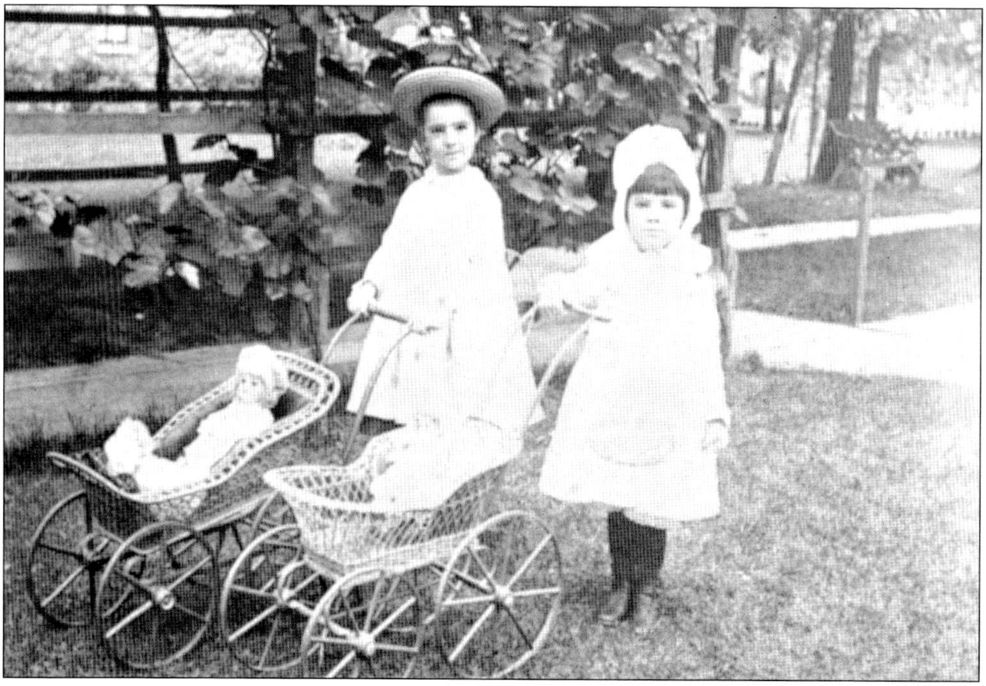

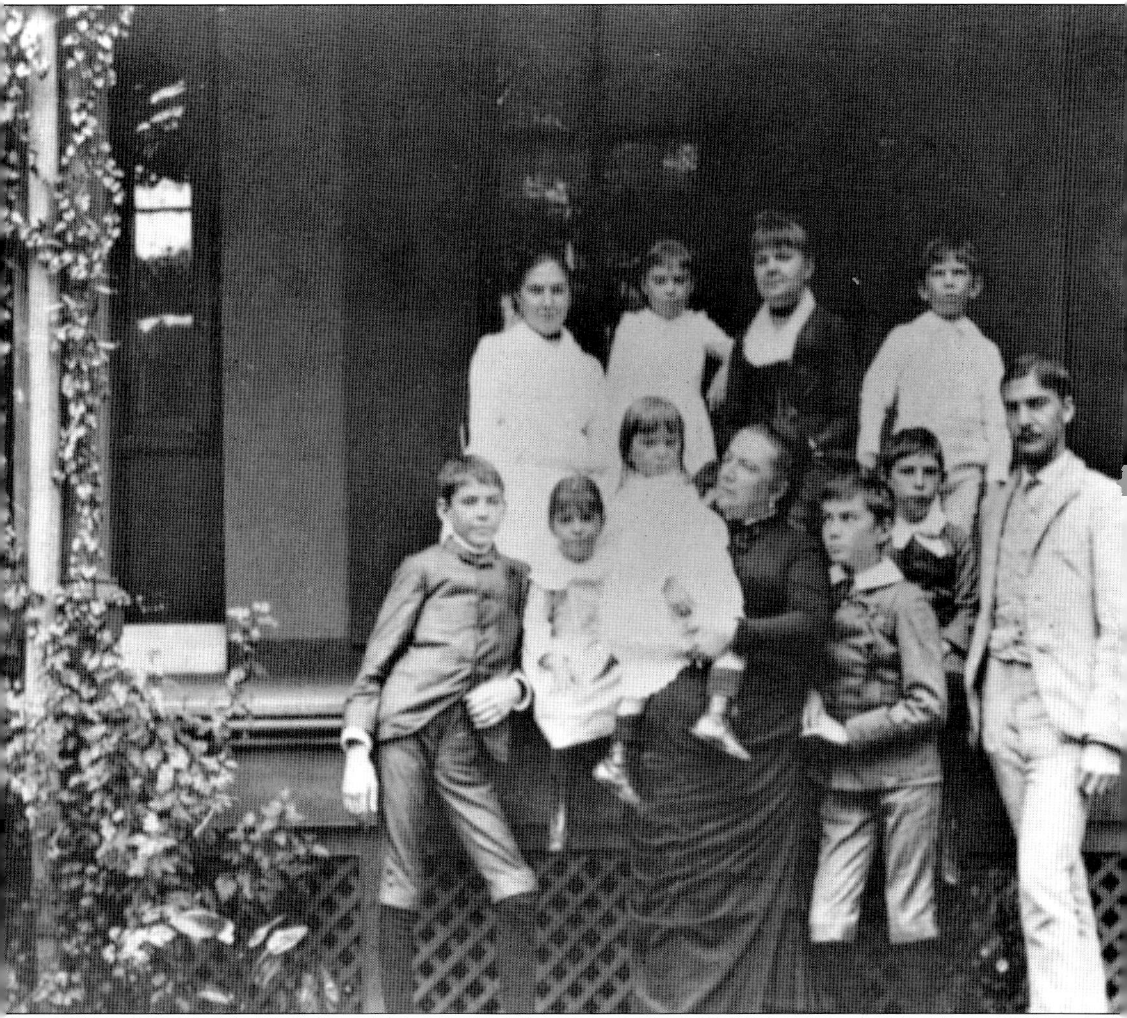

While little is known about Isabella specifically, it is likely that horticulture was highly valued within her family. Many of her siblings, seen here with their mother outside their Philadelphia home, developed large estate gardens in Delaware. Most notable of these is her eldest brother, Pierre S. duPont, who is seen at the far right of this image at the age of 16, who would later found Longwood Gardens, one of the country's preeminent horticultural institutions. Pictured to his left is Irénée, who at age 15 designed the home and some of the grounds for his mother's Wilmington estate, St. Amour. His home, Granogue, boasted elaborate gardens and greenhouses. Third from left in the back is Louisa d'Andelot duPont, whose son Lammot duPont Copeland, along with his wife, Pamela Cunningham Copeland, founded the Mt. Cuba Center. These estates are all clustered near Gibraltar in northern Delaware's Chateau Country. (Hagley.)

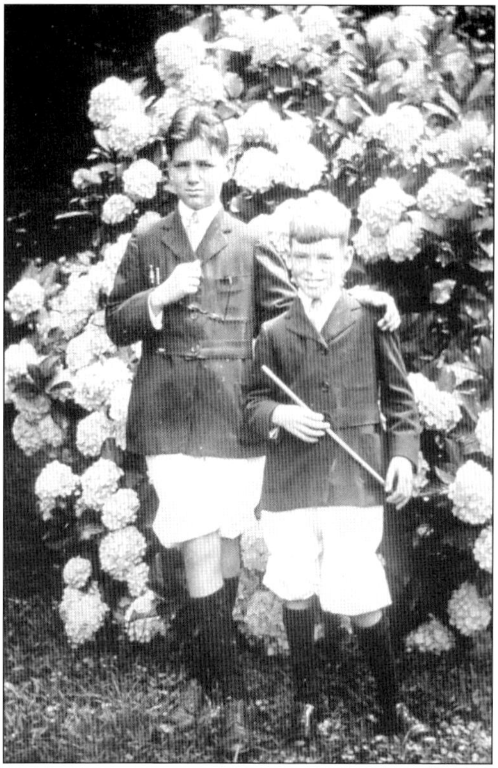

The Sharps had four children while living at Gibraltar. Seen in these images are the oldest three, (at left) Hugh Rodney Sharp Jr., born in 1909; and Bayard, born in 1913; and (below) Anne, born in 1915. These images are believed to have been taken on a family trip to Japan around 1920. The youngest child, John Mathieu, was only three or four at the time, so he was likely left with a nanny. Only H. Rodney and Bayard Sharp survived into adulthood, and both remained committed to the family's charitable causes as contributors to the University of Delaware and other organizations. (Both, Hagley.)

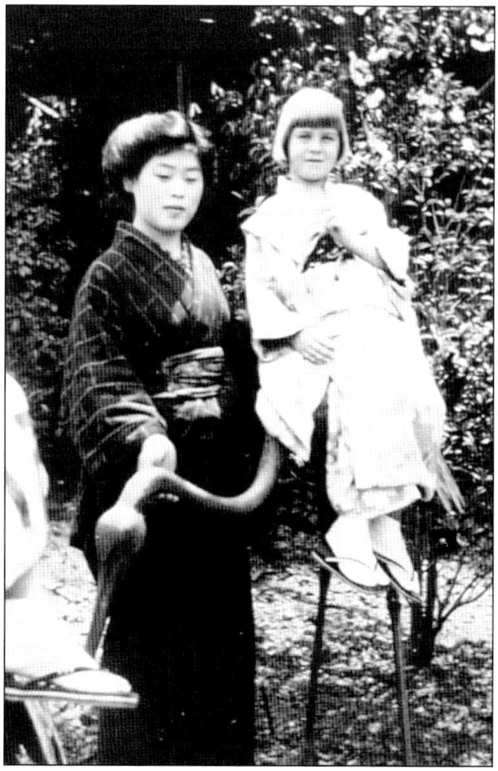

Three

The Gardens at Gibraltar

The Sharps retained Marian Cruger Coffin in 1916 to complete a garden for Gibraltar. This was Coffin's first of many formal commissions within the state of Delaware. She immediately began work on a series of four terraced garden rooms and the grand staircase, which was designed to connect the terraces and navigate the steep slope. The experience of enjoying the rooms starts on the rise at the house and follows to the south side of the estate. Coffin returned two years after completion of the rooms to design and install the teahouse, which terminates the bald cypress allée, as well as the winding driveway approach to the house. While the gardens at Gibraltar seem almost rigidly traditional, Coffin's design, like many of her works, cleverly warps the design conventions of the time. In a reverse of what was expected, the most formal garden areas, such as the flower garden and bald cypress allée, were located farthest from the house. More intimate spaces like the flagstone patio and evergreen terrace were located at the top of the house's precipice, providing views to the gardens below. The design was perfectly suited for the site and its inhabitants. Coffin worked with existing structures to provide service areas and designed around existing trees and statues purchased by the Sharps on their travels. Over time, while the area outside the garden walls changed, Coffin's garden has endured through periods of care and neglect. It remains one of the best remaining examples of Coffin's work.

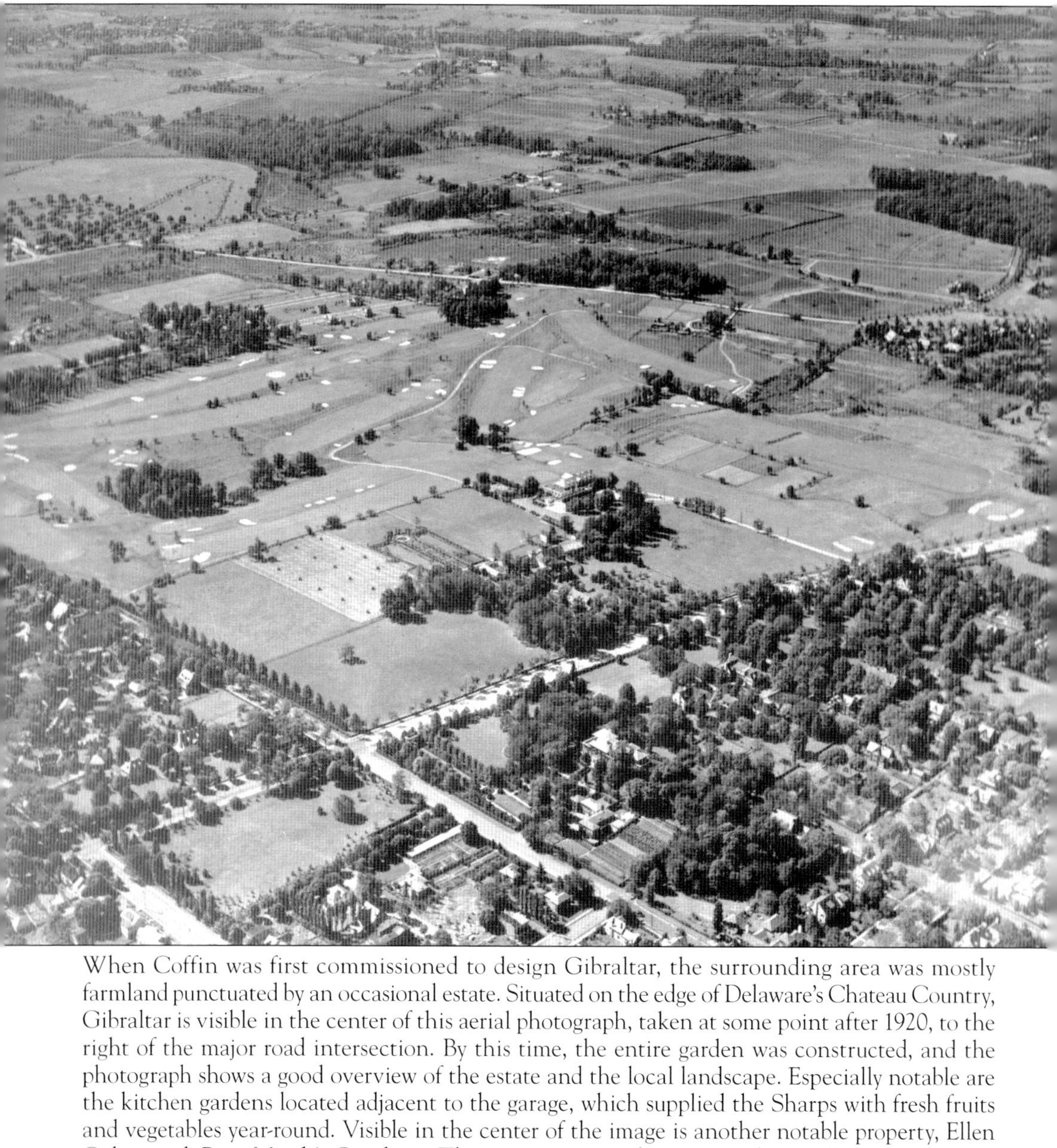

When Coffin was first commissioned to design Gibraltar, the surrounding area was mostly farmland punctuated by an occasional estate. Situated on the edge of Delaware's Chateau Country, Gibraltar is visible in the center of this aerial photograph, taken at some point after 1920, to the right of the major road intersection. By this time, the entire garden was constructed, and the photograph shows a good overview of the estate and the local landscape. Especially notable are the kitchen gardens located adjacent to the garage, which supplied the Sharps with fresh fruits and vegetables year-round. Visible in the center of the image is another notable property, Ellen Coleman duPont Meeds's Goodstay. The owner prior to duPont Meeds was illustrator Howard Pyle. Also visible nearby is the original clubhouse of the Wilmington Country Club. (Hagley.)

Marian Coffin's initial design for Gibraltar comprised three garden rooms, which one would pass by on a grand staircase leading from the home. The three rooms were arranged as terraces in order to retain the steep elevation change from the house to street level and all the associated viewsheds. Here, one can see Coffin's overall garden plan, as well as her first pass at the plantings for the flower garden, the lowermost and most formal garden room. Coffin's plantings, for the most part, were in formal beds bisected by flagstone pathways and lawn. The beds were color-curated, with central beds planted in blue, white, and yellow; southwest beds in pink, white, and yellow; and the northern end dominated by bronzes and oranges. While individual flowers would change from season to season, the color palettes remained standard. (Both, Sharp family.)

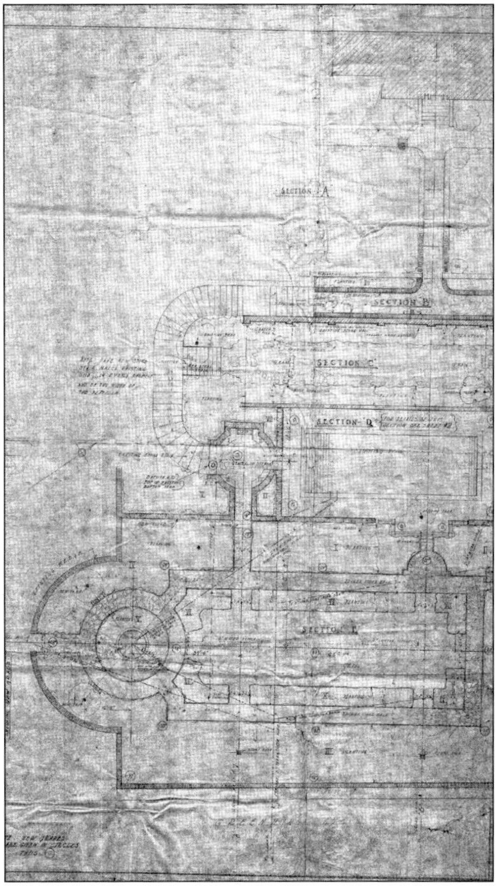

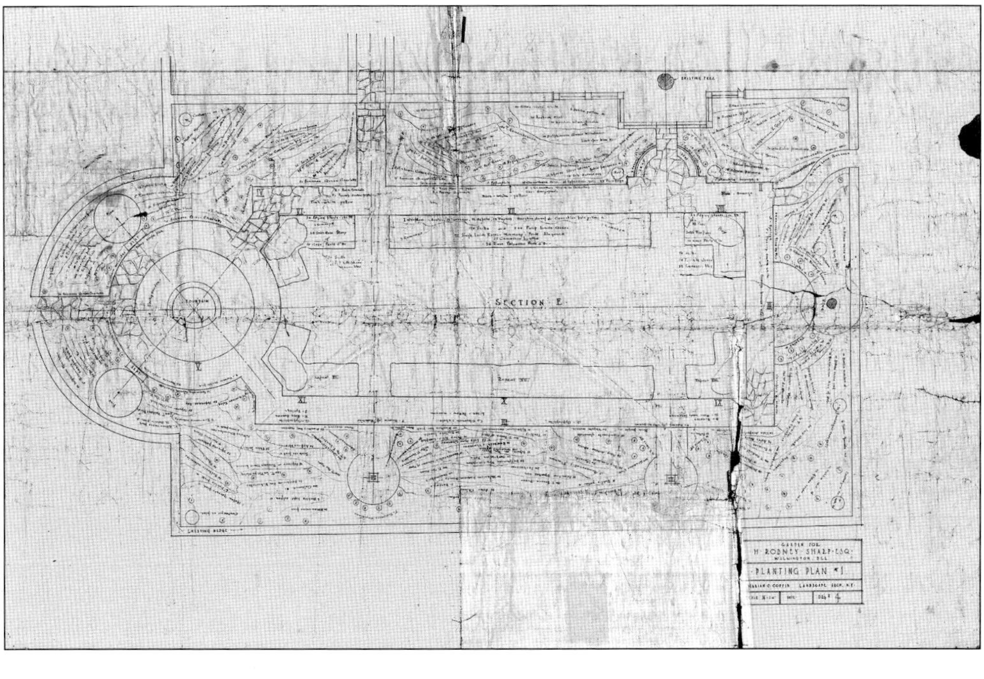

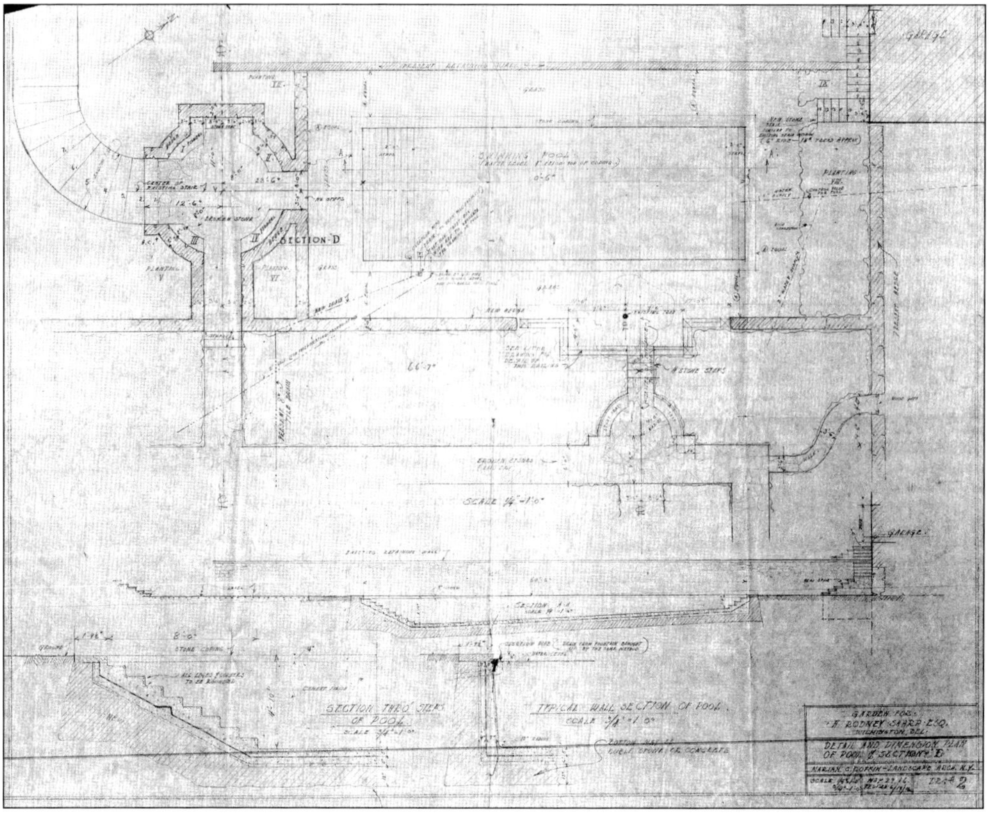

Marian Coffin was known as a "one-stop shop" in terms of landscape design. She did not just design the artistic design elements—plant palettes, statue placement, and water features—but the more functional aspects of landscape planning as well. Here, one can see two of her more technical designs for Gibraltar. Above is a plan for the stone walls, which surround the property and separate the garden rooms. The design is detailed, including materials, measurements, and where new walls should attach to the old. Below is the design for an area across Greenhill Avenue from the main estate, used by the Sharps as a kitchen garden and laundry yard. Looking at this design, which focuses mainly on the placement of sewage, it is almost hard to remember that they were made by the same person who made the garden plans. (Both, Sharp family.)

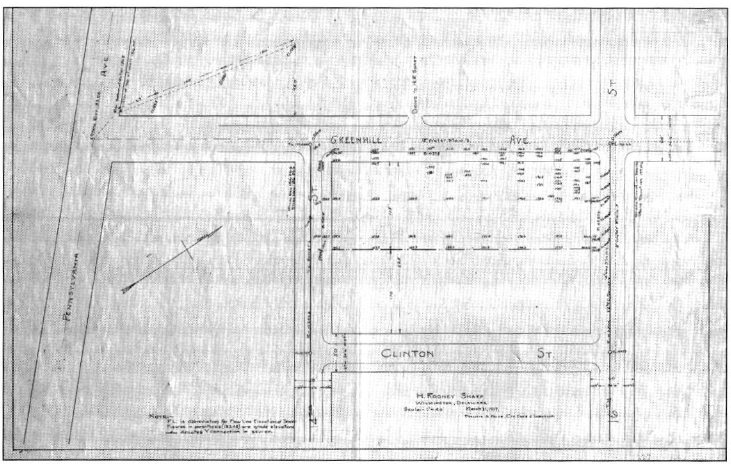

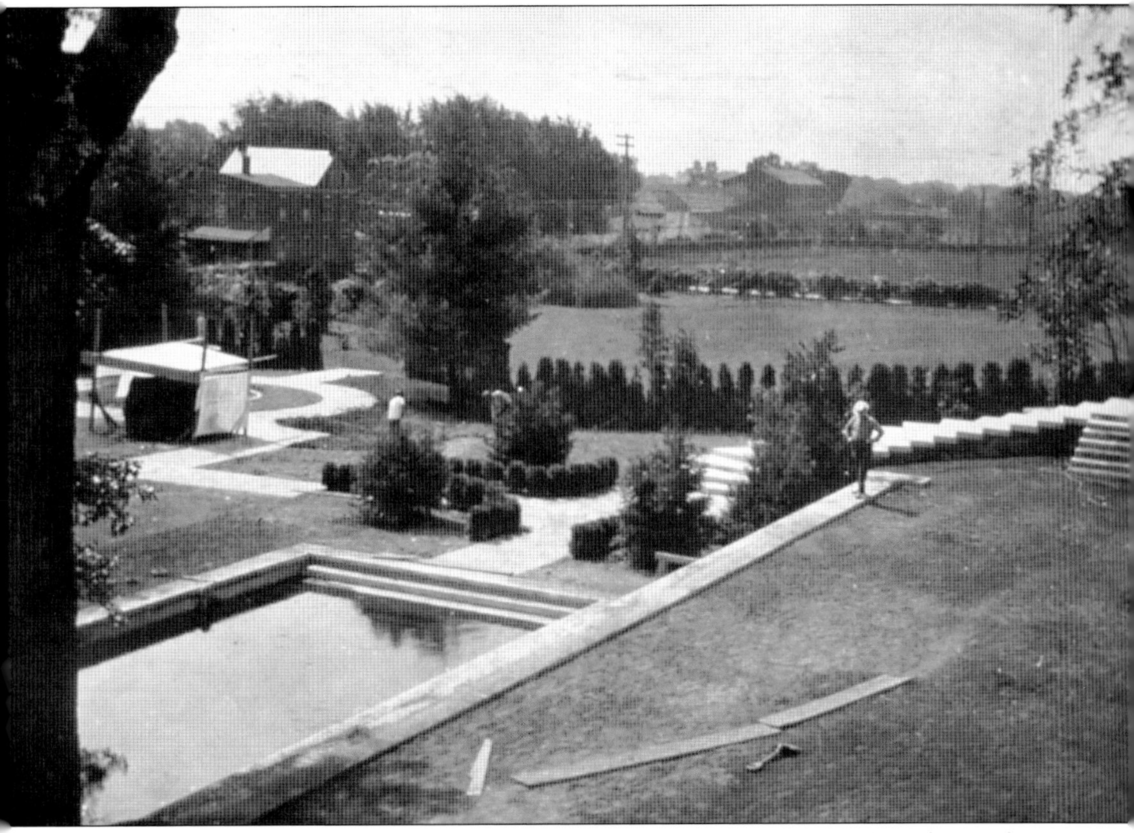

This image is the earliest known of Coffin's design at Gibraltar. It appears to have been taken from the corner of the flagstone terrace around 1917, when construction first began. Coffin usually recommended the more architectural foundation plantings be placed before any herbaceous plants, hence the presence of only boxwoods (*Buxus sempervirens*) and evergreen shrubs. The large boxwoods at each corner of the formal garden, seen on the left side of the image under a shade, were quite expensive due to their size. However, this would have been considered a necessary expense to achieve the desired garden effect within a quick time frame. The small boxwood hedges along pathways were likely temporary until the stone wall, that later separated the garden rooms, was built. This temporary placement was not unheard of in designs of the time as the construction of an estate was a multiyear effort. (PDI.)

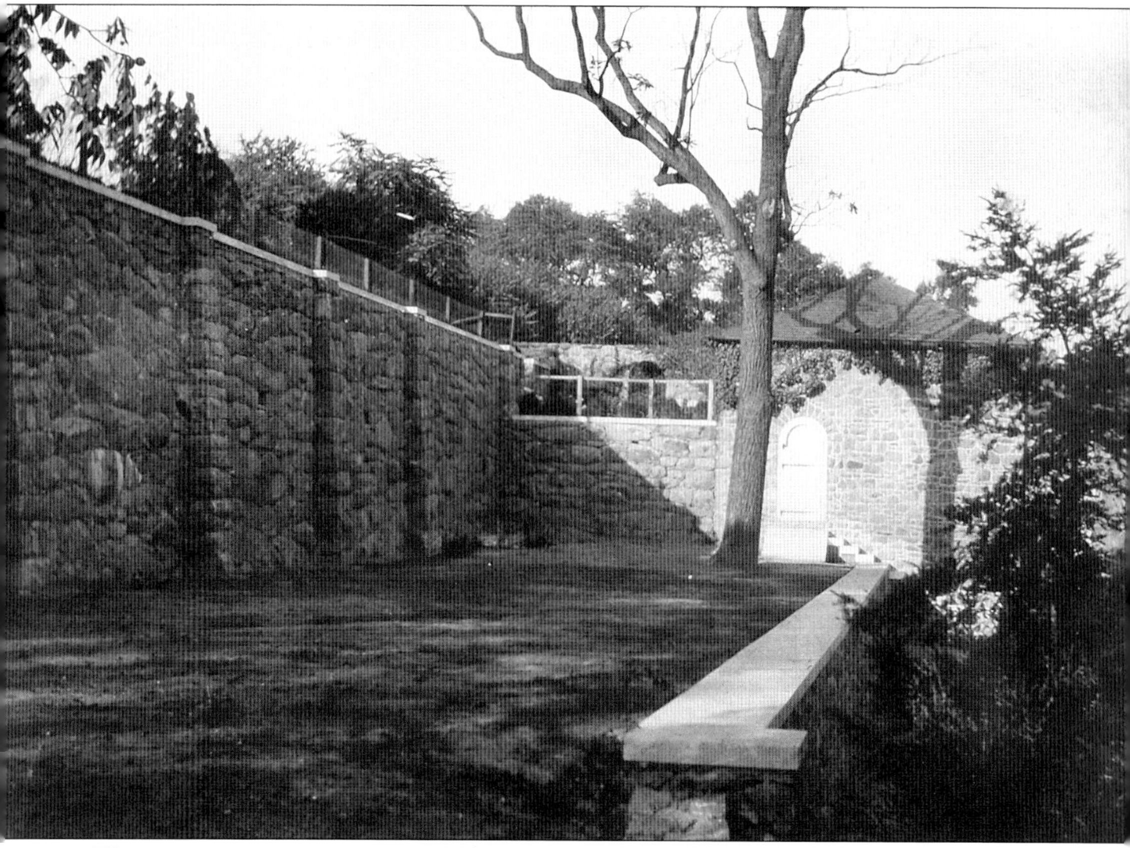

The evergreen terrace prior to any planting. Coffin often went to great lengths to incorporate large existing trees when designing her gardens, frequently designing around them. She firmly believed that trees were the most important part of a design, but an often neglected element, saying in her book that "too much emphasis has been laid by gardening books on the ephemeral value of color and color schemes, and too little on the enduring importance of sculptural form, which is given by trees and trees alone." Indeed, surviving letters advocated for shifting perennials and small shrubs around when needed, something one cannot do with trees. At Gibraltar, the layout of paths hints at the presence of standing trees at the time of the design, most notably this black walnut (*Juglans nigra*) on the evergreen terrace, and a large tree near the entrance to the pool, which she flanked with benches. (PDI.)

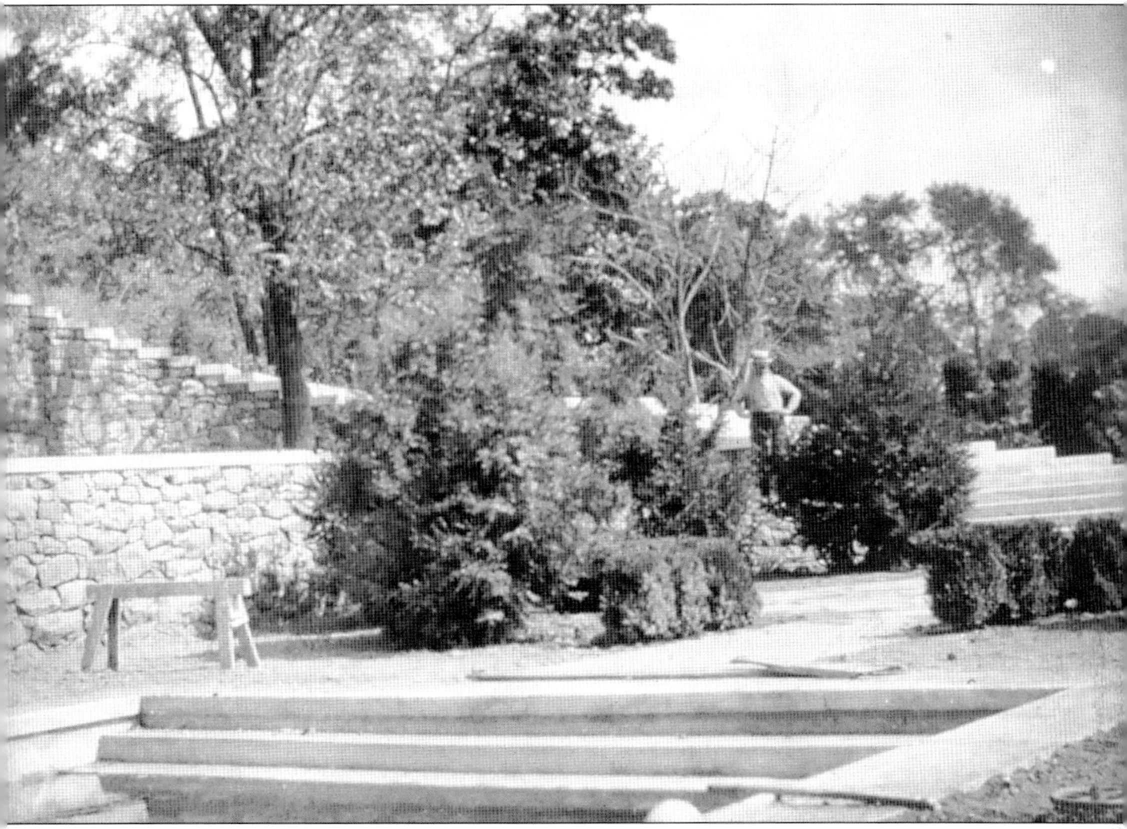

This early image of the garden, taken facing the grand staircase from the pool area, shows a view of the boxwoods, which Coffin used for screening and as architectural elements prior to the construction of the large stone walls, which was eventually constructed to separate the different garden rooms. The large, conical shrubs in the center foreground are also boxwoods, but these were larger specimen plants, designed for impact. Also visible is a large tree, documented in original plans as a magnolia, that likely dated to the Brincklé period. Later, wisteria (*Wisteria sinensis*), tulips, and climbing roses were added, and the roses were allowed to climb up the back wall. As the pool was meant for recreation, not as an area in which to promenade or reflect, the planting in this area was relatively simple. (PDI.)

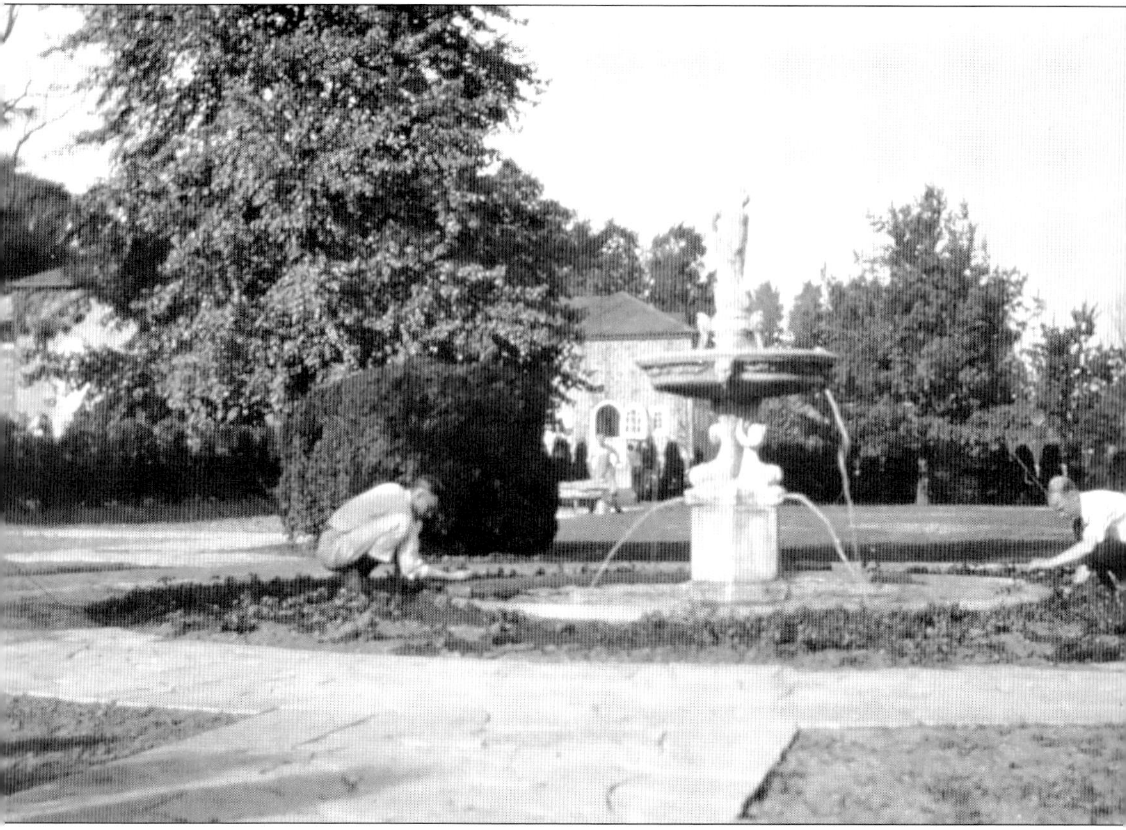

Pictured here are two members of the estate staff planting pachysandra (*Pachysandra terminalis*) and English ivy (*Hedera helix*) around the base of the "Bathing Venus" fountain early in the garden's construction. While the Sharps employed 12 gardeners at any given time to maintain their garden, finding the names of these persons proves difficult. Known gardeners include Joseph Galeski, a Polish immigrant who lived directly across Greenhill Avenue from Gibraltar and worked at the estate from at least 1920; Joseph Coleman, a Maryland native; a George; and J.C. Numbers, believed to be a supervisor. Coffin mentioned the names of the latter two, along with Galeski, in letters to the Sharps detailing the construction of the allée. While the rest of the workers' names or much about their lives are unknown, they left an indelible mark on the landscape. (Sharp family.)

When choosing plants for her garden designs, Coffin ordered from suppliers herself, before billing her clients and sending the orders to their estates. For Gibraltar, Coffin ordered heavily from two relatively local nurseries: Henry A. Dreer's in Riverton, New Jersey, and Farr Nursery Company in Wyomissing, just outside of Reading, Pennsylvania. It is likely she consulted the 1916 catalogs, the covers of which are presented here, while planning the landscape. Neither company is still in operation, but both had large impacts on the horticulture industry. Dreer's was one of the first nurseries in America, established in the early 1800s on the site of what is now Woodlands Cemetery in Philadelphia, and Farr's was one of the first to use full-color illustrations in their catalogs. (Both, US Department of Agriculture.)

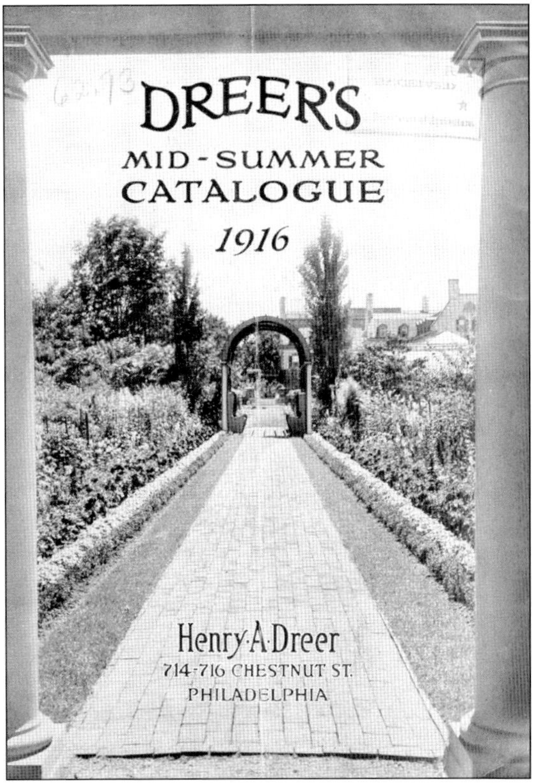

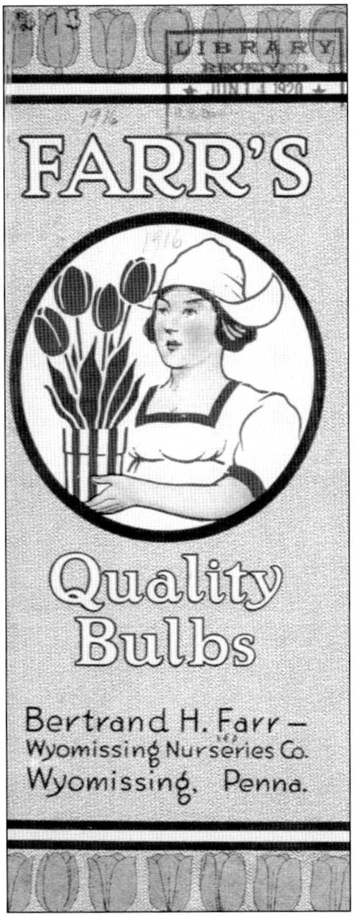

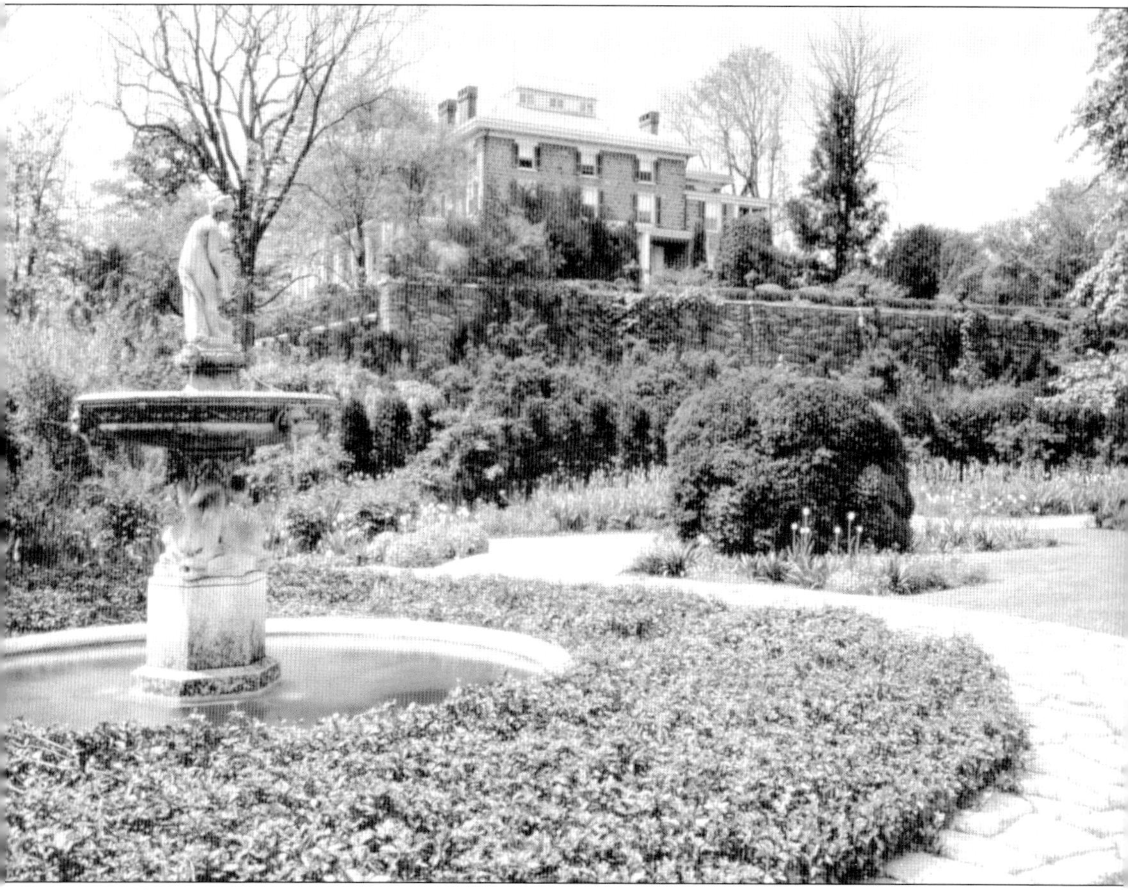

Coffin's Beaux-Arts training put a heavy emphasis on Italianate design. Despite being 10 years out of college at the time of this commission, the influence is highly present in her Gibraltar design. Terracing, a frequent component of Italianate design, was a stylistic way to navigate the steep coastal or mountainous terrain common in Italy's mainland, and it proved useful in Delaware's rocky Piedmont region. The view shown in this photograph from the lower terrace shows the house sitting high on a hill, with a series of garden rooms partially hidden in the space below. One of Coffin's biggest strengths was the near-seamless integration of the house and landscape through garden rooms. Gibraltar is an outstanding example of this practice in which the garden visitor seamlessly moves from room to room upon the terraces easily as if navigating the inside of a building. (PDI.)

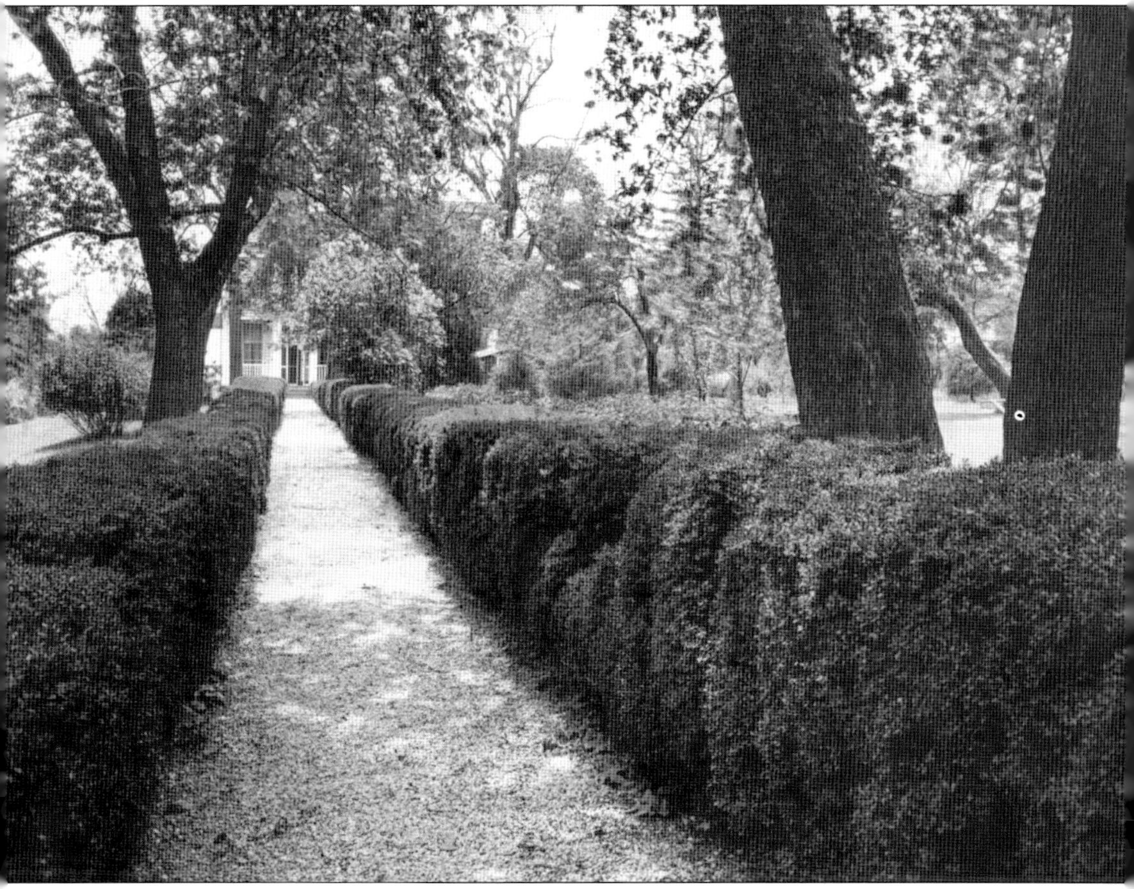

The upper gardens at Gibraltar comprise the area surrounding the house. These gardens are more restrained than those farther down the grand staircase. Indeed, the fact that this 1922 image is labeled "old box hedge" lends credence to the theory that this area dates to the Samuel Brincklé period of the home, during which time the highly curated but informal "gardenesque" style pioneered by Andrew Jackson Downing was in fashion. The hedge seems to match one present in descriptions by Julia and Gertrude Brincklé, the final occupants of the house before the Sharps. Coffin was a fan of using existing infrastructure and plantings if it aligned with her and her clients' needs. Here, the formality of the hedges is offset by the pea gravel of the path and accentuated by what appear to be scarlet hawthorne (*Crataegus coccinea*) and ornamental cherry trees (*Prunus sp.*). As this was a side entrance out of view from the main garden, overt decoration was not required. (Hagley.)

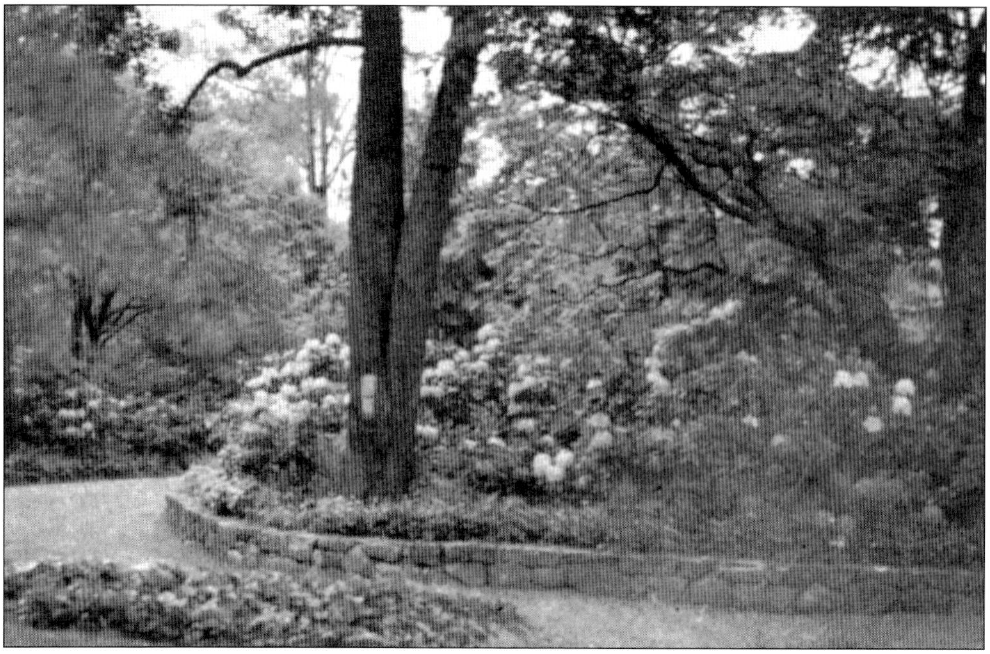

In a way, the design Coffin conceived of for the gardens at Gibraltar is backward. A common design theory in the 1920s called for placing the most formal garden areas closest to the house. Yet, Coffin chose to allow a naturalistic style for this area to remain. Her final design employed a winding drive leading to the house, accented by copses of rhododendrons and woodland trees, as seen here. When viewed in conjunction with the formality of the lower gardens, this winding woodland area showcases Coffin's breadth and talent and her diverse abilities, which pays homage to her client's existing site conditions. (Both, Hagley.)

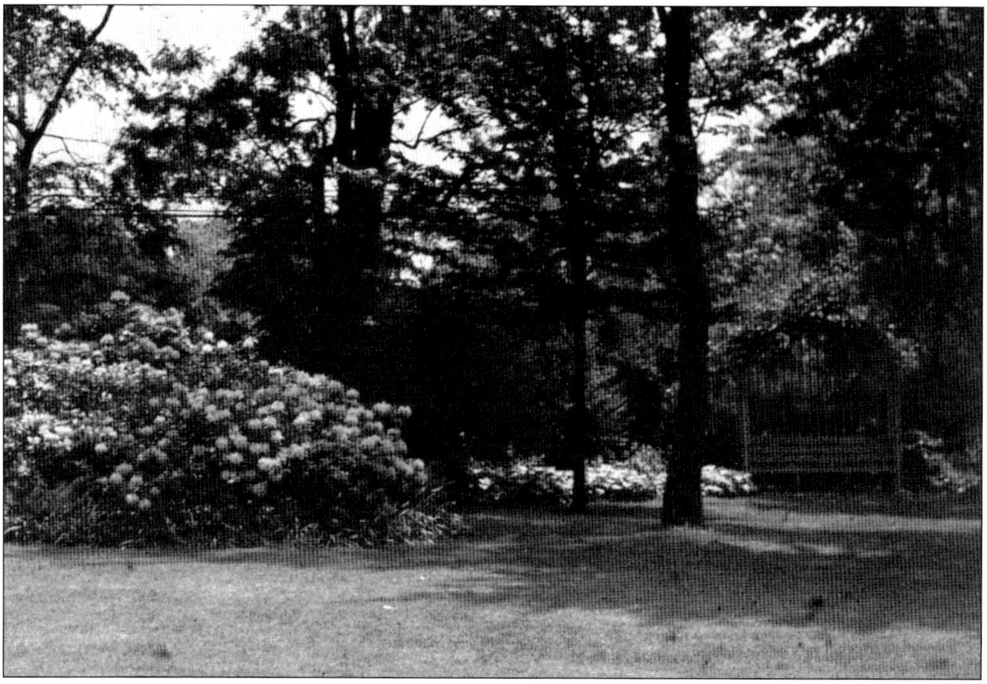

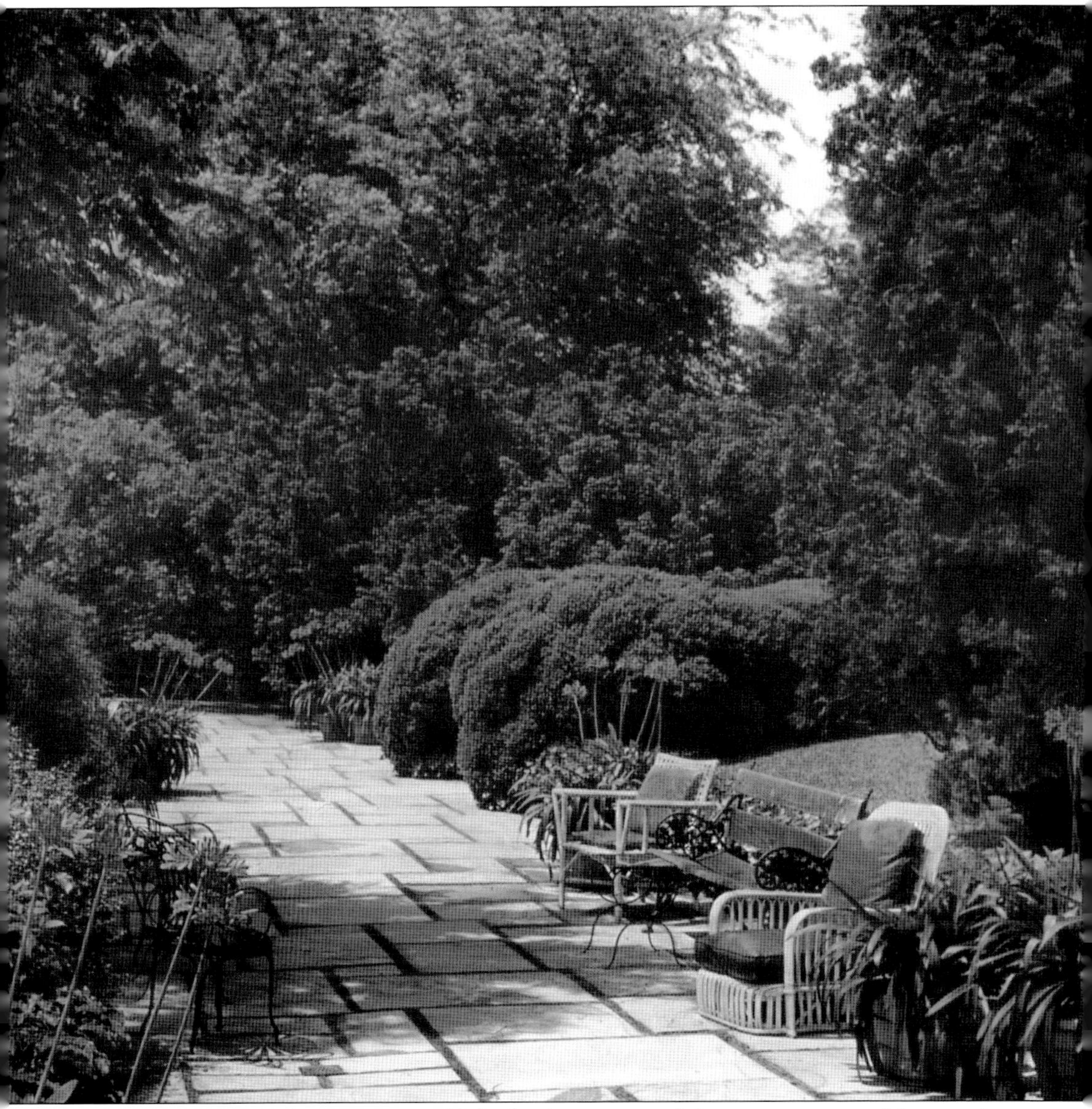

The flagstone terrace is the uppermost of Gibraltar's terraces and the starting point of the grand staircase. It is adjacent to the mansion and was located down a short path lined with tall, bulbous boxwoods. Alternatively, the terrace was accessed via a small path leading from the service and greenhouse area, likely used only by the gardeners and staff. The family and their visitors could relax on the terrace and gaze through an ornate iron railing to peer down into the rest of the garden and the city beyond. Because the area primarily provided prospect, it was relatively simple in design, as seen in the above image. The only decor gracing the marble flagging were simple cane or iron chairs, pots of lily of the Nile (*Agapanthus*), and, for a time, a stone eagle statue on either end. Later, the eagle statues were moved to the allée gateposts. (Smithsonian Archive of American Gardens.)

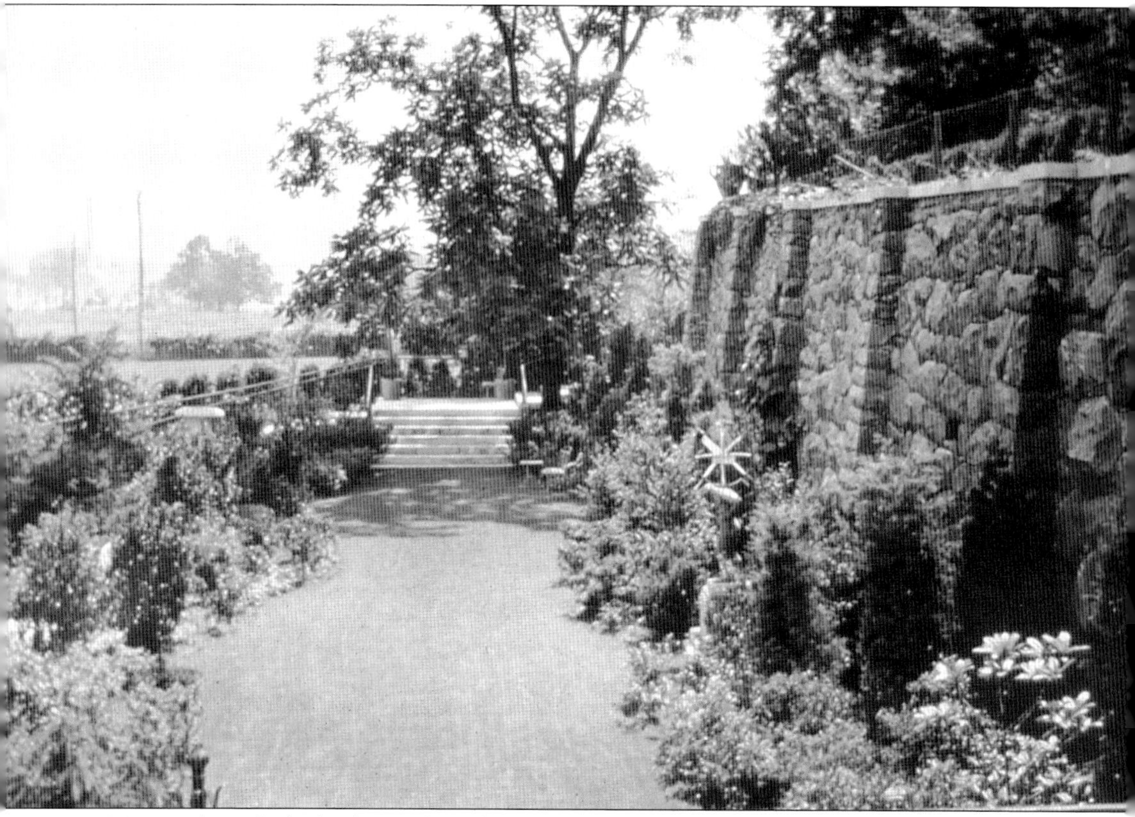

Moving through the landscape from the uppermost flagstone terrace, visitors entered the evergreen terrace by descending to the midpoint of the grand staircase. This garden room is an example of what Coffin called a "green garden," a stylized garden of evergreen shrubs. Coffin describes green gardens as being "equally successful in sunlight or in shadow; in a formal design or in an informal one; near the house or far from it." At Gibraltar, this terrace is a transitional space between the relative informality of the area adjacent to the house and the formal areas (see plan below). Enjoyed year-round, the plantings were mostly members of the *Ericaceae* family, including rhododendrons, laurels, and heaths, accented with ferns. Southern magnolia (*Magnolia grandiflora*) and a black walnut tree provide structure. (PDI.)

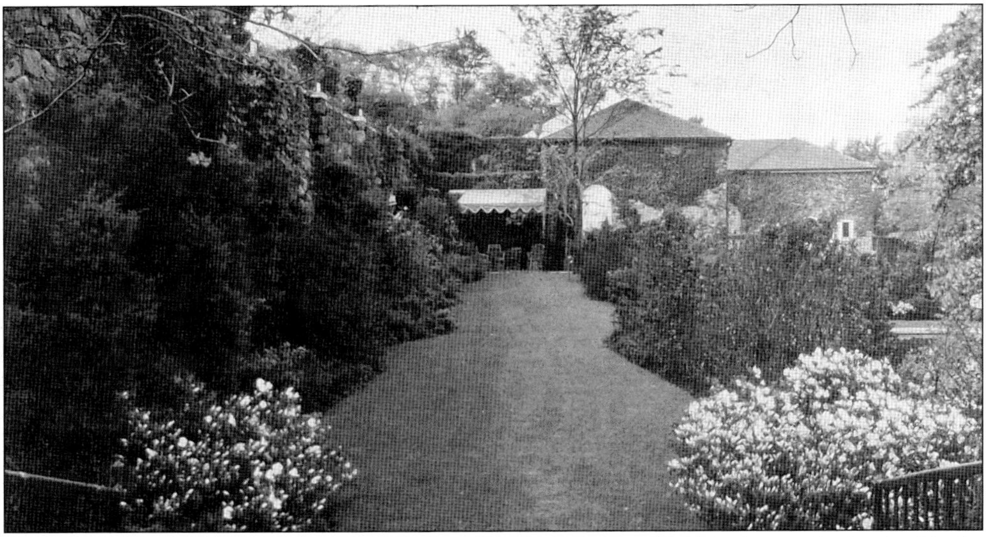

Coffin was conscious of making her gardens, though ornate and highly designed, also livable for her clients. Hence, the awning at the end of the evergreen terrace seen above and the vestibule shown on the plan below at the entrance to the pool, where the Sharps and their guests could relax. From these tucked-away corners of the garden, the family could serve refreshments while guests looked out to enjoy the lush plantings or warmed up after a swim in the pool. The above image, taken from the grand staircase, also shows the unusual design of the planting beds on the terrace, which included uneven bed lines likely meant as a stylized version of naturalism, as in a perfectly groomed woodland. As informal as they may look, keeping the ornamental plants looking seemingly wild, and the curved path perfectly imperfect would have required frequent trimming, mowing, and shaping by the Sharps' landscaping staff. (Above, PDI; below, Sharp family.)

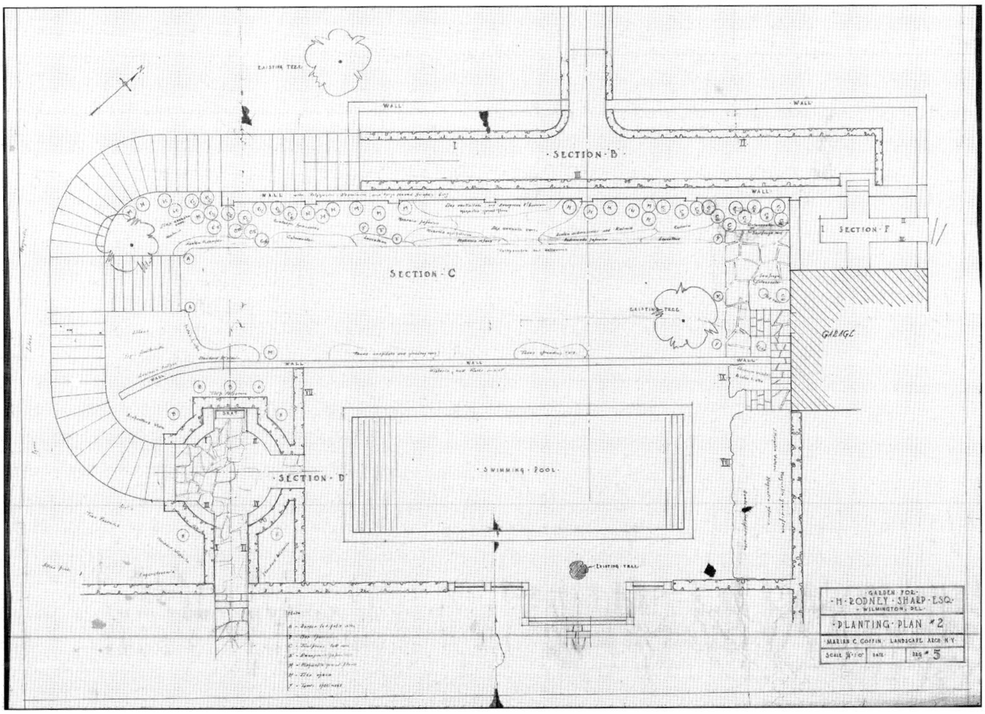

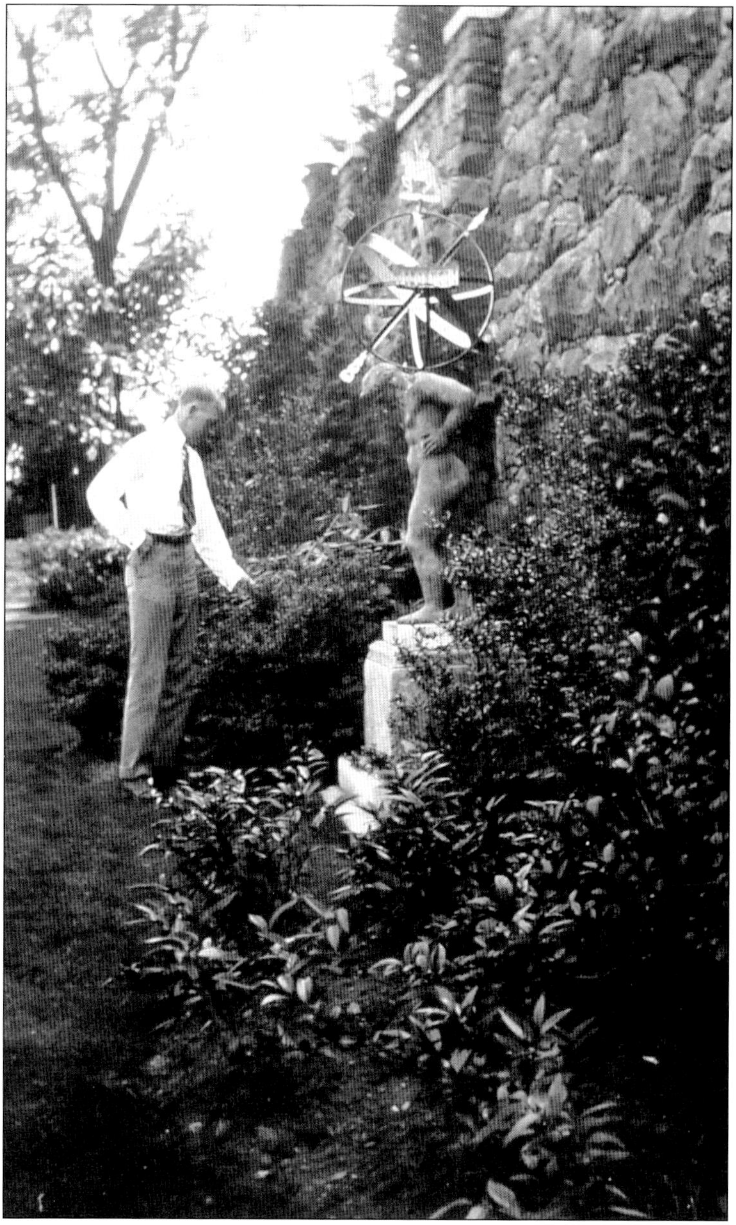

The main decorative element, and one of the only formal features on the evergreen terrace, was this statue of Atlas. A Titan in Greek mythology, Atlas was punished following a great battle with the Greek gods to forever hold up the universe. At Gibraltar, however, he was simply tasked with holding up an armillary sphere containing a sundial. The man in this image is thought to be a member of the Sharp family, possibly Hugh Rodney Sharp, who himself took a very hands-on approach to garden ornament. Atlas was likely purchased by the Sharps at some point in the 1910s from an English manufacturer of iron ornament, H. Crowther, which is still in business today, flanking it with two stone urns decorated with carvings of lion heads. Atlas was damaged by a falling tree in 1995, at which time the statue's body was disconnected from its feet, which remained on the pedestal. All parts of the sculpture are now lost, and Mercury, another member of the Greek pantheon, stands in its place (PDI.)

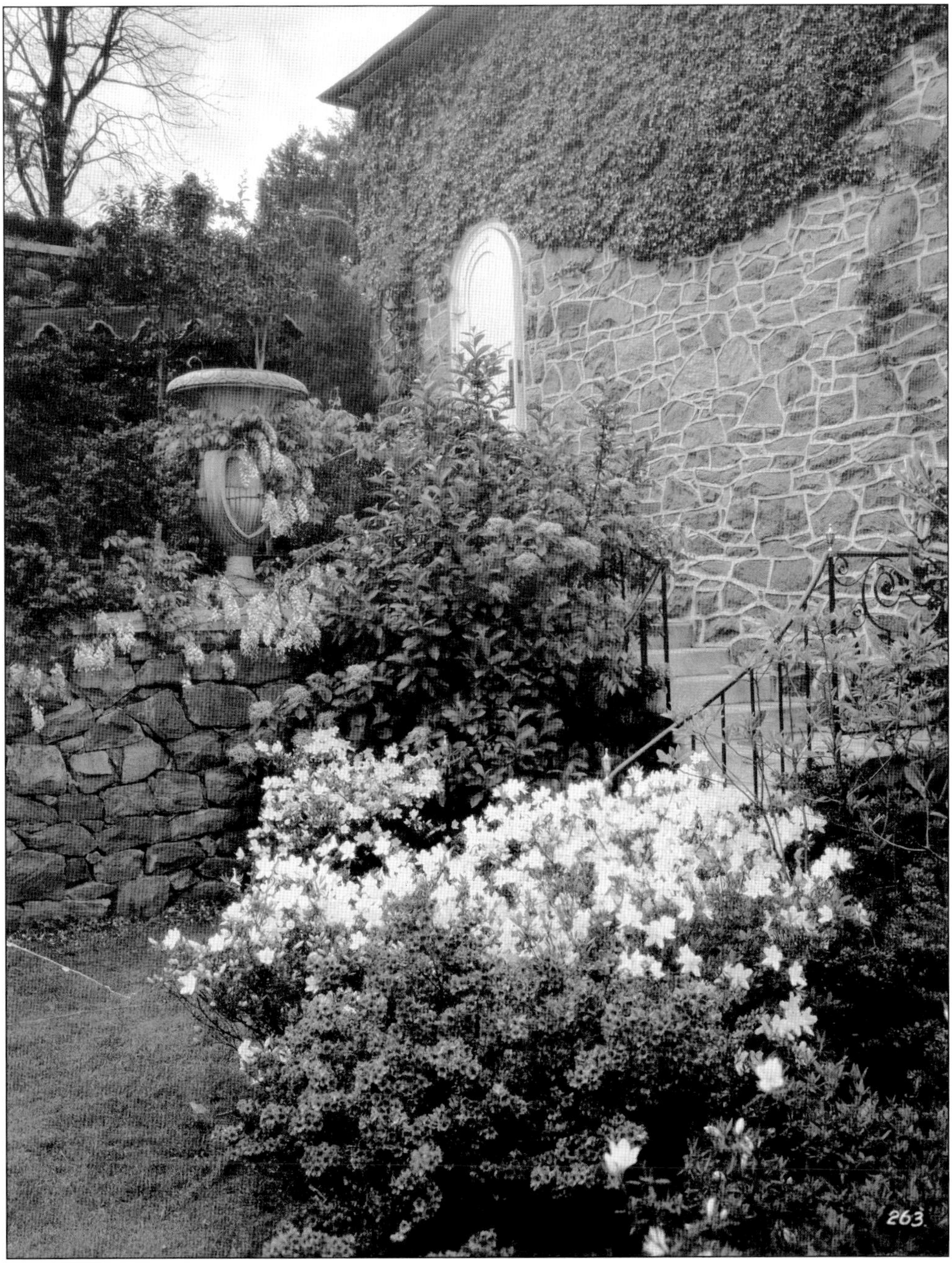

Coffin was proud of her design at Gibraltar, and this image of the gardens became the frontispiece for her book *Trees and Shrubs for Landscape Effects*, published over 20 years after she finished her work at Gibraltar. She chose to highlight a tucked-away corner of the garden—the stairway to the bathhouse. Despite this space's small footprint, the design is still magical and carefully composed, with a classical urn accented by viburnum, azaleas, and wisteria. The bathhouse began its existence as a Brincklé-era carriage barn, but it was converted by the Sharps when the larger service structure and greenhouse were built. Of note is the English ivy climbing above the door. Coffin was no fan of ivy climbing up walls but conceded to the Sharps' tastes. (Winterthur.)

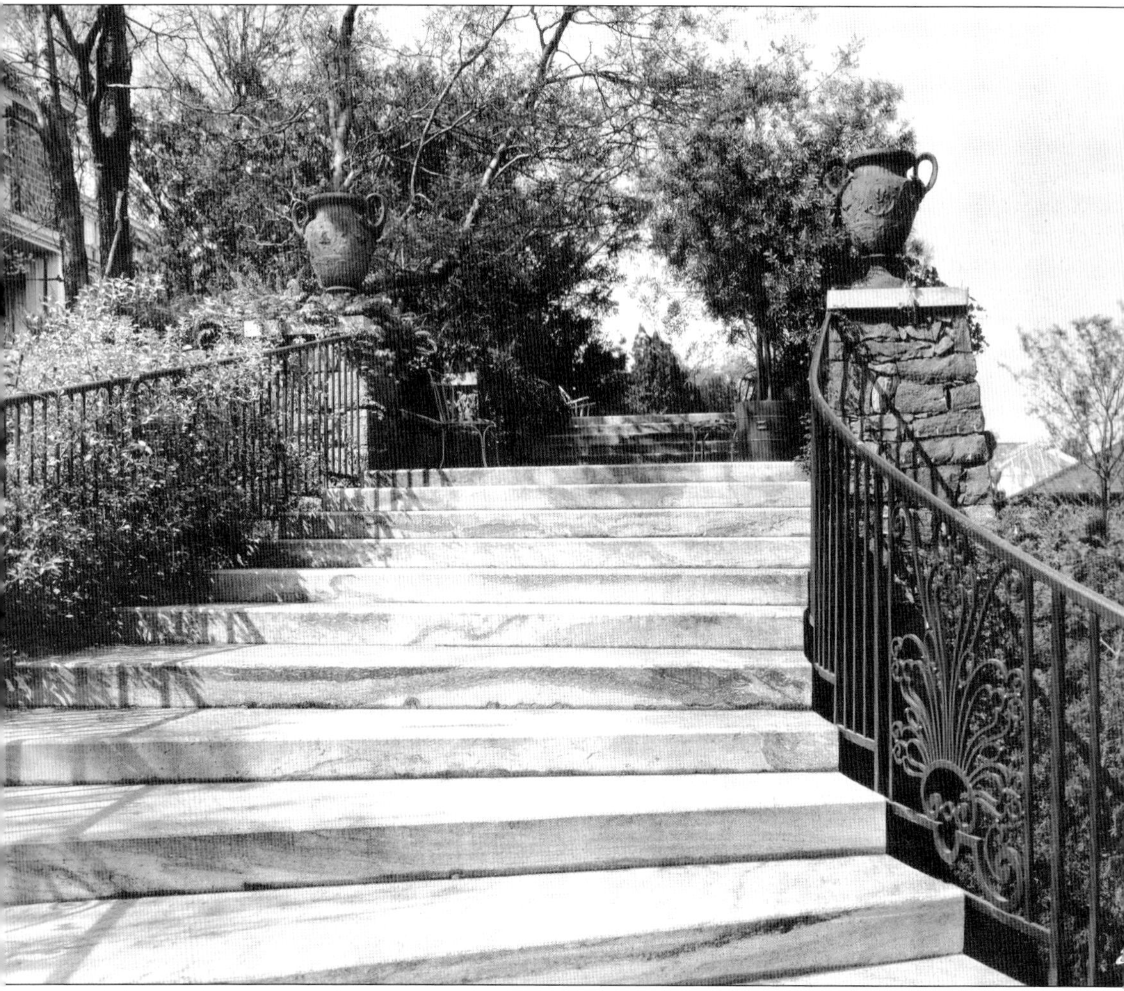

The grand staircase is the centerpiece of Gibraltar's garden. An obvious focal point, the staircase's marble construction included relatively austere iron railings. Overall, this feature would have been wildly expensive to install, and although no cost estimate survives, it would have dwarfed the cost of the marble flagging for pathways, which cost $820—an exorbitant sum in 1916. However, the grand staircase was not just decorative, as it both linked each terrace and gracefully navigated the steep slope that gave the estate its name. Coffin likely took inspiration for the stairs, as well as the terraces it linked together, from Italy, where terracing was used to negotiate the steep, rocky slopes of estates around the Apennine Mountains. She may have learned this technique on a trip she took to Italy with Henry Francis duPont shortly after finishing her course of study at MIT. (PDI.)

In her designs, Coffin was conscious of incorporating prescribed viewpoints, places from which the garden was meant to be viewed, and often suggested seating placement based on these viewpoints. Rarely would she directly build seating into significant design elements, as seen in one instance at Gibraltar. This stone bench, built into a landing near the top of the grand staircase, provides a vantage point to see all the garden rooms of the original design. The decorative urns were made of cast lead and are decorated with classical imagery, including figural handles meant to look like snakes. They were frequently moved around the garden. (Right, Winterthur; below, Hagley.)

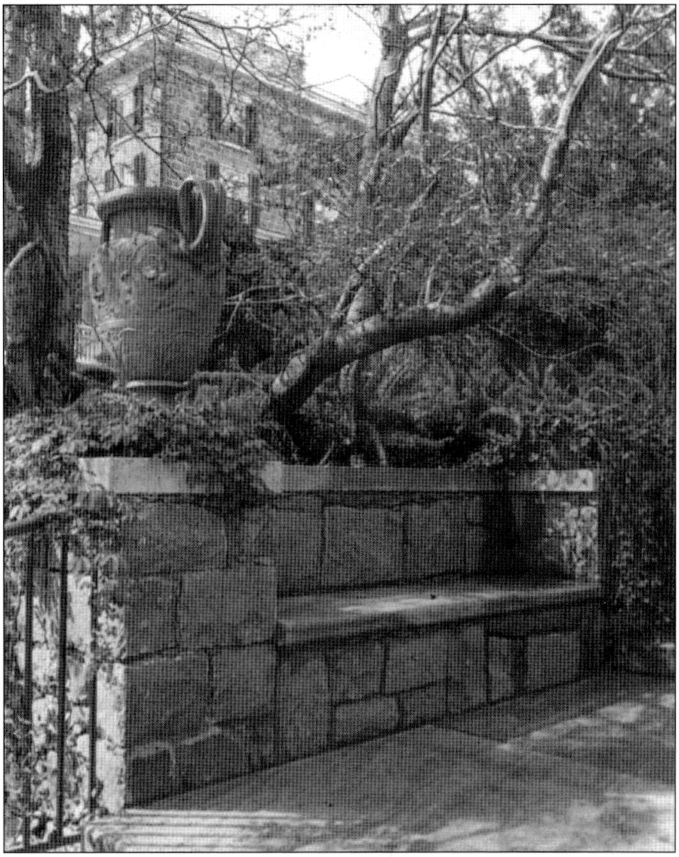

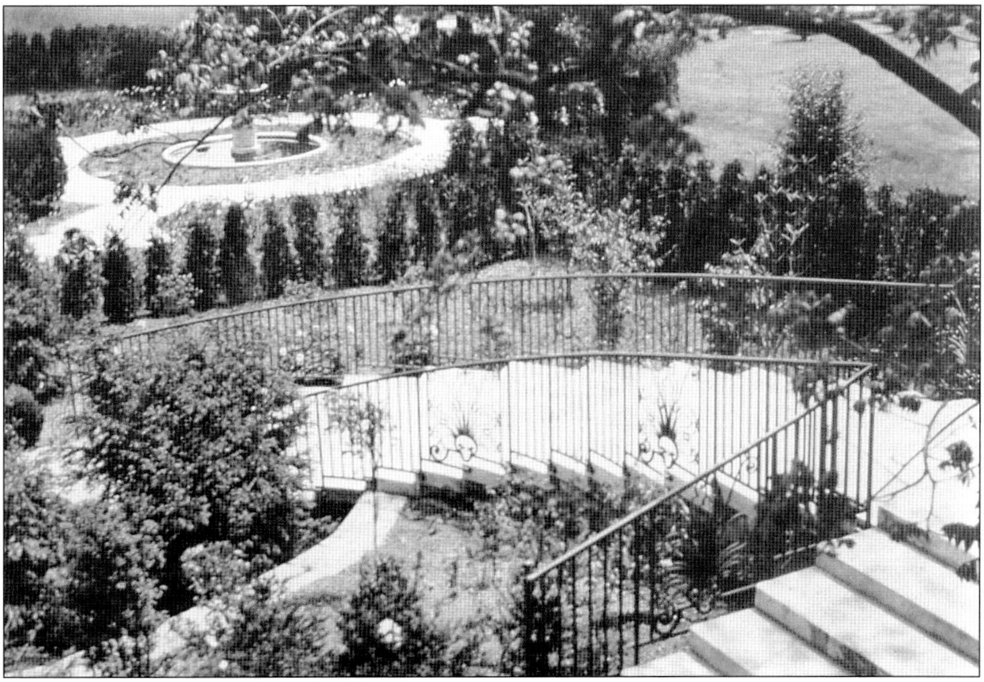

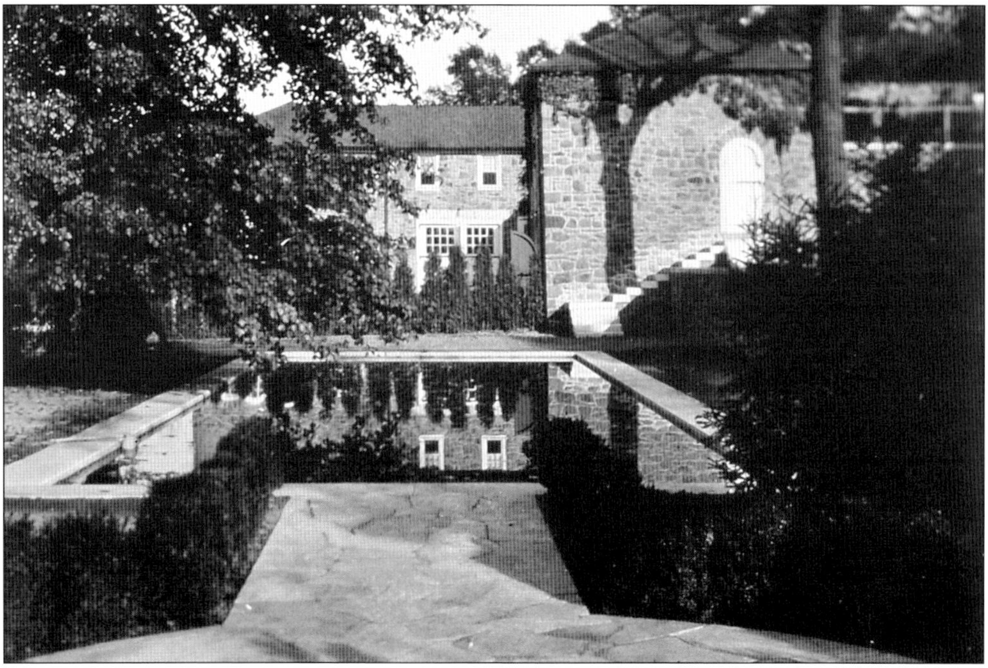

At the bottom of the grand staircase, a 40-by-60 foot pool served as both a swimming pool—entered by a set of inlaid stairs—and a reflecting pool. The planting in this area was relatively sparse, owing to the active nature of the space. An existing maple tree shaded the space, and Coffin added white azaleas and magnolias near the bounding wall. The entire area was lined with hedged boxwoods. Lily of the Nile was kept in pots near the pool for seasonal color. Below, a small ornament is seen at the pool adding a stream of water. This feature was later replaced by a sculpture consisting of two cherubs and a dolphin that was restored in 1999 and remains today. (Both, PDI.)

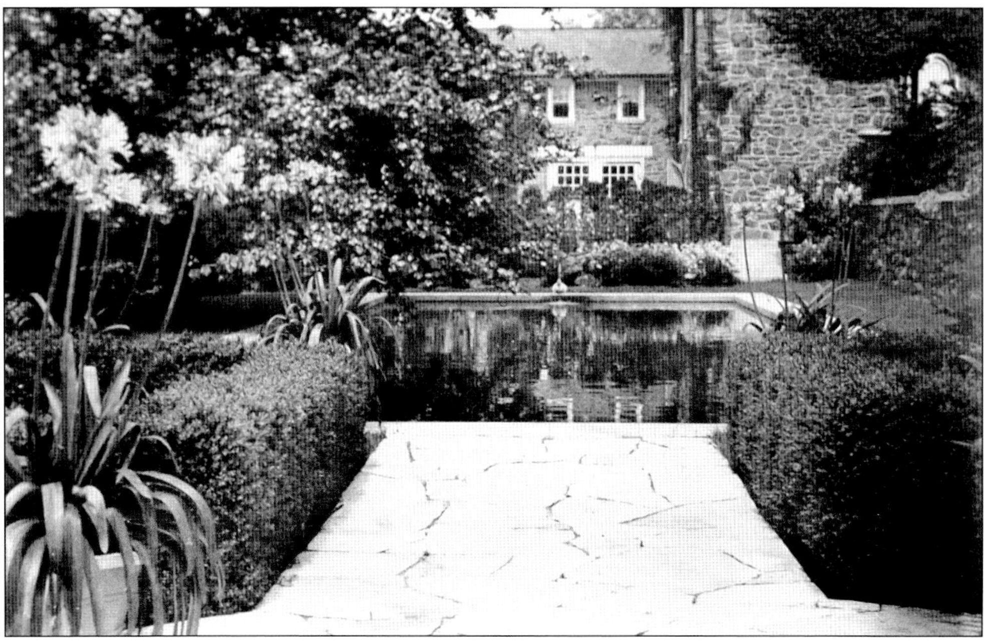

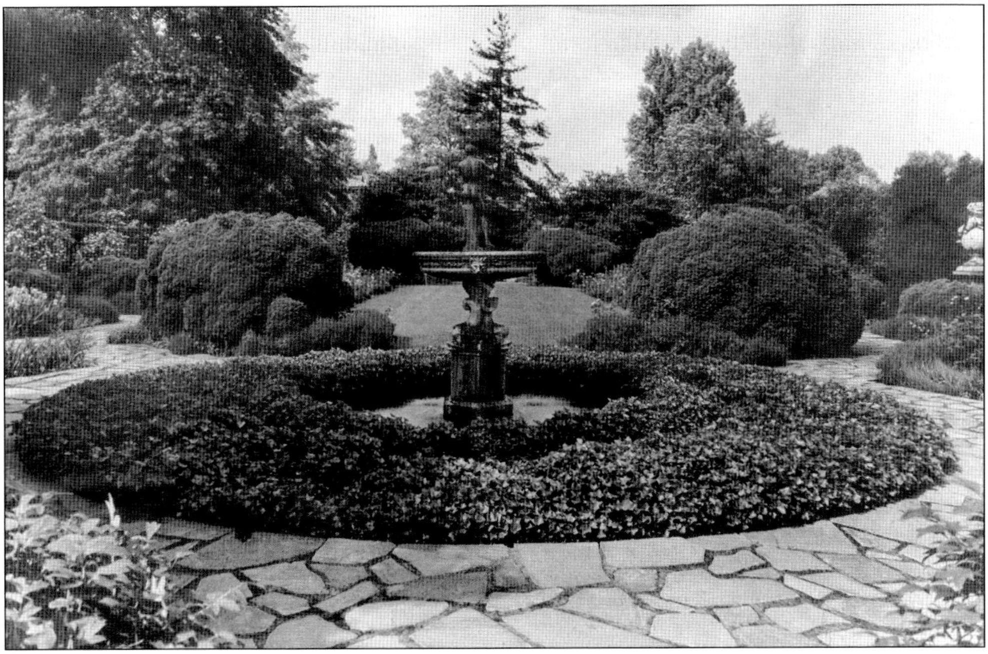

The centerpiece of the flower garden is the two-tied marble fountain. While it initially featured a statue of Bathing Venus on the top tier and three dolphins on the bottom, it appears at some point before the 1960s the Venus was damaged and replaced by the cast-lead statue of Mercury, which would later move to the evergreen terrace. (Winterthur.)

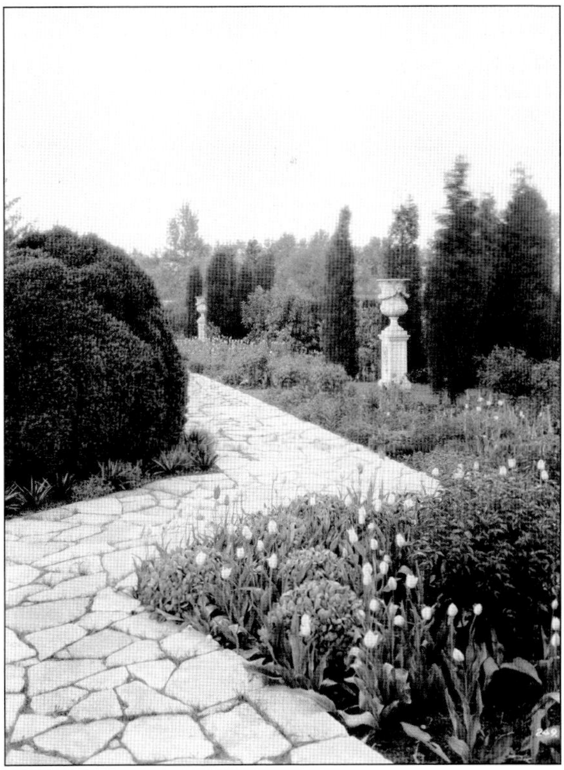

The statue of Mercury was not the only statue at Gibraltar to move around. These cast-stone lion mask urns had a home in the flower garden where they echoed lion motifs on the focal semi-circular bench. Later they were moved to the evergreen terrace, their niches replaced by a pair of stone putti (representations of chubby infants popularized during the Renaissance, often meant to represent cupid or cherubs). (Winterthur.)

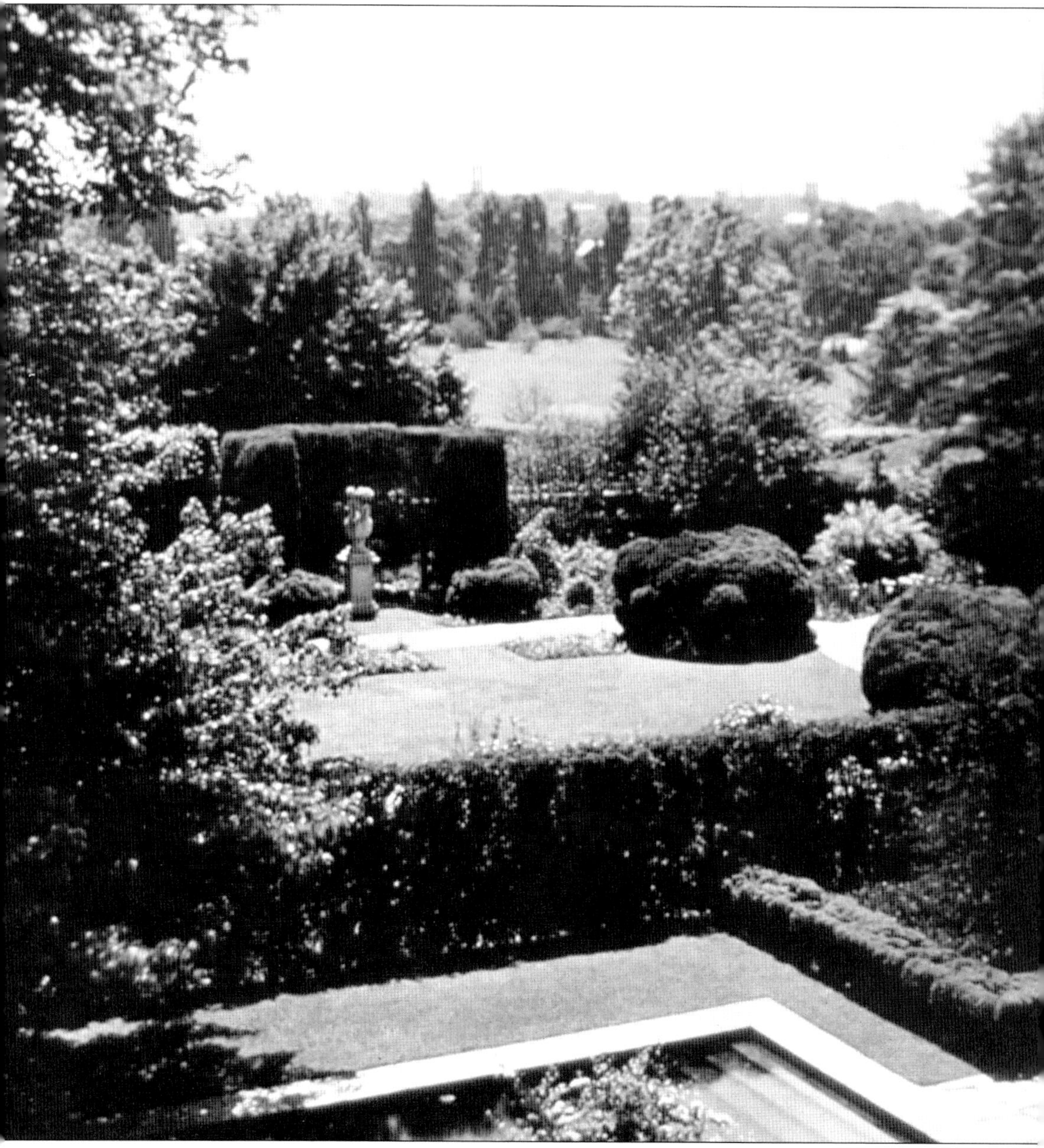

This image shows the garden from the evergreen terrace, shortly after the lion mask urns were replaced by stone putti. From this angle, one can see the easternmost putto, who holds a basket of nondescript flowers and fruits. This cherub is likely representing spring, while its partner, who holds roses in his basket, represents summer. Also visible within this viewshed is the columnar eastern red cedar (*Juniperus virginiana*), which Coffin used to form niches to frame the statuary. As seen in her design at Clayton (Chapter 1), one of Coffin's more playful design trademarks is her use of woody plants to echo forms of Italianate architecture. In this case, the hedge has the added benefit of acting as an extension of the stone wall surrounding the estate, shielding anyone in the street-level flower garden from those on the surrounding lot. (PDI.)

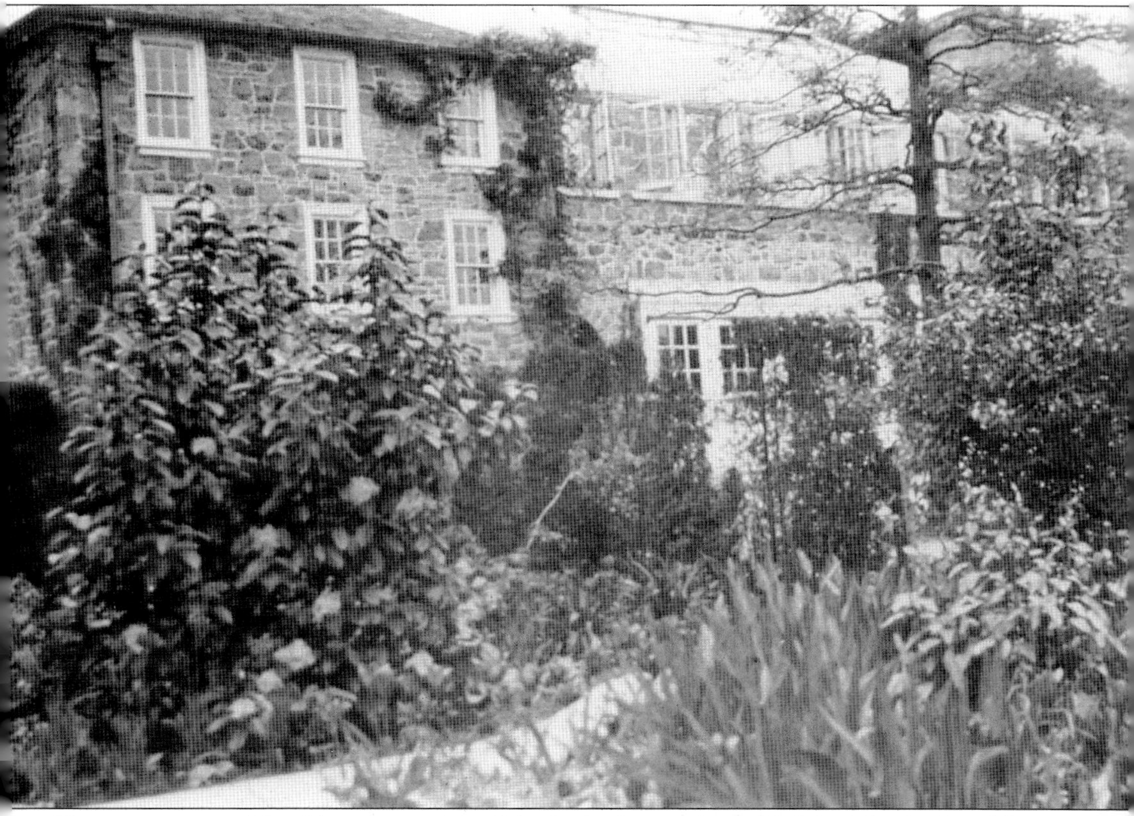

The garage is one of the oldest structures on Gibraltar's property. It was likely built by the Brincklés early during their tenure at the property, during which time they used it as a barn for their carriages and horses. Sharp enlarged this building, adding a two-story "arm" shown to the right in this photograph, which included a chauffeur's apartment and a greenhouse. The taller section was used by the family as a bathhouse where they or their guests might change before using the pool. Visible plants include a patch of out-of-season iris (*Iris sp.*) in the foreground and a viburnum in the background. This corner of the garden would not have been of high design priority, as it led to a "service" area of the estate. Still, the symmetrical nature of the design and the small size of the property meant it could not be hidden, as would have been desirable at that time, hence the lush plantings and, later, the addition of an ornate iron gate. (Courtesy of Preservation Delaware.)

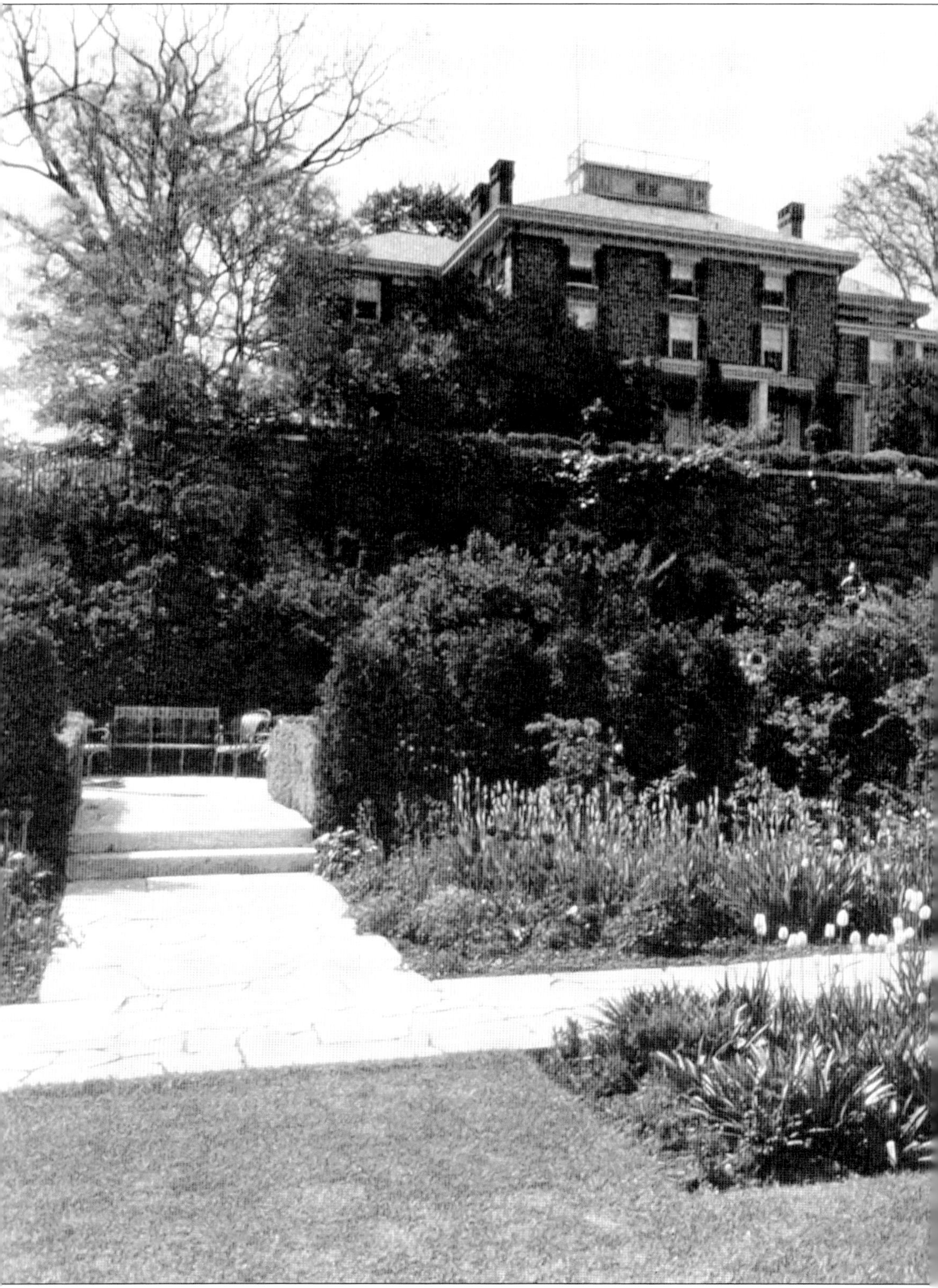

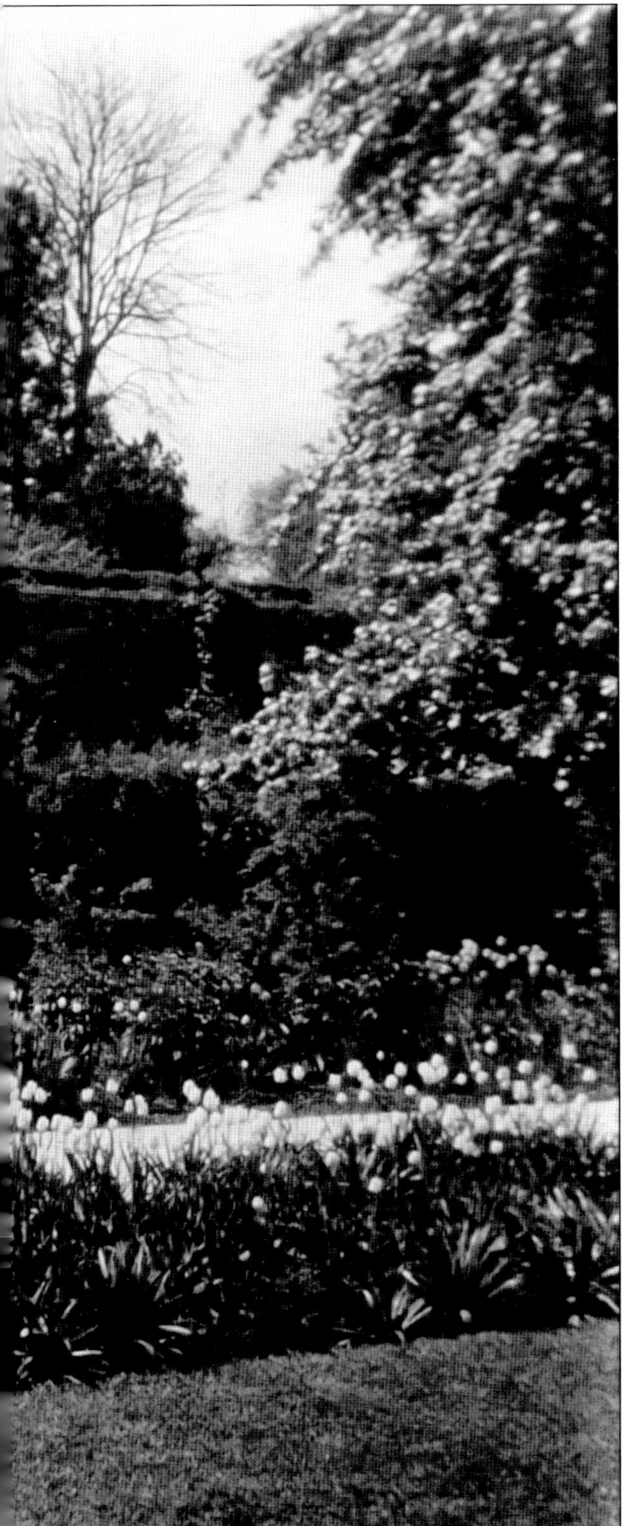

The lowermost terrace, and the most formal garden area at Gibraltar, is the flower garden. Located directly on what is now Greenhill Avenue, the flower garden is incredibly characteristic of Coffin's unique design style: informal cottage-style planting beds so full as to almost seem wild, placed within a matrix of strict neoclassical structures, such as parallel pathways; rectangular lawns; and Greco-Roman statuary. Of note in this image is the view of the mature boxwoods, which Coffin used to anchor each corner of the lawn. These were purchased from Lewis and Valentine, a firm specializing in the transplantation of large trees and shrubs, for a sum of $250 each (about $6,000 in 2020). (Winterthur.)

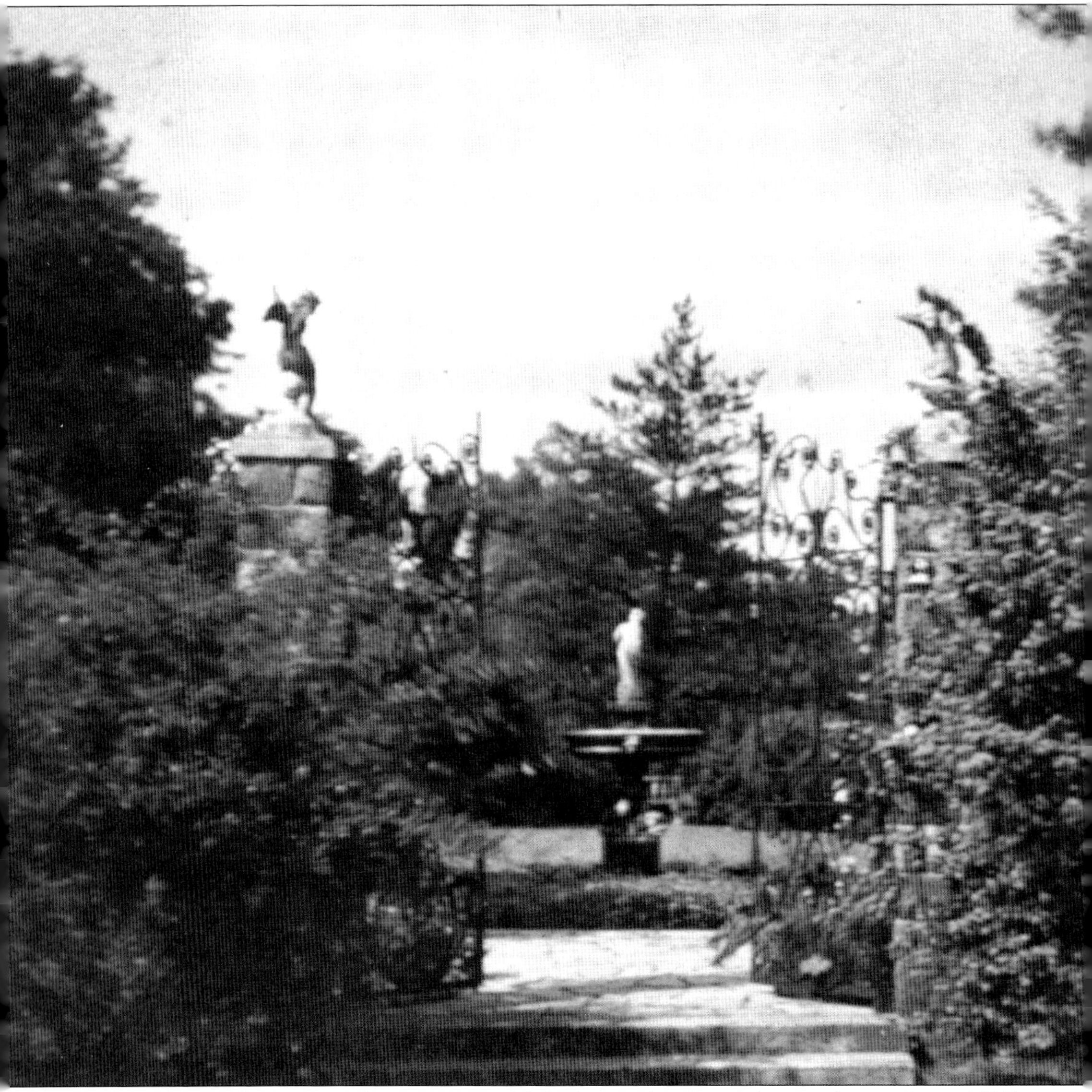

The set of garden gates in this image were likely designed and made by metal artist Samuel Yellin. Here, they are shown prior to the 1923 construction of the allée. Yellin, whose studio also was responsible for the grand staircase and flagstone terrace railings, immigrated to the United States from Ukraine in 1905, and quickly set up his own smithy in Philadelphia, where he employed up to 250 artisans at one time. Correspondence between Yellin and Sharp shows a substantial back-and-forth, with Sharp pushing for simpler designs than Yellin and his studio typically furnished. Still, the two men seemed to get along, as Sharp would go on to order everything from gates to candleholders to an iron table with a green marble top from the studio. While most of these pieces are lost, the stair rails and garden gates, having been restored in 1999 (see Chapter 5), remain in place. Yellin's other work can be seen across the East Coast, from the National Cathedral in Washington, DC, to Winterthur, to the Met Cloisters in New York City. (Hagley.)

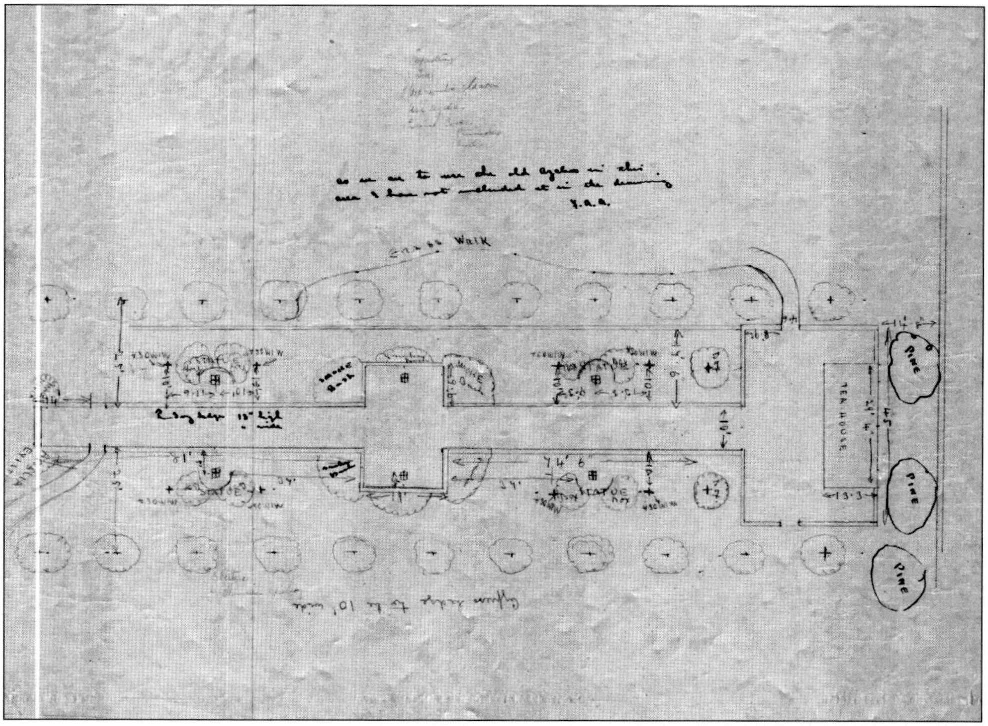

In 1920, Coffin returned to Gibraltar to design two additional areas—a sweeping drive leading to the back of the house and a formal allée located beyond an iron gate already built behind the formal garden's fountain. Her original design, seen here, bears little resemblance to its actual implementation. Instead of a stylized woodland, Coffin conceived of a formal walkway culminating in a teahouse. While the pathway remained essentially the same throughout the design process—consisting of bald cypress trees (*Taxodium distichium*), azaleas, and English ivy—these two images show how the teahouse changed from an octagonal building surrounded by a flagstone patio to a rectangular building with a grass plaza. (Both, Sharp family.)

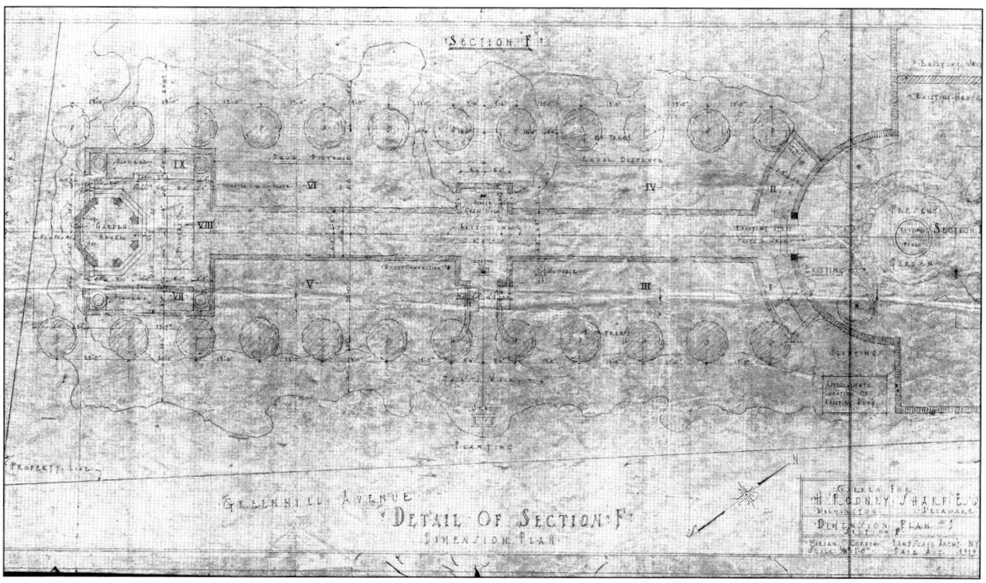

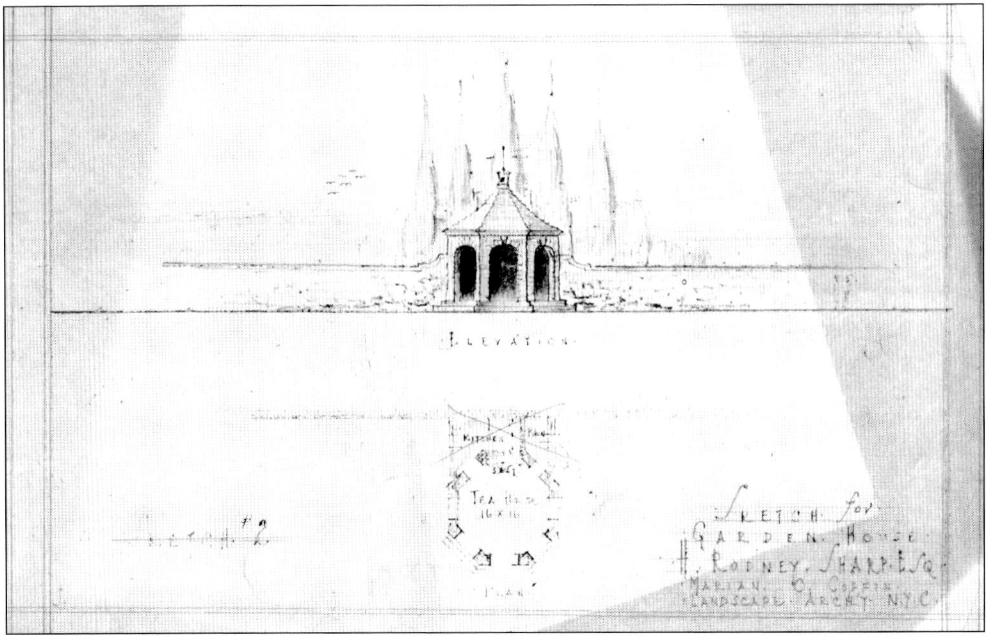

These sketches, dated to around 1920, show Marian Coffin's initial plans for the teahouse. Originally, she conceived of an octagonal brick structure open on all sides via arches, with a pointed roof and weathervane. With a backdrop of tall pencil cypresses (*Cupressus sempervirens*). Evidently, the Sharps did not see this design as fitting within their landscape. Indeed, it would look much more at home at an 18th century Colonial home than within Gibraltar's Italianate gardens, and the material (brick) does not reflect the existing design vernacular. Accordingly, the teahouse was replaced by a rectangular casino-type structure by the time the design was finalized. That is not to say that the Sharp family did not like the design, however; a similar structure could be found at their Florida home. (Both, Sharp family.)

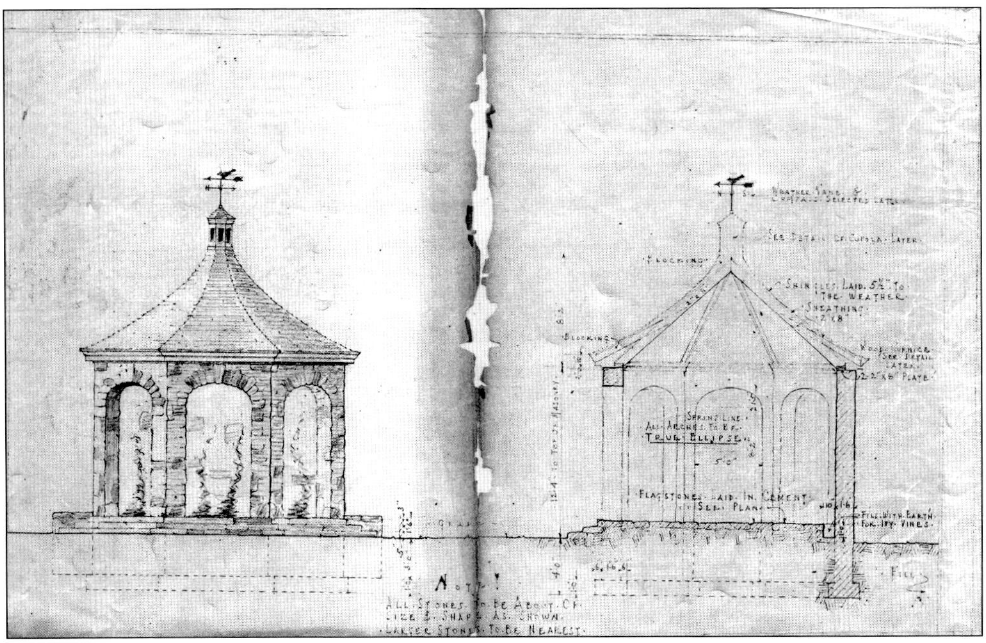

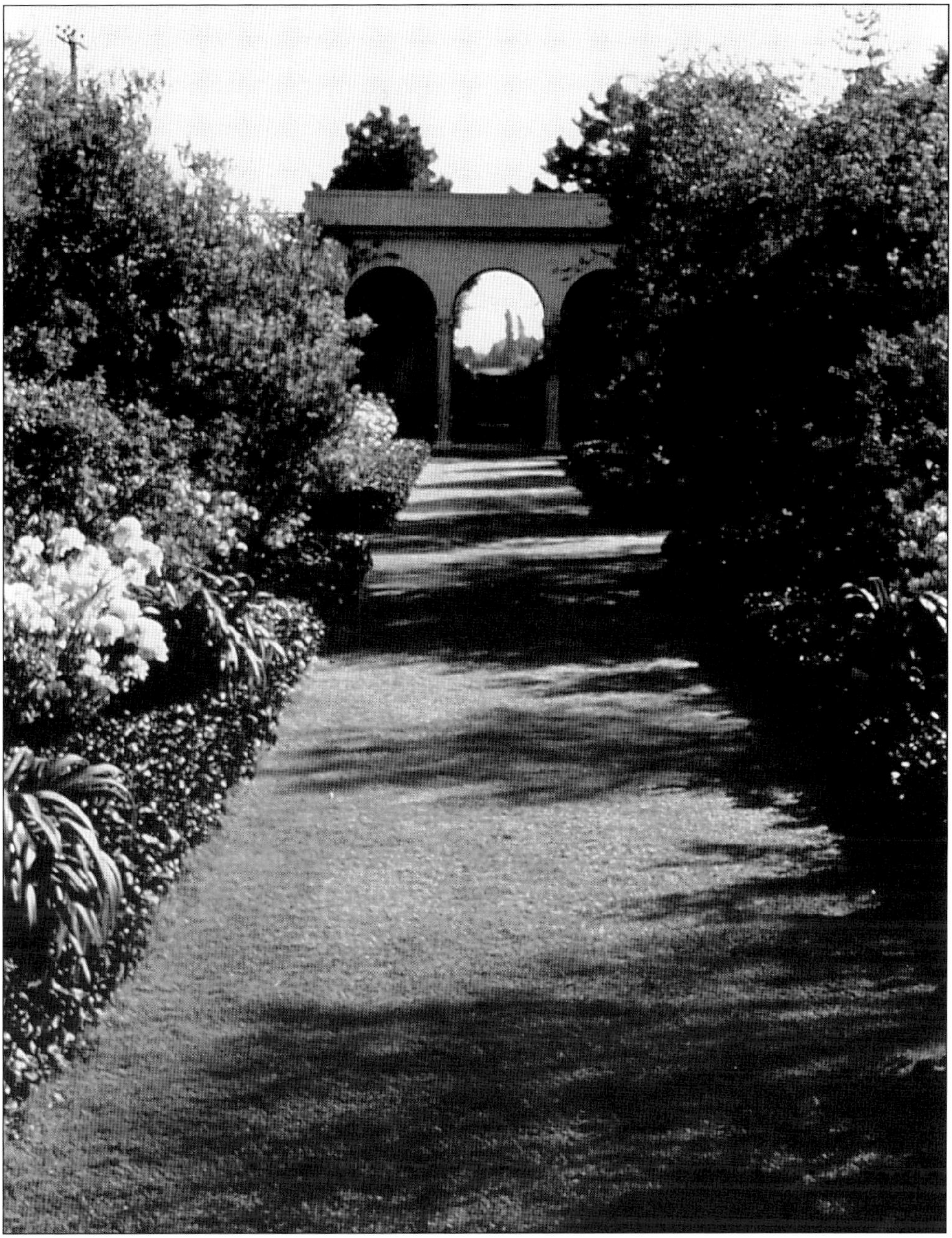

In her 1940 book, Coffin attributes the "not . . . so very formal" look of the bald cypress allée to the use of a variety of mixed shrubs, trees, and vines, which serve as a counterbalance to both the inherent formality of the teahouse and a series of four cast-stone statues and two urns, which one would pass on the way there. She achieved a feeling of enclosure by edging the garden room with layers of plants including bald cypress trees and tightly clipped English ivy bordering the path. Between these two, she planted azaleas (*Rhododendron sp.*) in a color gradient from white to pink to yellow to orange, accented by rugosa rose (*Rosa rugosa*) and blue squill (*Scilla siberica*). In fall and winter, four smoketrees (*Cotinus coggygria*) grouped at the center of the walk, and underplantings of evergreen periwinkle (*Vinca minor*) provided color. (PDI.)

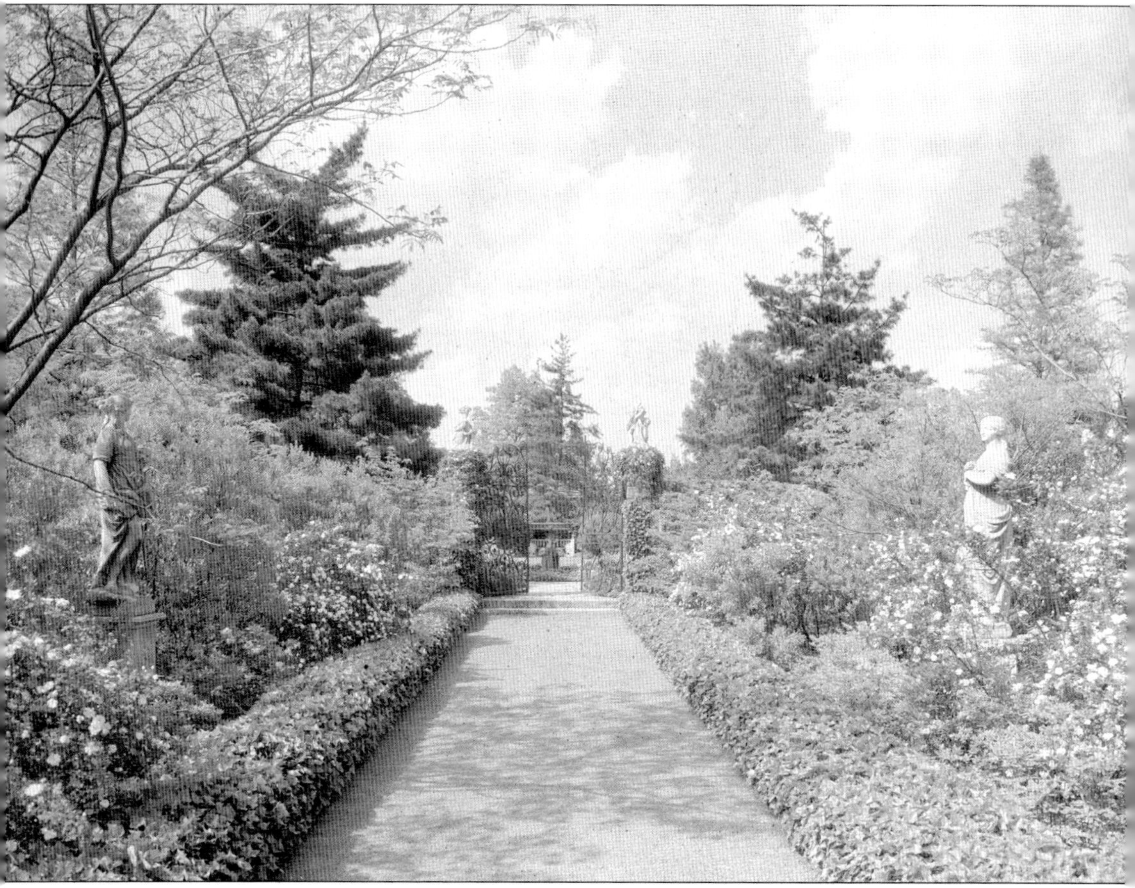

The bald cypress allée's statuary, two of which can be seen in this image, are interesting in their own right. The Sharps were avid travelers, and according to Coffin, they purchased these figural statues while on tour in 1922 in Italy, where they decorated a summer house along the Brenta. The Brenta, as a connector between the cities of Venice and Padua, was a common location for country estates and became a popular source for those who wished for antique statuary. Four in total, these cast-stone statues are allegorical in nature, each representing a season. Winter and Fall are paired closest to the teahouse, and Summer and Spring are closest to the gates. Between the pairs of seasons sit two large urns decorated with masks of Bacchus, the Roman god of wine. Scientific and documentary analysis performed in the 1990s shows that these were likely purchased from a Florentine stonemason on the same 1922 trip on which they sourced the seasons. (Library of Congress.)

The bald cypress allée was the last part of Gibraltar to be installed, and the end of this naturalistic planting was an Italian teahouse, constructed in 1923. It became a favorite spot for the family, where they would arrange chairs and decorative rugs in the summer and entertain guests. The 12 gardeners at the site would put tropical plants from the greenhouse in the teahouse when weather permitted, such as bird of paradise (*Strelitzia sp.*) and fiddle-leaf fig (*Ficus lyrata*). One can imagine how lovely the teahouse would be in summer, sitting in the shade and hearing nothing but the birds and the bubbling fountain. (Both, PDI.)

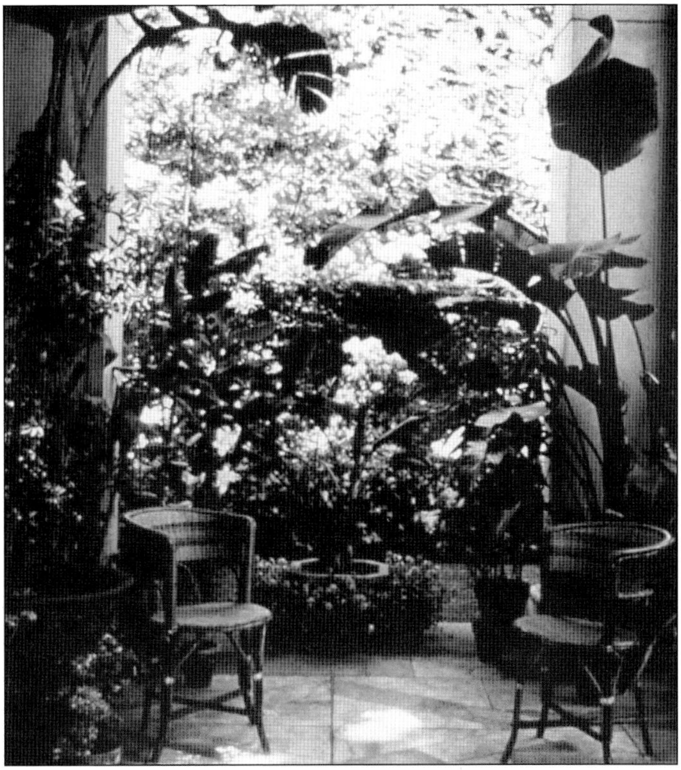

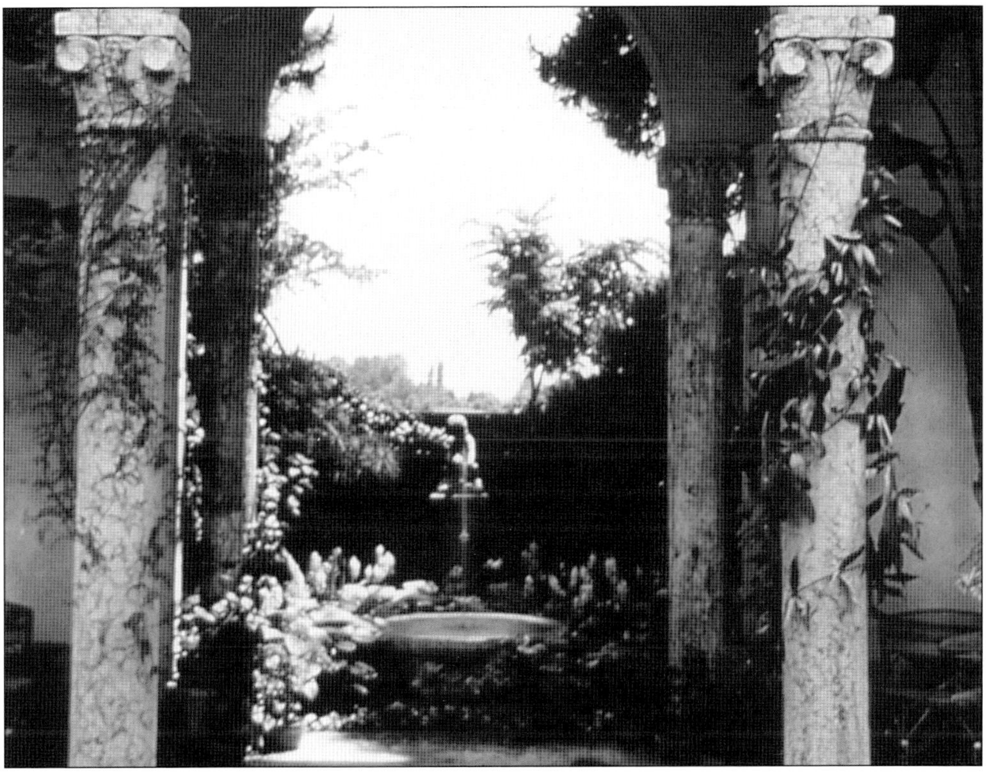

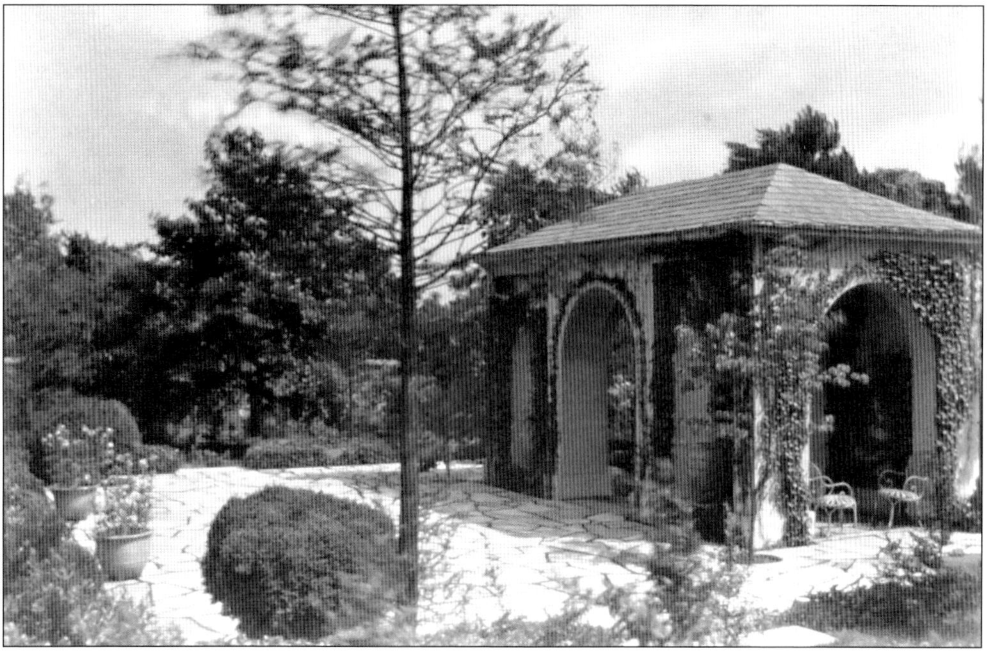

Gibraltar technically has had two teahouses. The original teahouse was closer to an Italian casino, with a vaulted ceiling, hipped roof, and ornate tiled floor. The walls were closed, with niches in the front to hold potted plants, and ivy crawling up the sides. Surrounding the casino was a marble-tiled patio, anchored in each corner by a boxwood. The first structure was built in about 1923 and remodeled shortly after into what stands today—a much simpler structure with the niches substituted for an open front and the roof flattened. It is likely that the Sharps came up with the idea of both the original and remodeled teahouse on a trip to Italy, taken in 1922, during which time they also sourced the four statues that now grace the allée. (Both, PDI.)

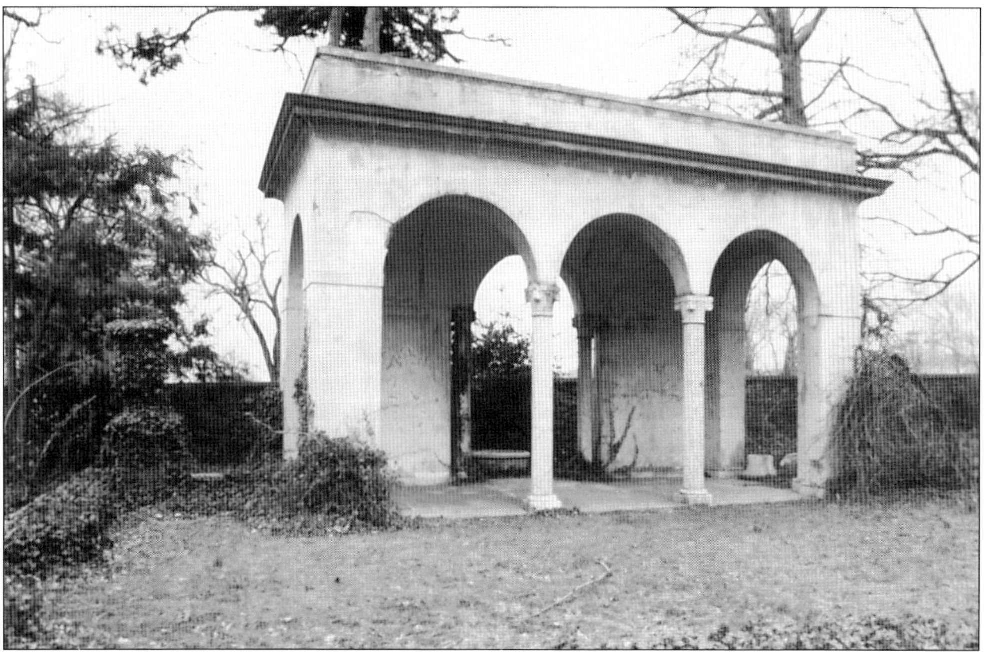

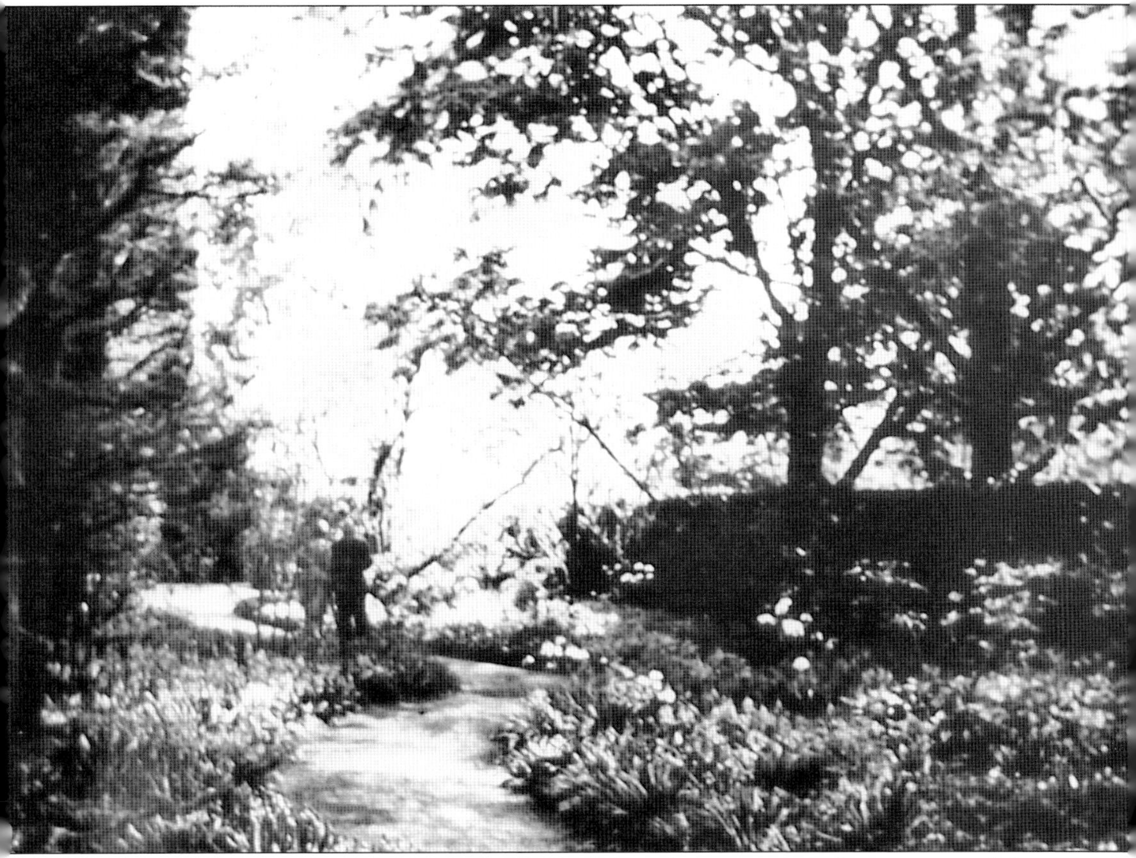

Despite being close to the road, the Woodland Walk is the most "tucked away" area of the garden. Nestled between the stone wall on Greenhill Avenue and the back of the bald cypress allée, visitors enter either near the teahouse or along the side of the flower garden's fountain. The woodland walk's style is more simple than even Coffin's more naturalistic works, such as the grove at Winterthur or the woods at the Oaks, both discussed at other points in this book. The botanical palette is an extension of the plants seen in the bald cypress allée. This image, a hand-tinted black and white photograph, appears to show the garden in mid-spring, with blue squill ground cover and an orange shrub, perhaps the same azaleas used in the allée. Deciduous trees provide further structure and protection along the roadside. (PDI.)

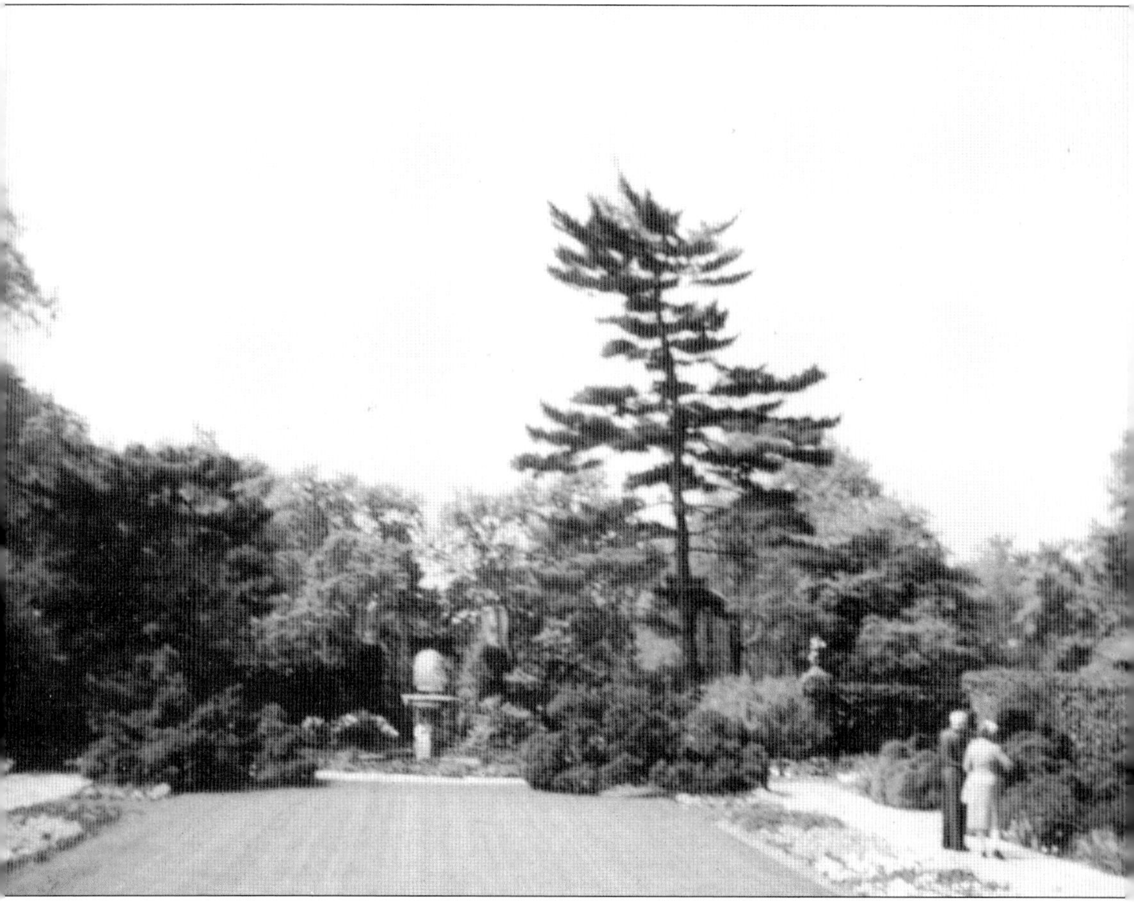

In this image, Gibraltar is seen in a state of transition. Following World War II, to combat a lack of available labor, Sharp simplified the garden maintenance. The statue that sat on top of the fountain is gone, and the ornate mixed perennial beds are removed in favor of low-maintenance annuals. These elements, in addition to the clothing of the woman in the foreground, seem to indicate that this image was taken during either a Wilmington Garden Day in the 1950s or potentially a Garden Club of America tour, which occurred in 1963. A description of the garden in the latter tour's pamphlet praises the garden's "tranquility and protected nature" and calls it "one of Wilmington's most distinguished formal gardens." This tour would take place less than five years before Hugh Rodney Sharp's death, which occurred while he was returning on a steamboat from Italy. His funeral was held on-site, with the coffin draped with ivy from his beloved garden. (PDI.)

Four

Marian Coffin's Related Commissions

While Gibraltar was both Coffin's first Delaware commission and her first commission for a person within the duPont family, it certainly was not her last on either count. Coffin completed nine more commissions in Delaware's Chateau Country, most for duPont family members, in addition to three additional family properties as far away as Florida. These commissions, which spanned the rest of her career, included estates, vacation properties, working farms, college campuses, family cemeteries, and historic house museums. Some projects were small, like a single parterre at the Corbit-Sharp House, while others were large, such as the Winterthur estate, which Coffin revisited over a period of 40 years. When viewed together, these designs show Coffin's consistent design vocabulary and her incredible range. While certain design motifs and plants are repeated, each design reflects the preferences of the original owner.

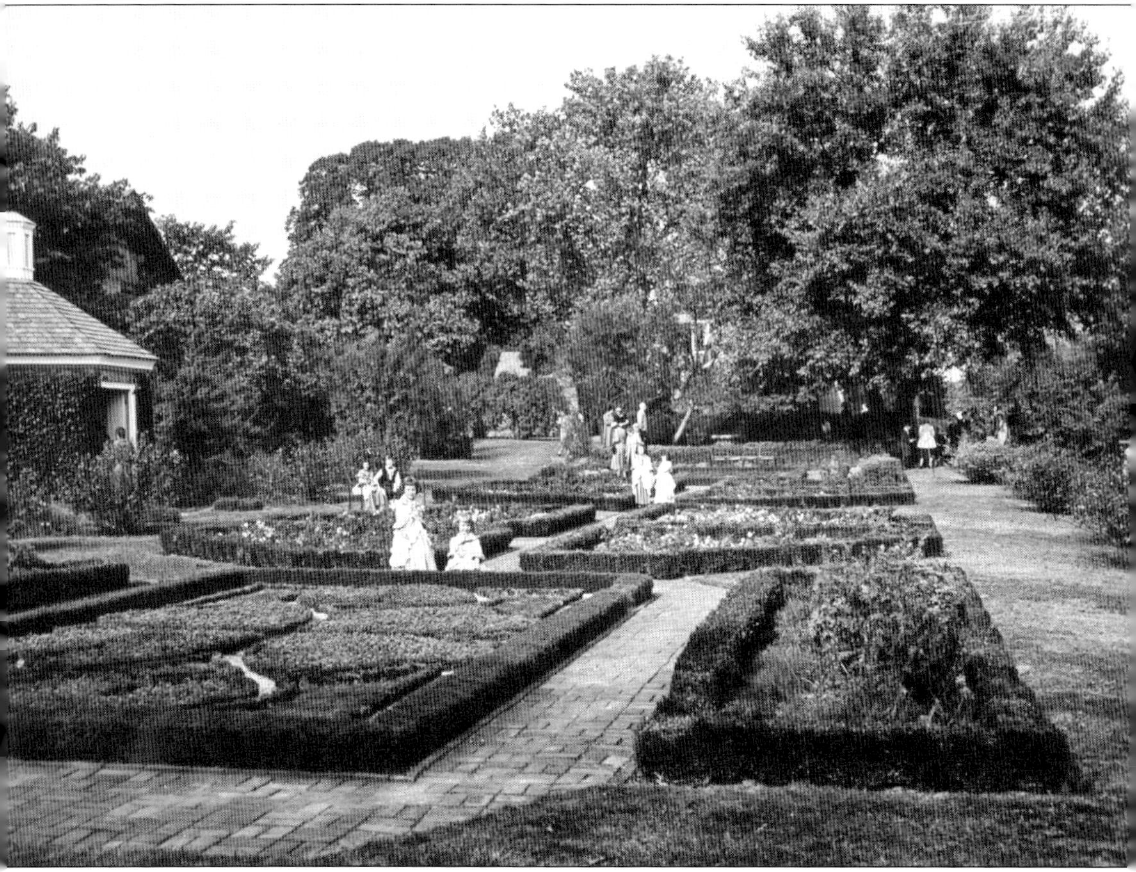

Coffin designed garden areas for three houses owned by the Sharp family, the most unusual of which was likely the Corbit-Sharp House. In 1938, Hugh Rodney Sharp purchased the Odessa property and, in the following two years, restored the property for use as a historic house museum. As part of this effort, Sharp enlisted Coffin's help in designing a traditional Colonial Revival garden. This was not Coffin's only design of this type, but it was certainly outside of her normal vernacular. The design, which is strongly axially and bilaterally symmetrical, is relatively restrained compared to her other works. It features boxwood-lined brick walkways, fruit tree accents, and planting beds filled with herbs and annual flowers. The site was frequently used for education events, as seen in the image below. (Winterthur.)

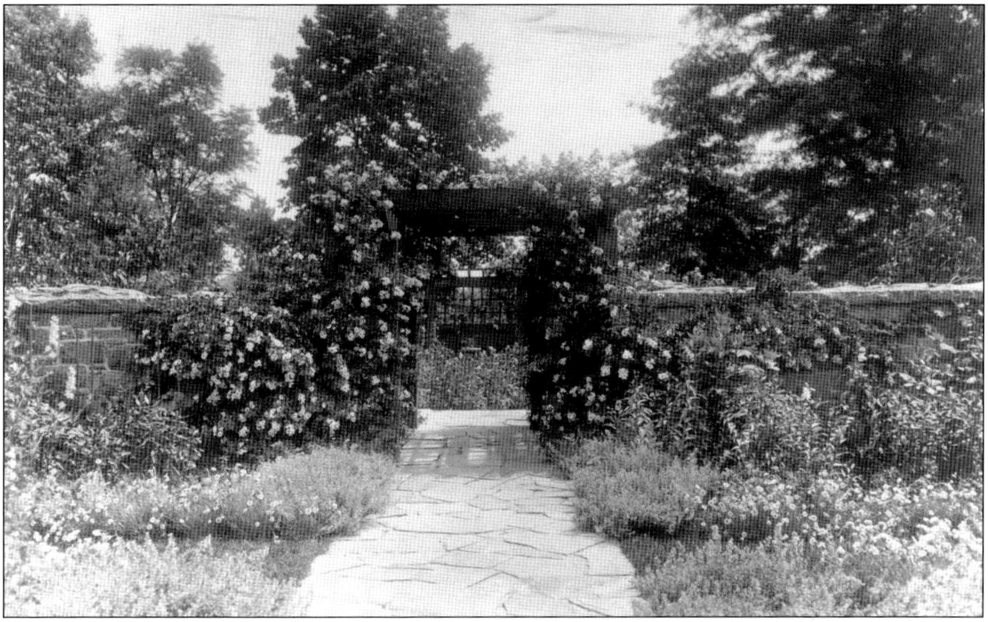

Coffin's walled garden design at St. Amour, with its wall fountains, espaliered boxwoods, and pale roses, is highly conforming to the theories taught at the *École des Beaux-Arts* ("School of Fine Arts"), which influenced Coffin's designs. In all fields—architecture, painting, and sculpture—the École des Beaux-Arts and derivative programs taught an idealized and modernized retelling of classical and renaissance design. This theory was clearly at play in the St. Amour garden. The walled fountain is reminiscent of medieval cloister gardens, and the central boxwood garden takes inspiration from 18th-century parterre design. Like some of Coffin's designs discussed elsewhere in this book, it is likely this central feature was meant to be viewed from above, where the ornate scrolling could be best appreciated. The young child seen balancing on the built-in stone bench is unidentified but was likely a grandchild of Mary Belin duPont and therefore a niece or nephew of Isabella Sharp. (Both, Winterthur.)

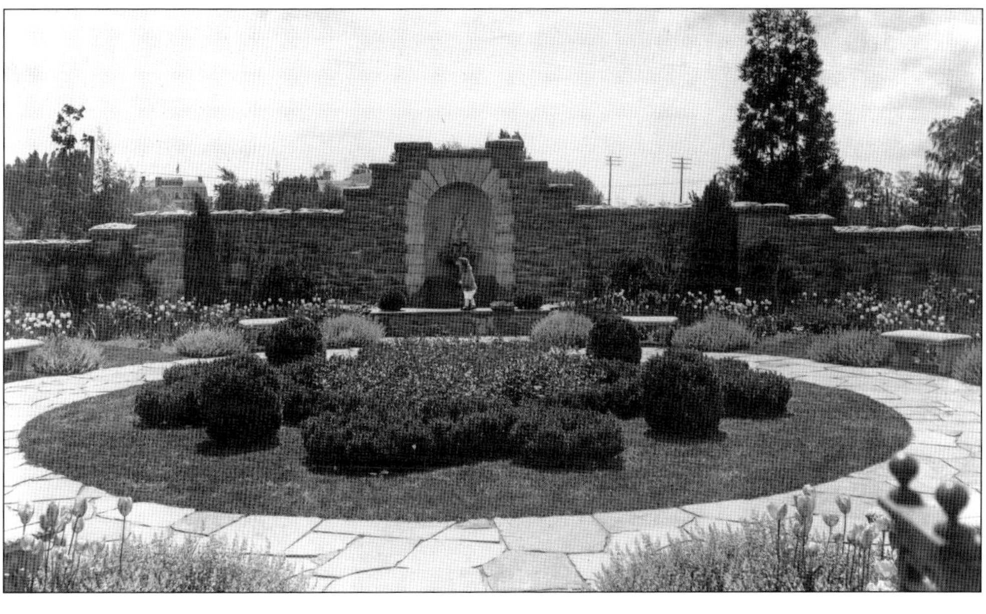

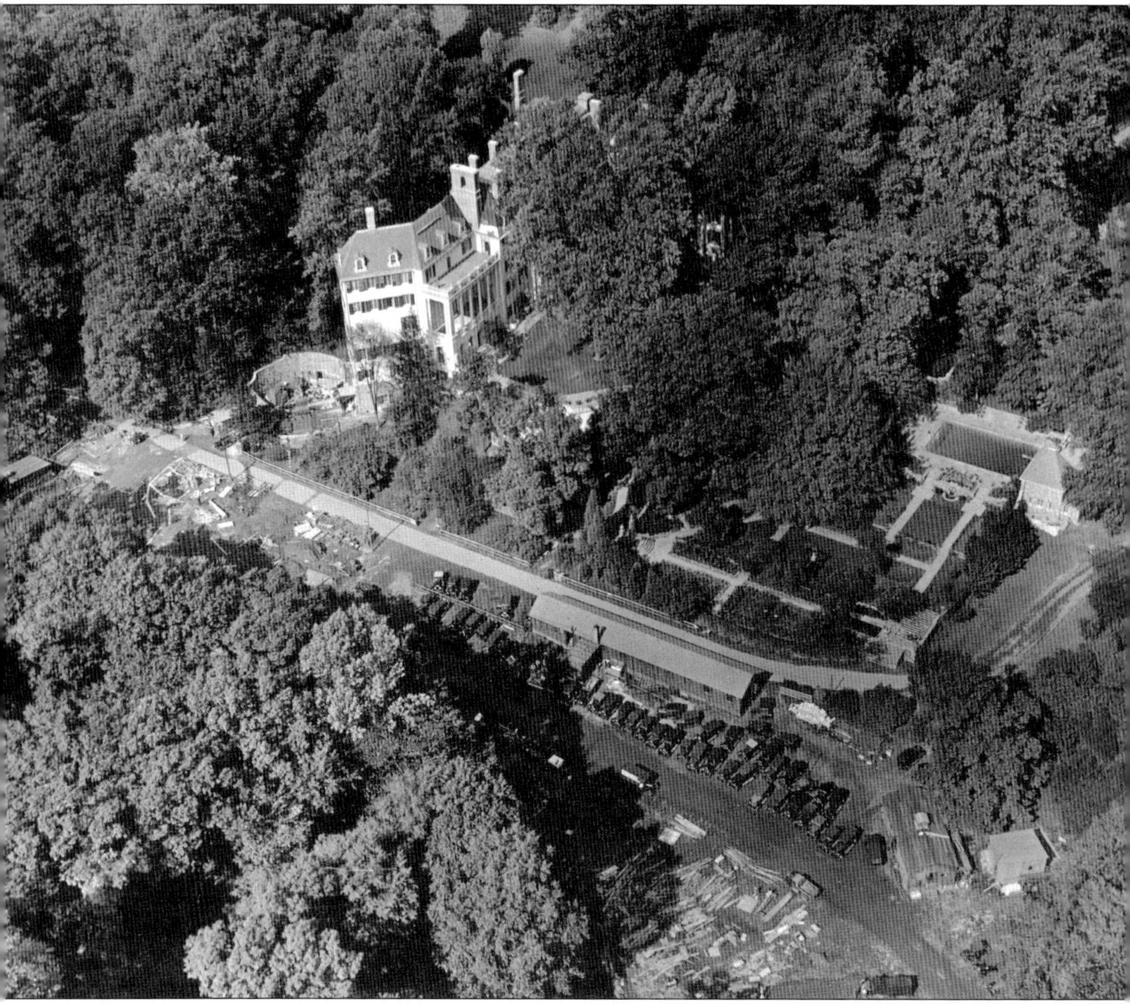

Winterthur was the estate of Henry Francis duPont, Marian Coffin's longtime friend. DuPont was the gateway to many of her Mid-Atlantic commissions, Gibraltar included. At its height, Winterthur occupied over 2,400 acres of land, although the gardens (as seen in this aerial photograph) only occupied 60 of those acres. Coffin's first exposure to the estate was as a small child during a visit in 1896. Years later, in the late 1910s, she sent one of her earliest staff members to oversee work on duPont's trial garden. Her formal design work began at Winterthur after duPont inherited the estate in the late 1920s. Over the ensuing 30 years, Coffin visited the estate more than 46 times—more than any other nonfamily guest—having nearly as great an impact on the bucolic landscape as the owner himself. (Hagley.)

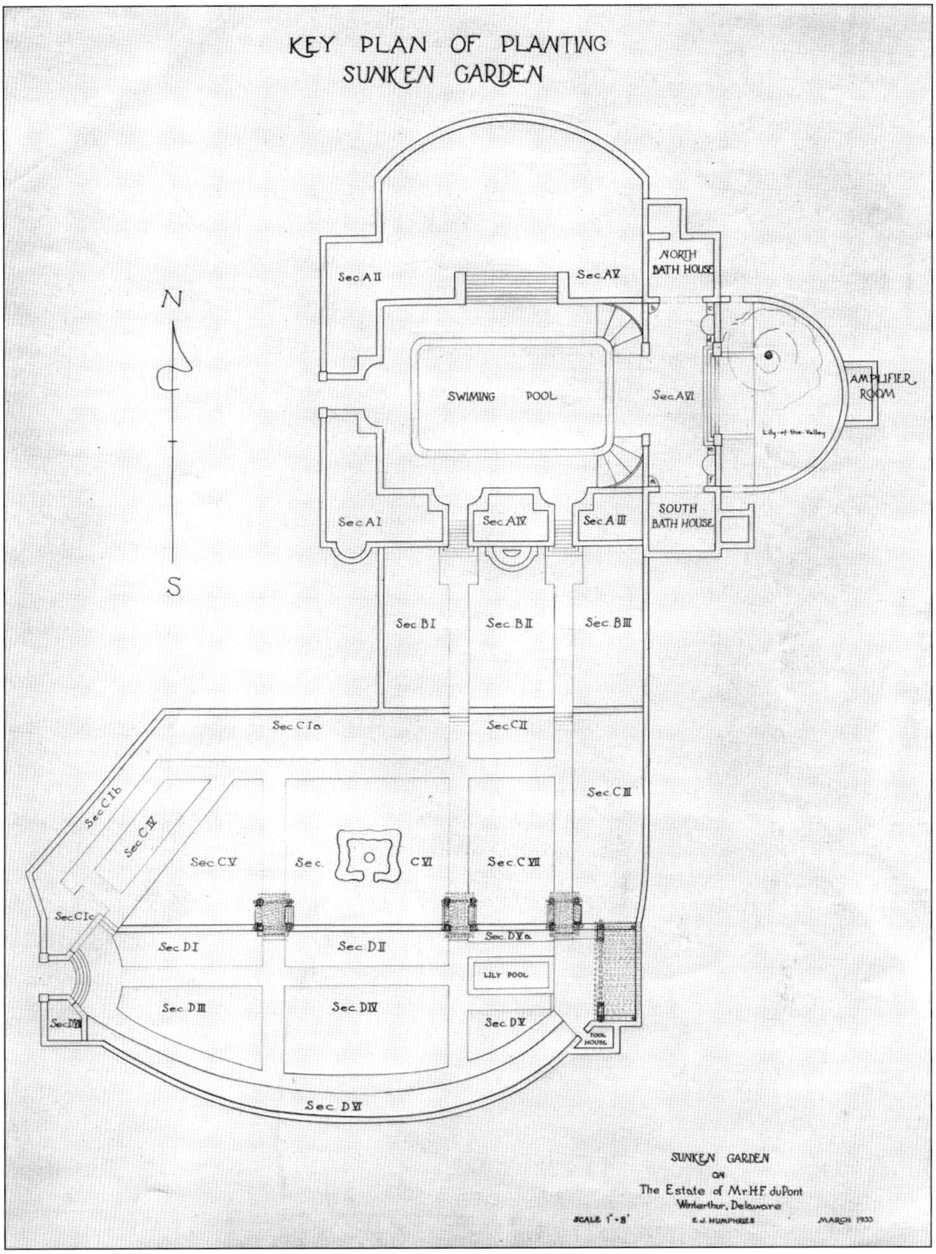

Perhaps Coffin's most extensive and adventurous design is at Winterthur. She began designing at the estate in 1928, only one year after H.F. inherited the property from his father. When duPont was dramatically enlarging the home to accommodate his museum collections and period rooms, the existing gardens were demolished out of necessity, creating a need for new designs. Coffin had done some work for duPont previously, working on his Southampton home, but it is at Winterthur that their relationship shines. It is clear that H.F. trusted Coffin's instinct and was willing to pay whatever it cost to implement her design. However, she deferred to him when it came to plant selection, as a favorite hobby of duPont's was collecting, testing, importing, and breeding bulbs and azaleas. She would design at Winterthur on and off for almost 30 years, from 1928 until 1955, when she died. Here, Coffin's overall estate layout is seen. (Winterthur.)

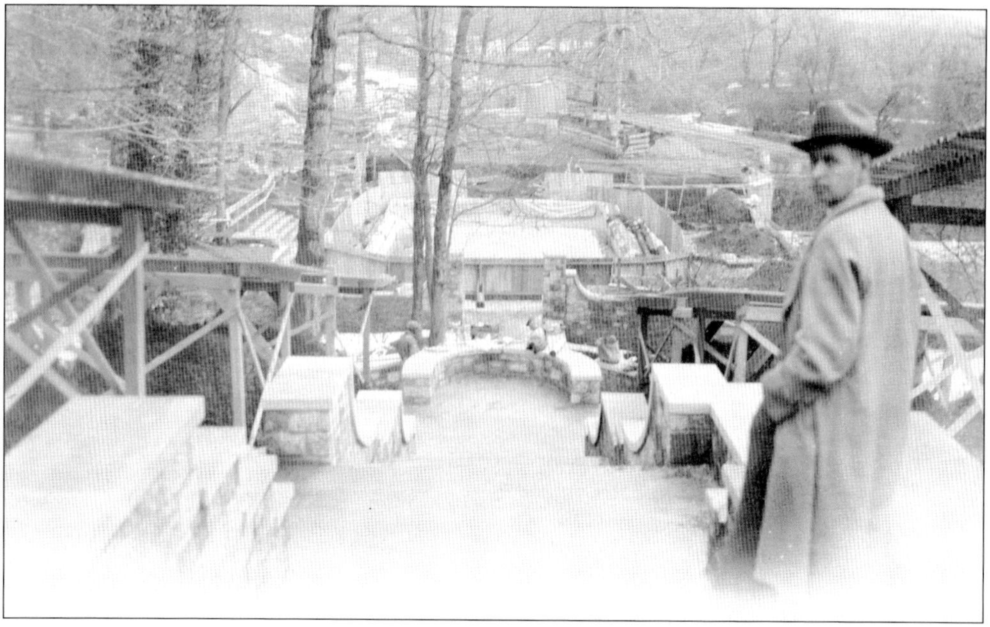

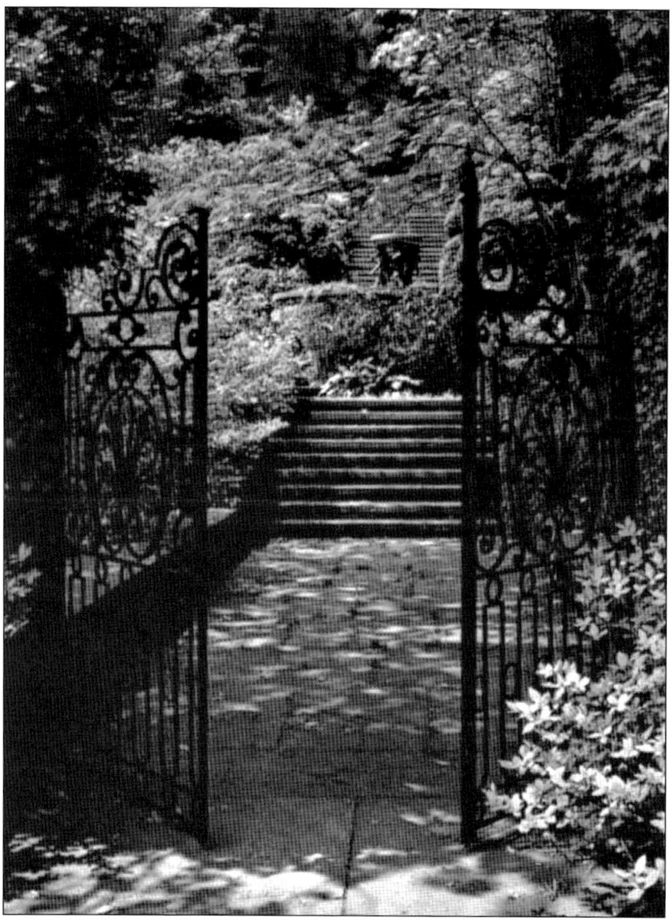

Coffin did not work alone, and in addition to employing female design assistants, many of whom went on to landscape design careers of their own, she also worked closely with architects to oversee technical aspects of implementing complex structures and hardscapes. One such architect was James Scheiner, who joined Coffin's practice in the early 1910s. Despite service in World War I and later founding his own practice, Scheiner worked with Coffin for more than 20 years. Here, Scheiner is overseeing the construction of the staircase at Winterthur. Not only a lifelong friend, Scheiner often acted as a mediator, using his privilege to help integrate her into the male-dominated architecture field. (Above, Winterthur; below, Delaware Public Archives.)

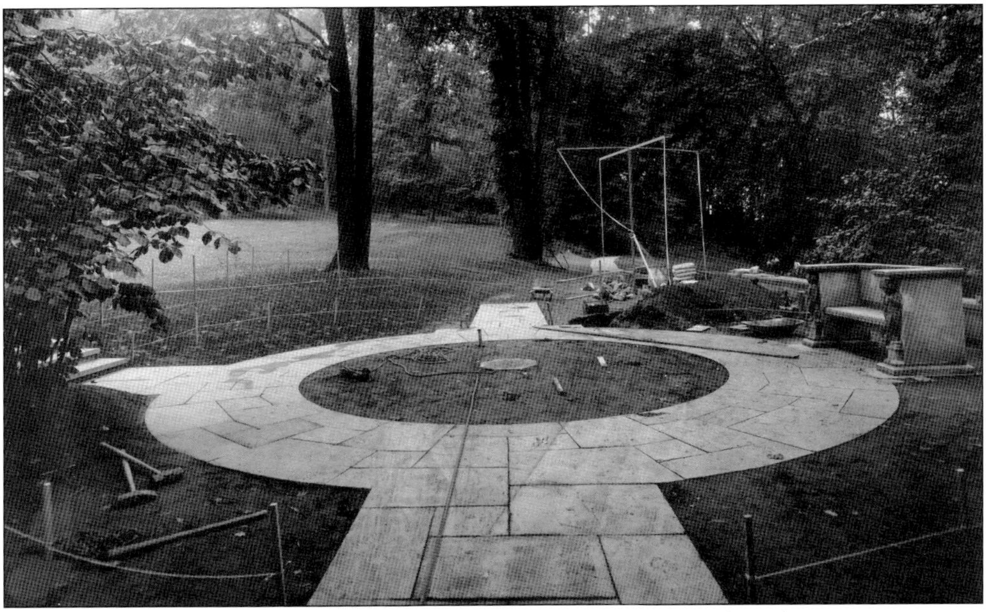

Coffin designed a sunken, terraced garden for Winterthur, which allowed visitors to start at the house and descend into the landscape. The first of the constructed areas became what is now called the "boxwood scroll garden." A feature best viewed from above, the space includes a classical fountain surrounded by two concentric circles of ornately swirling European boxwoods. The outer circle was inter-planted with white and pale-yellow tulips chosen by H.F. duPont, a bulb aficionado who enjoyed testing new cultivars in his kitchen garden. Here, one can see the area before and after construction. The rope-and-stick devices seen in the background were used by Coffin to estimate the heights of larger shrubs before they were ordered. This visualization tool allowed her to tweak the design as needed before placing the plants. (Both, Winterthur.)

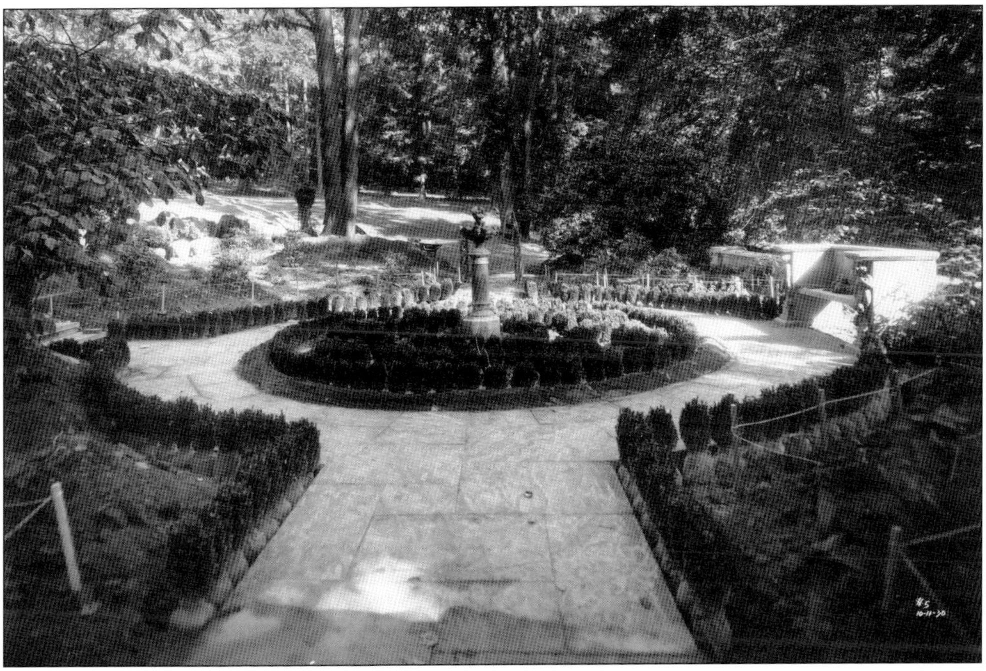

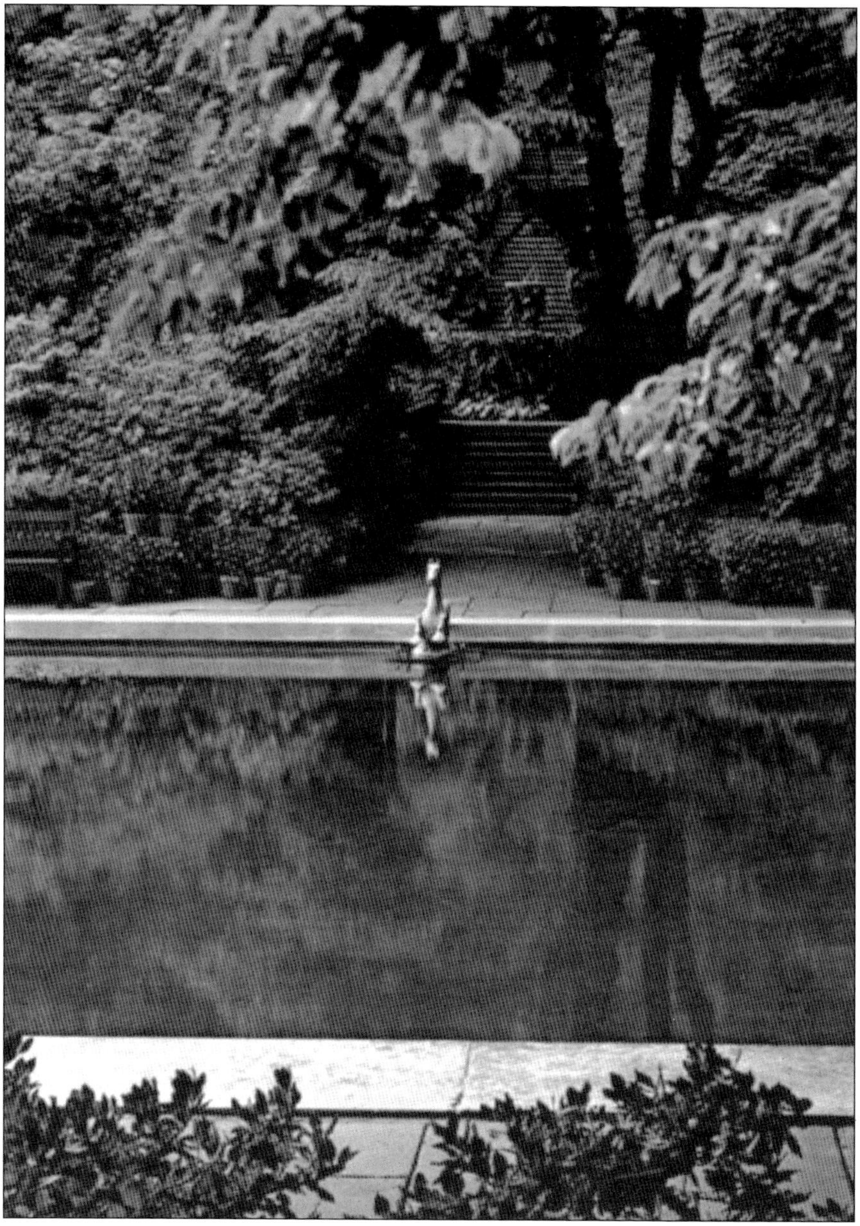

The main axis of Coffin's terrace design led visitors from the house, through a grove of tulip poplars (*Liriodendron tulipifera*), down a grand staircase flanked with boxwoods, to the pool area, seen here. When the estate was owned by H.F. duPont's father, Henry Algernon duPont, the area was used as a forecourt (a place where visitors and guests could be received), but Coffin reimagined it as a rectangular swimming pool within a flagstone patio. The pool was flanked at the far end by two pool houses—one for men and one for women. A speaker system hidden by decorative grates in the middle allowed music to be played for guests. A cross-axis led via grand staircases to the formal Italianate garden on the south side and the glade garden, which is still extant, on the north. While the pool was converted into a reflecting pool once the property was made into a museum, Coffin's original plant palette of azaleas and potted seasonal tropical plants remains today. (Delaware Public Archives.)

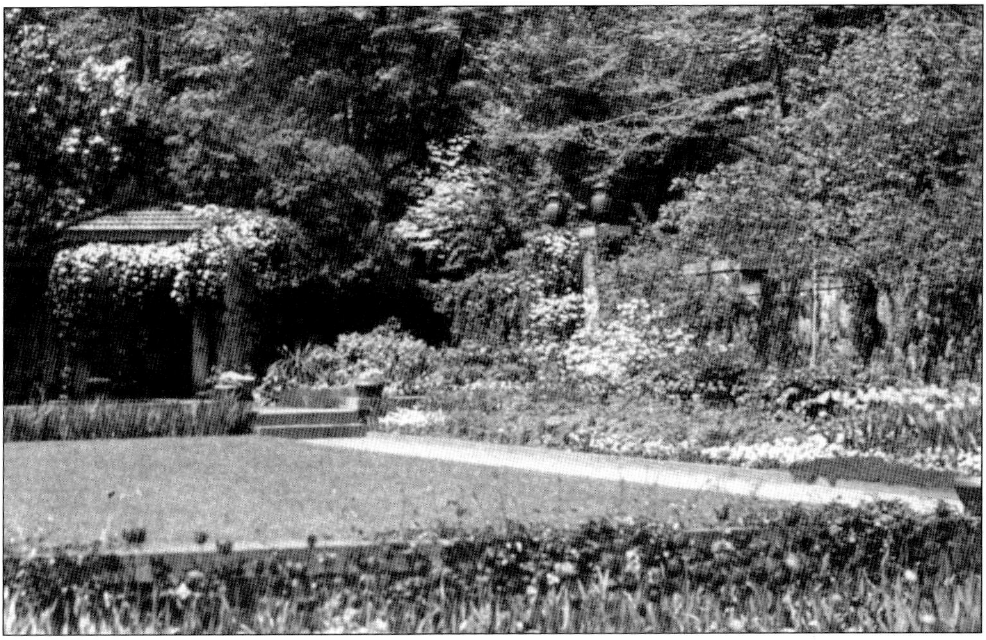

While Coffin's design at Winterthur is remarkably well-preserved, one formal garden room she designed at the site no longer exists. Directly south and slightly west of the pool area was a formal Italianate garden featuring a wisteria-covered pergola. To reach this area, guests could take parallel pea gravel paths edged with mixed planting borders. A lawn graced in the center of it all, which perhaps was the original home of the armillary sphere now in the sundial garden. This garden, which resembles one of Coffin's earlier designs for Jonathan Godfrey at the Oaks in Bridgeport, Connecticut, was demolished for the 1969 construction of the Crowninshield Research Building. The stairway to the garden survives, as does one surrounding wall. (Above, Smithsonian Archive of American Gardens; below, Hagley.)

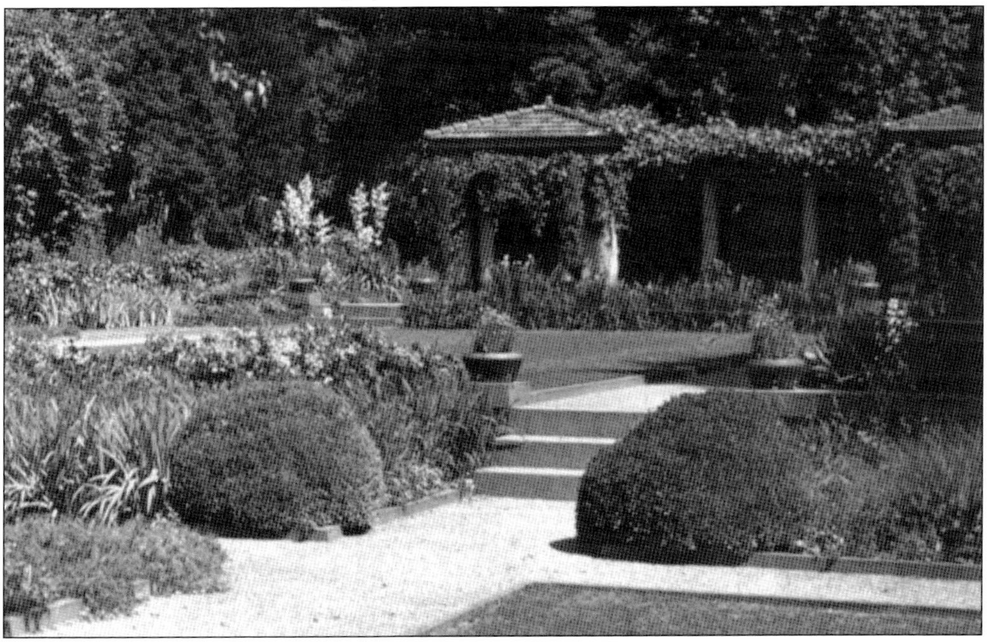

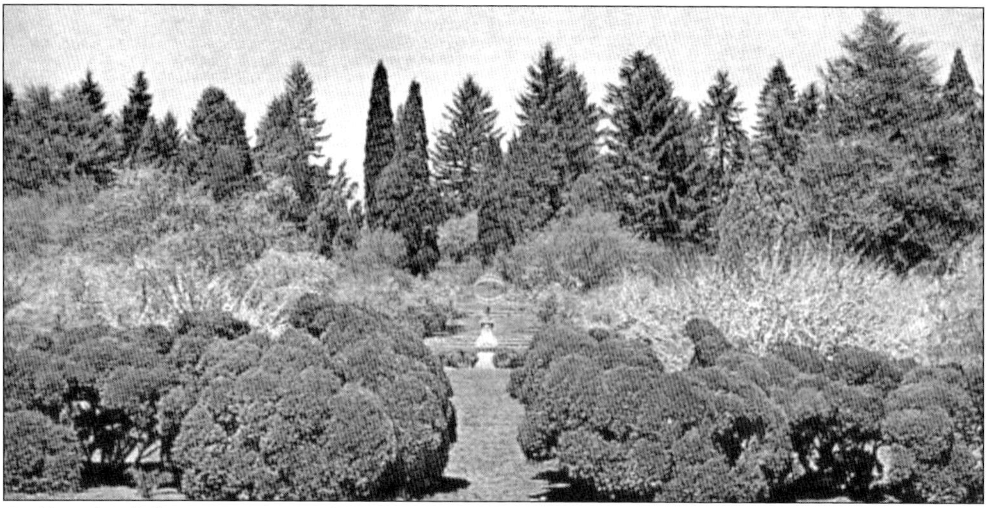

Coffin's final design at Winterthur, which she created during the last years of her life, was the sundial garden. As H.F. duPont began to transition his home into a museum, he determined that the location of the sunken flower garden was the best location for his research building. Many of the garden's elements were placed into storage for the next 50 years until they were repurposed in the Enchanted Forest newly designed by W. Gary Smith. However, the focal point of the garden, the sundial, was made the centerpiece of a new garden at the former site of the family's roque courts. For this garden, Coffin chose to focus on spring-flowering shrubs and trees, with the landscape dominated by flowering quince (*Chaenomeles sp.*), dogwood (*Cornus sanguinea*), and forsythia (*Forsythia x intermedia*), among others. (Both, Delaware Public Archives.)

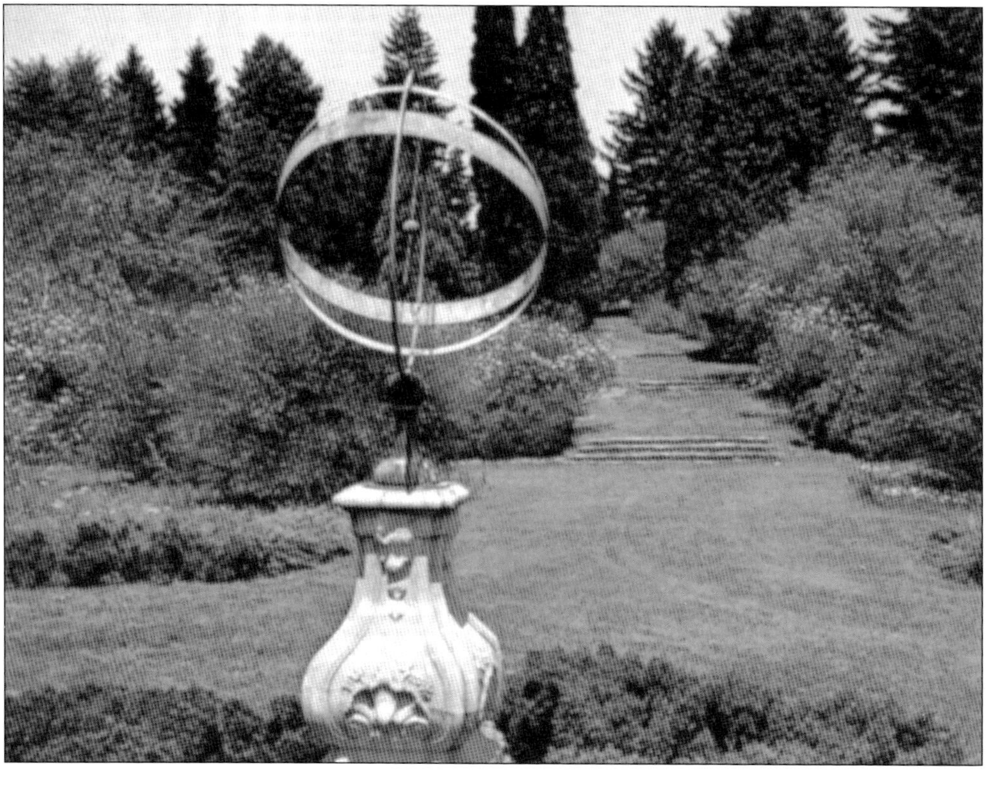

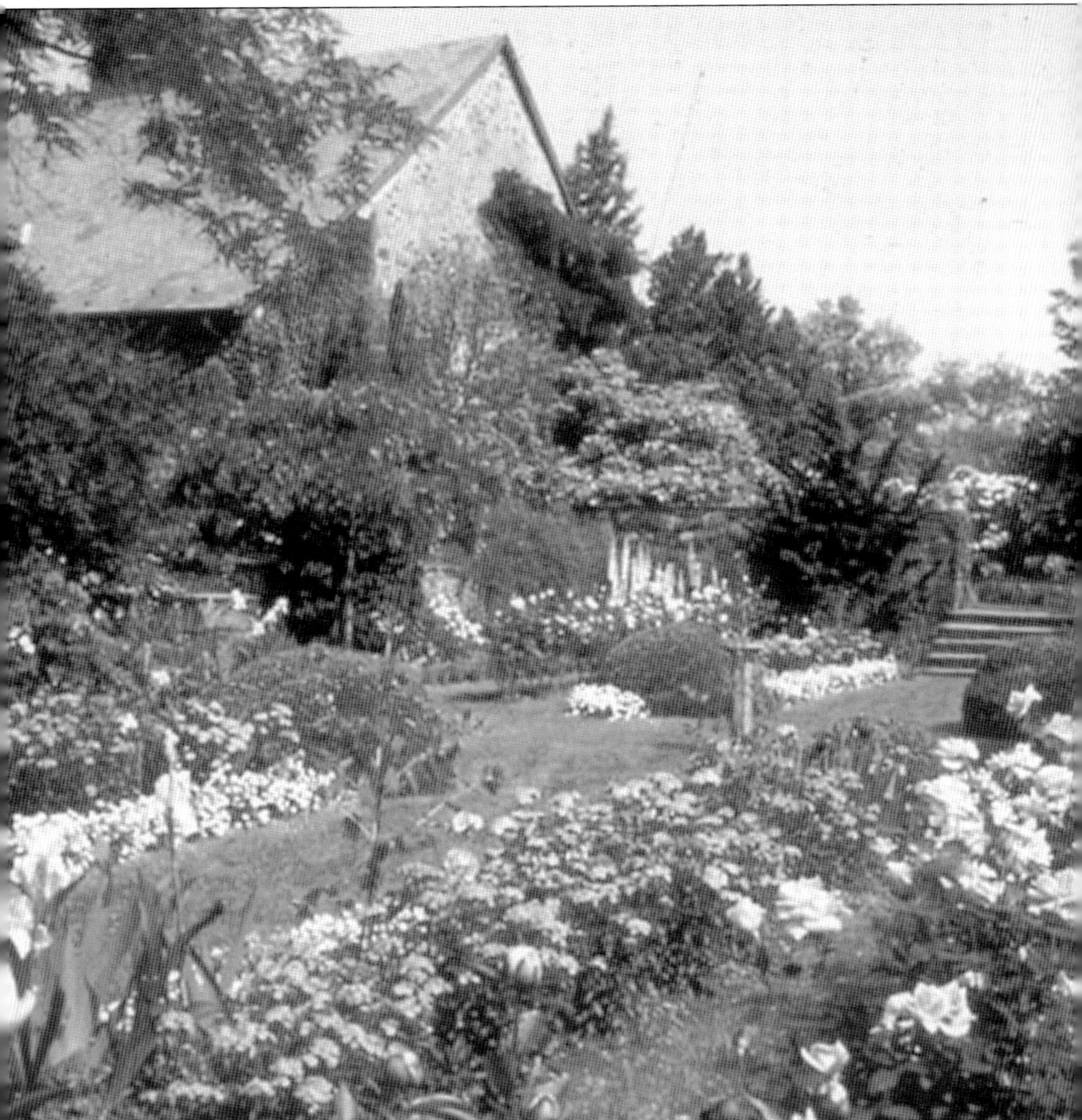

Coffin's smallest commission in Delaware was at Applecross, home of Wilhelmina duPont and her new husband, Donald Ross, a businessman who would later found Delaware Park. Their estate was located on land adjacent to the Winterthur estate, given to the couple as a gift. While a majority of the grounds was designed by architect Noel Chamberlin, Coffin made some significant additions in 1953. Following the death of her mother, Ethel, in 1951, Wilhelmina Ross inherited her large collection of more than 100 tree peony (*Paeonia sp.*) species and hired Coffin to design a garden for their exhibit. The design was anchored by a summerhouse at one end and a standing crabapple tree at the other, with a thin rectangular reflecting pool in the center. The peonies were arranged, grouped by color, around the pool in two concentric series of beds, which together formed an oval. In this photograph, the pool is visible, and to this day, it exists alongside the house. However, it appears the tree peonies are now lost. The rest of the estate now makes up the Applecross subdivision. (Smithsonian Archive of American Gardens.)

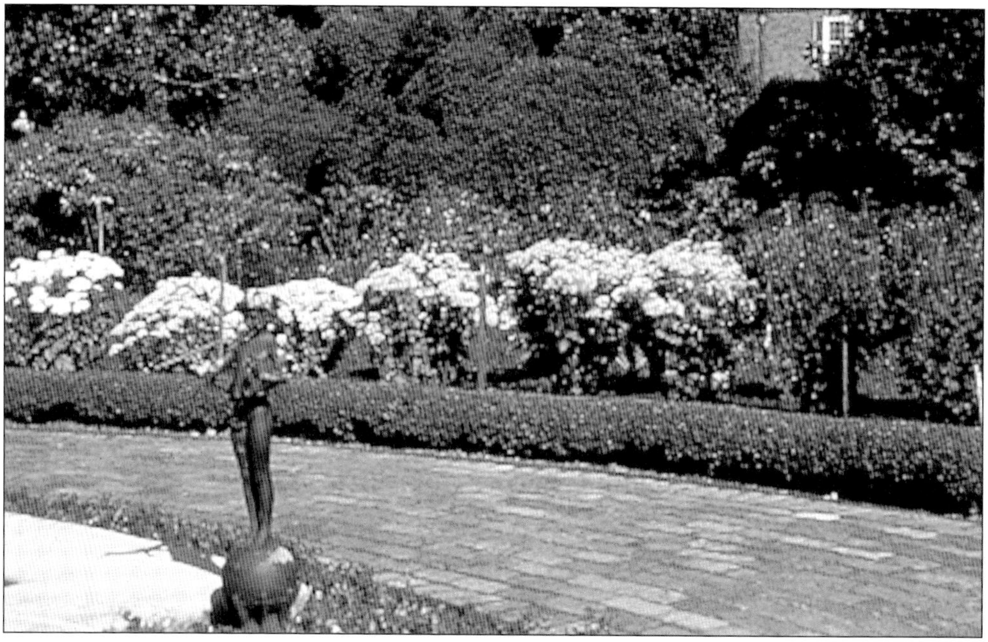

Mount Cuba was Coffin's final major residential commission in Delaware. Nestled within the rolling hills of the Piedmont, Mount Cuba was the estate of Lammot duPont Copeland, nephew of Isabella Sharp, and his wife, Pamela, who lived on the estate until her death in 2001. While a majority of the estate was kept naturalistic, dedicated to the propagation of Delaware's native flora, the Copelands hired Coffin in the early 1950s to redevelop the formal garden area directly adjacent to their home, including a round pool surrounded by brick walkways and beds of flowers. While the design was in keeping with the Georgian Revival architecture of the house, the plant content was less formal. The contents of the planting beds were in keeping with the character of the rest of the estate and included a mix of annuals and perennials, which are seen in this image. (Both, Smithsonian Archive of American Gardens.)

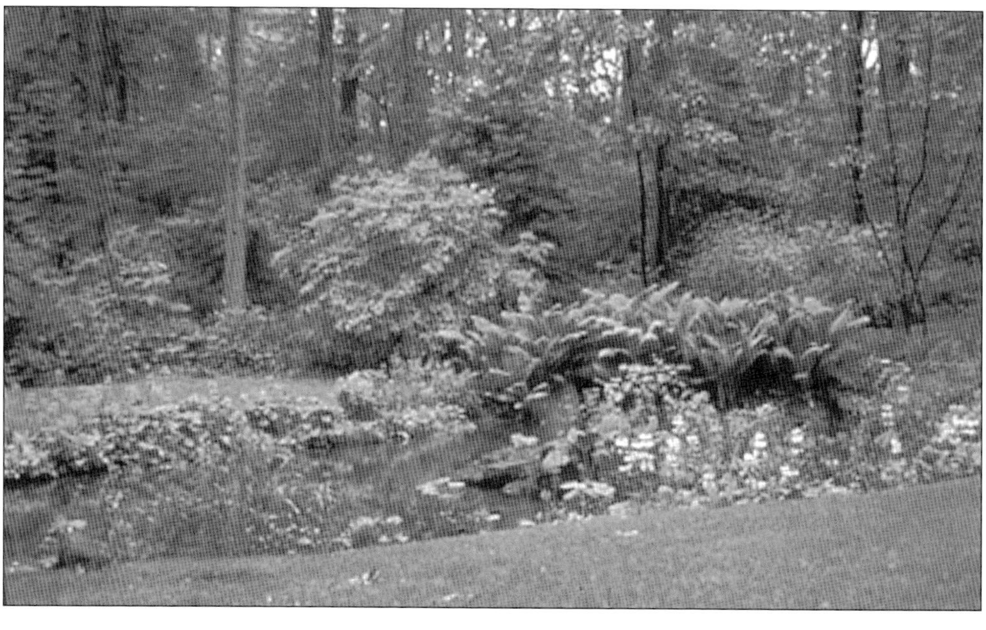

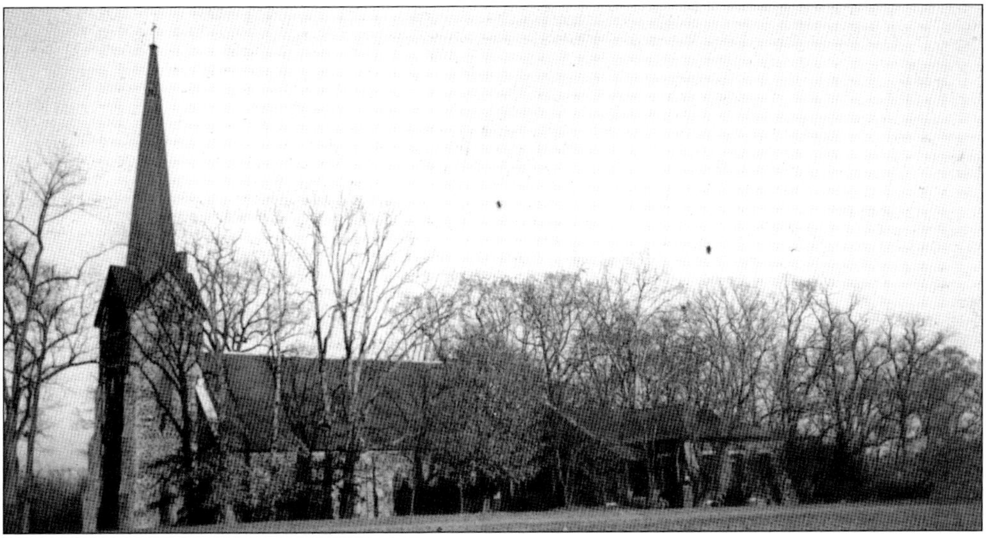

Shortly before the end of her life, Coffin completed a design for Wilmington's Christ Church. Coffin's design for the space bears little resemblance to her residential designs at sites like Gibraltar or Winterthur. Instead, it reflects Coffin's skill for designing institutional landscapes, something she honed in the years following the Great Depression. While much of Christ Church's campus is comprised of circular drives and motor courts to accommodate parishioners, the design also makes use of some of Coffin's staple plants including English yew (*Taxus baccata*) for year-round texture and azalea, forsythia, and lilacs (*Syringa vulgaris*) for seasonal color. The design was completed in 1952, coinciding with a renovation and expansion of the chapel. (Above, Winterthur; below, Hagley.)

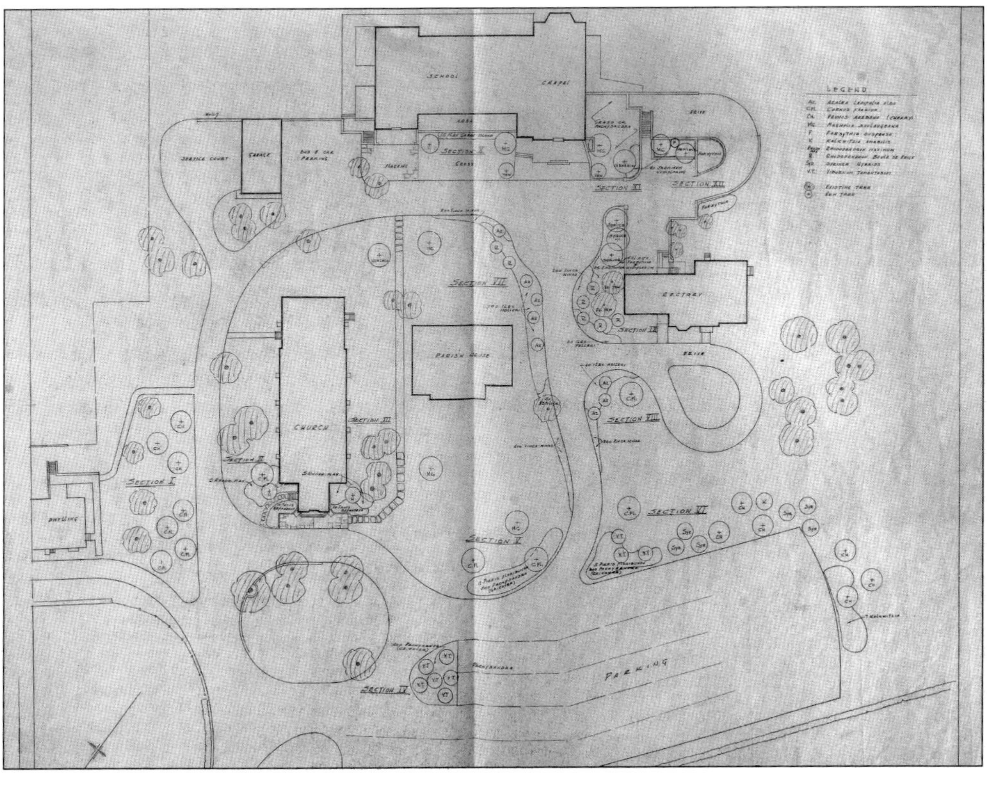

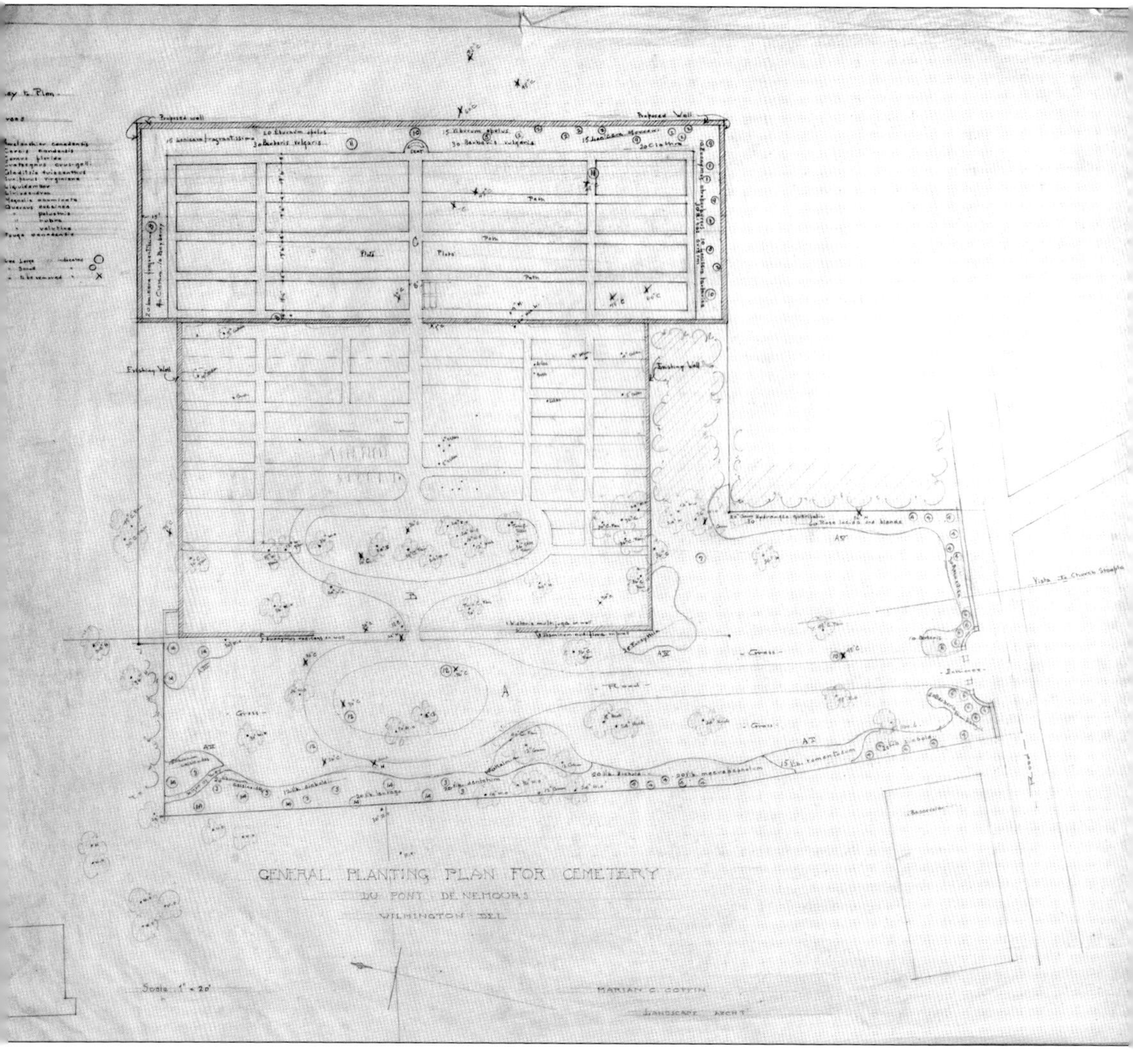

A testament to Coffin's closeness to the duPont family is her role in designing the duPont-Nemours family's burial ground near their Hagley estate. The location is notoriously private, known only to family, friends, and staff, and so the fact that Coffin was chosen to design it says a lot about her friendship. In designing the space, Coffin had a number of obstacles to consider, primarily the space's continuing use through time. The earliest burial occurred in 1830, with more likely occurring in undocumented locations, so Coffin's usual strategy of treating the soil, tilling it, and adding minerals was not feasible. Moreover, the presence of standing stones would make mowing difficult, and the space needed to be left open for future interments. Accordingly, Coffin chose plantings of trees, traditional low-maintenance shrubs, and simple ground covers such as yew (*Taxus baccata*), ferns, and pachysandra (*Pachysandra terminalis*). (Winterthur.)

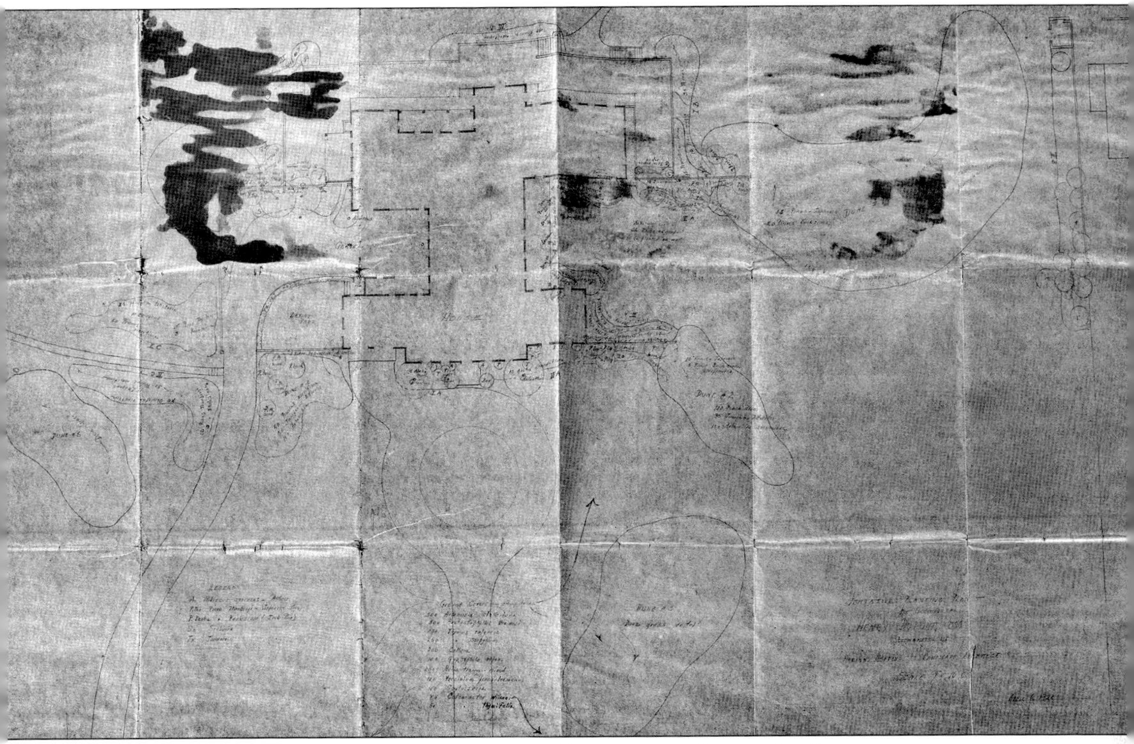

One of Coffin's most unique commissions was at Chestertown House, the Southampton summer home of Henry Francis duPont, named after the town in Maryland from where much of its interior decoration was obtained. The property was located on the beach, which imposed on Coffin a different consideration of soil and drainage than her prior works. Fortunately, the design documents at Southampton put more emphasis on constructed elements including walls, drives, and berms than on plantings. What plants are specified are mostly herbaceous perennials, which could survive in that climate, including ornamental grasses and moss roses (*Portulaca sp.*), among others. The home and its associated landscape no longer exist. The home, already expanded out of recognition by Baby Jane Hozler, was demolished in the early 2000s by Calvin Klein. (Winterthur.)

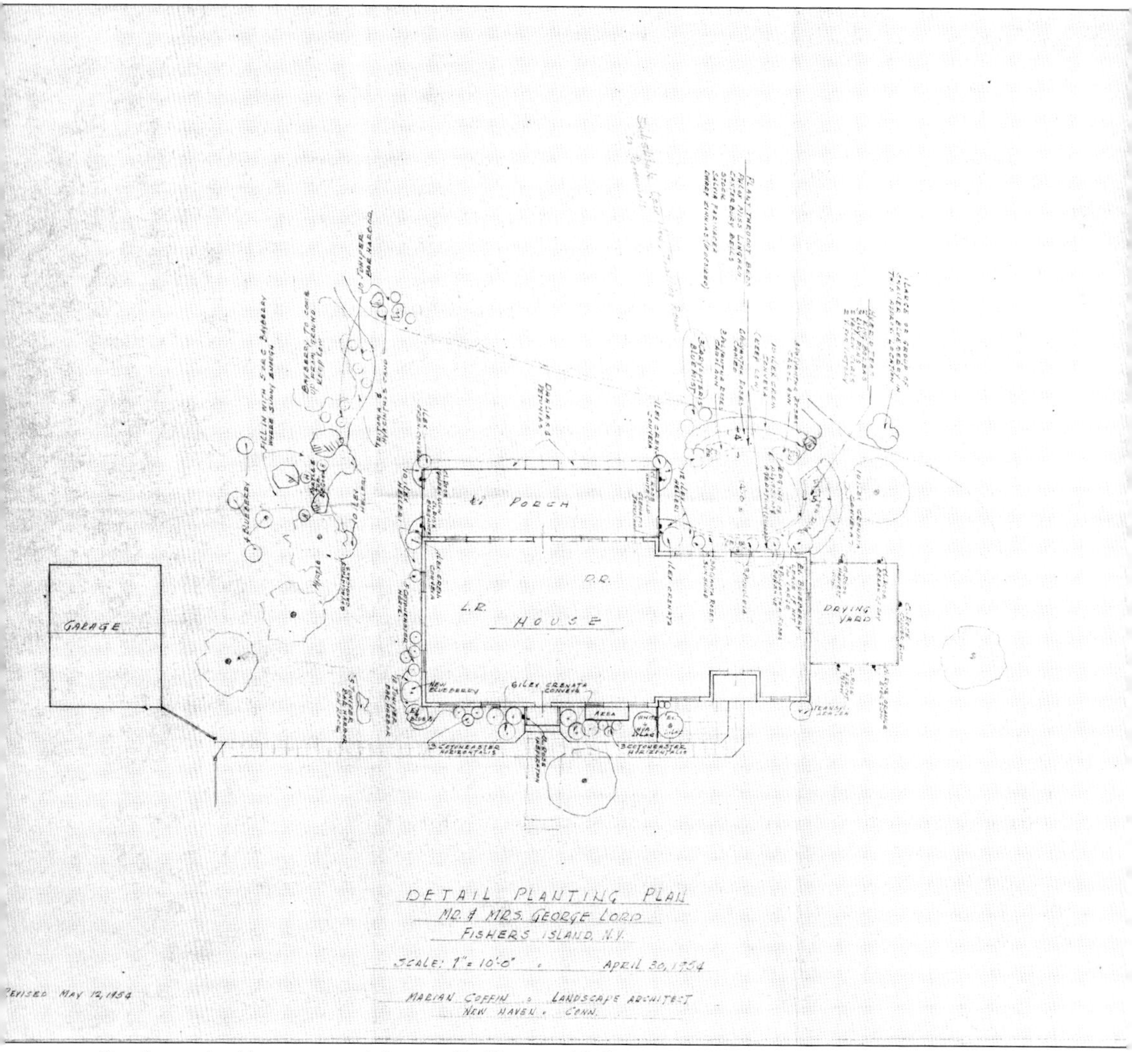

By the end of her career, Marian Coffin would design works for three generations of duPonts, including her close friend H.F. duPont's daughter, Ruth Ellen. While married to George deForest Lord, a Yale academic, Ruth commissioned Marian Coffin to create an estate plan for her home on Fishers Island, an island on the Connecticut border just north of Long Island, New York. The plan is incredibly detailed, comprising not just plantings but locations of roads and other infrastructure. Coffin also makes sure to include ample space for a play area for the couple's three small children. (Winterthur.)

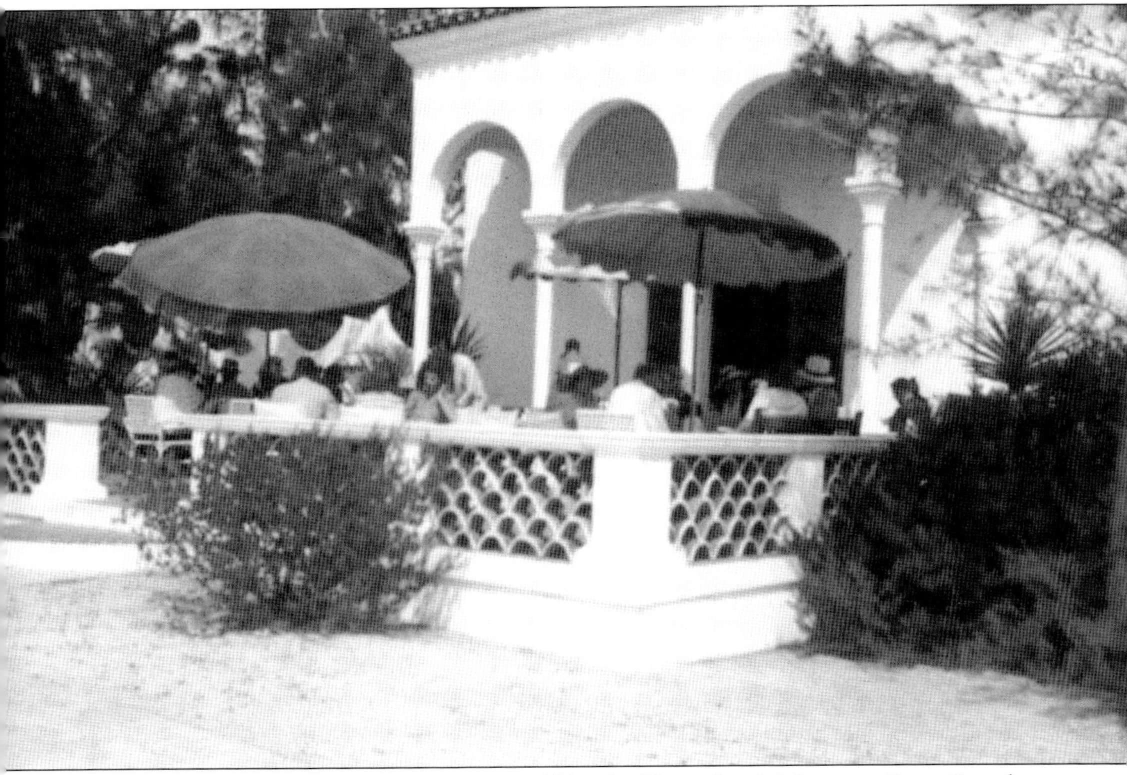

Marian Coffin's southernmost commission would be the Sharp family's home at Boca Grande, Florida, which they called "La Hacienda." The home was constructed in a combination Spanish/Moroccan style, which was a departure from many of Coffin's prior commissions. However, her design principles remain; while the plant palette is different due to the tropical climate, the landscape still has strong axial symmetry with naturalistic plantings. Coffin also had the opportunity to design not just a strolling garden as she normally did but also for the house's multiple interior courtyards. Major landscape features include a decorative garden rill water feature and a small gazebo, which bears more than a passing resemblance to Coffin's original concept sketches for Gibraltar's teahouse. (Hagley.)

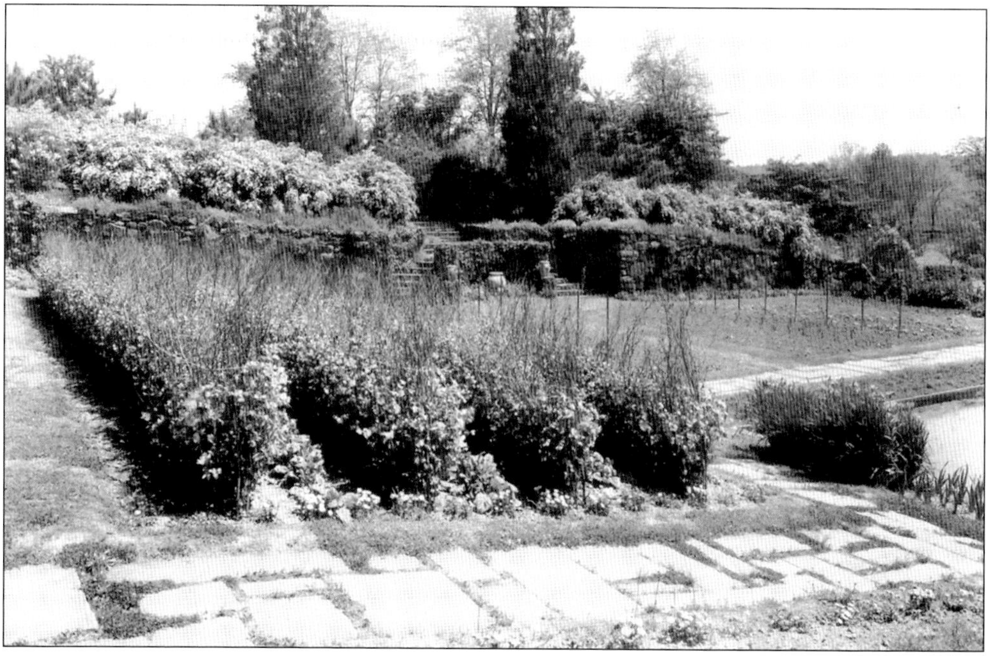

Hill Girt Farm, located in Chadds Ford, Pennsylvania, was, and still is, the working farm of the Haskell family, who commissioned Coffin to design a formal garden in the 1920s. The garden required both functionality and beauty, so this design proves to be one of Coffin's most unique. Here, we can see her ingenuity in turning the pond at the end of an existing, functional spillway into a lotus pond with echoes of ancient Persian gardening techniques. She surrounded the spillway with her characteristic natural mixed borders that included lupines (*Lupinus sp.*), Oriental poppies (*Papaver orientale*), and irises organized into complementary, but not completely matching, colors. (Both, Smithsonian Archive of American Gardens.)

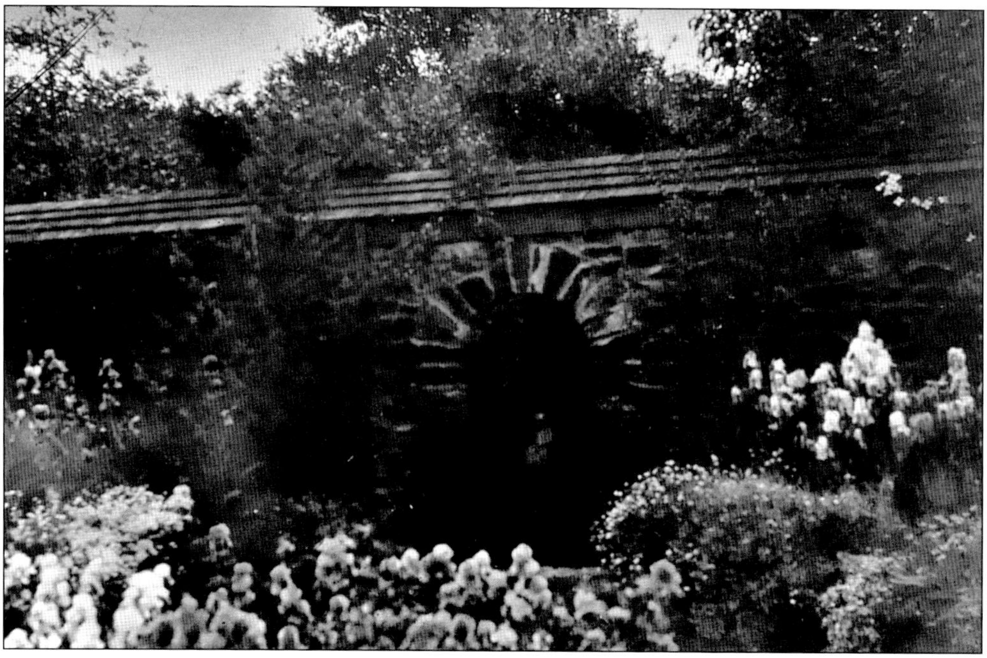

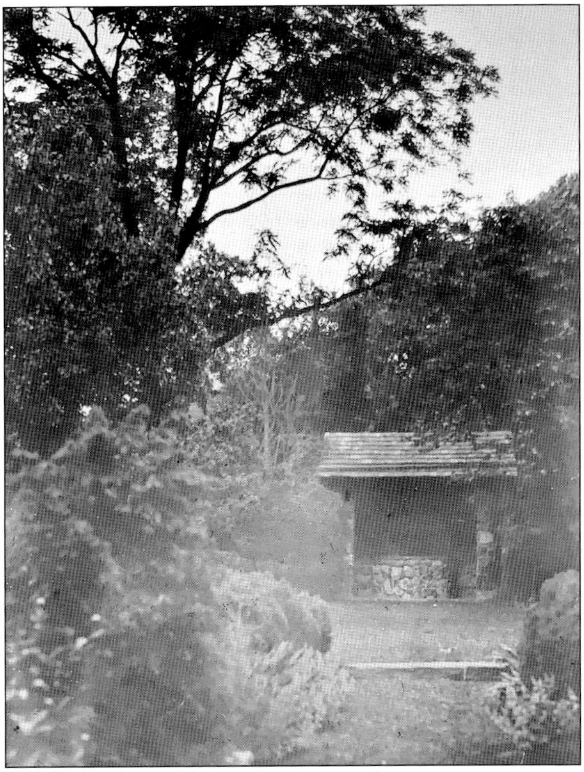

Hill Girt was also unique in that it challenged Coffin to work around existing landscaping and structures instead of starting with a blank slate, as was the case with many of her other commissions. The design showcases her ingenuity in the inclusion of her signature design touches, such as flagstone pathways and overflowing beds woven into the existing landscape fabric to incorporate the family's well, canal, and grape arbors. Her design for the site turned a working farm into a hobby farm, which would be both productive and aesthetically appealing for the family and their visitors. The farm and its landscape remain within the family. (Both, Haskell family.)

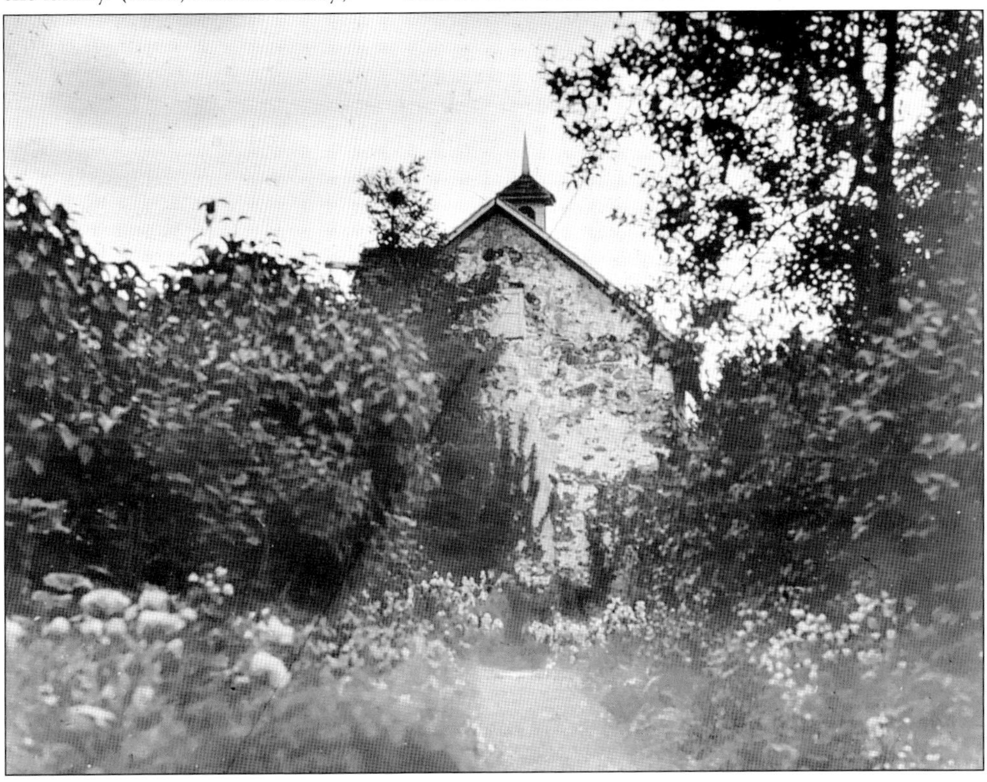

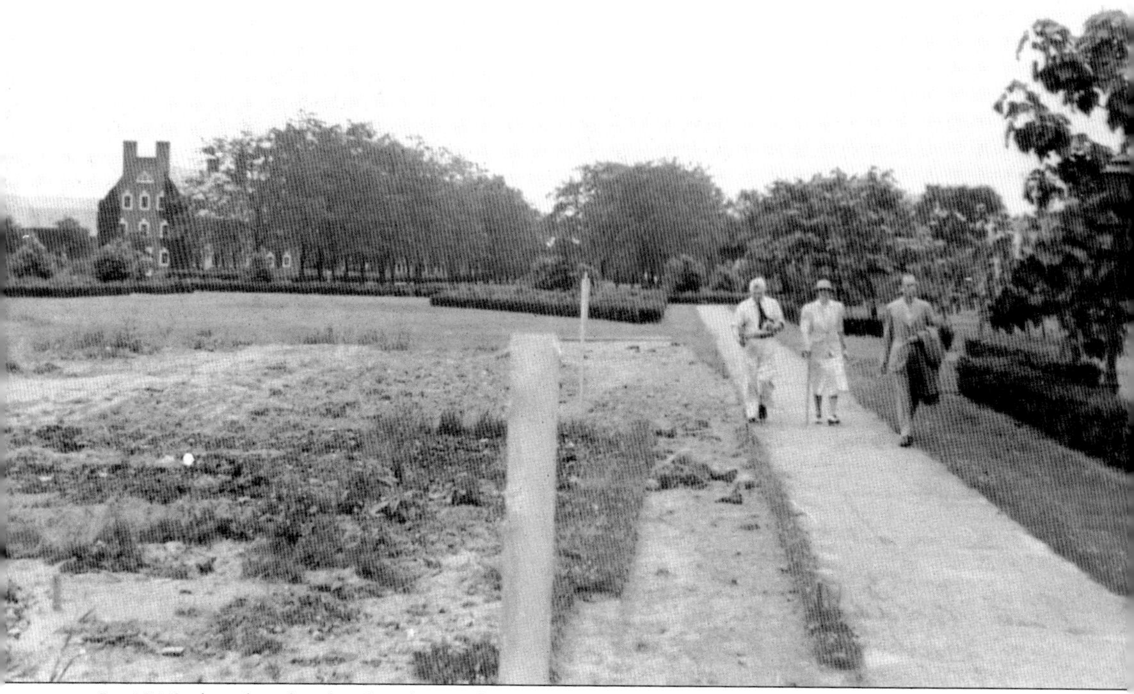

In 1915, shortly after his brother-in-law P.S. duPont made a hefty donation to the institution allowing its expansion, Sharp joined the board of the University of Delaware (UD). Five years after that, he worked with the board to commission Coffin to resolve the merging of two sides of the campus on what is now considered the university's central campus. While she had completed institutional work in the past, Coffin had a difficult job ahead of her at UD. Working within the site's existing design vernacular, she united the men's college, now called Old College, and the women's college, now south of Memorial Hall, which were laid out on different sides of the main thoroughfare with a non-axial alignment. Coffin completed the task with her usual mastery, using a central fountain feature, Magnolia Circle, to marry the two sides. Coffin worked as the campus' consulting landscape architect—laying out paths, suggesting locations for new buildings, and organizing plantings—for the next 40 years. Here, she can be seen walking on campus with Hugh Rodney Sharp and an unidentified man at some point in the 1940s. (Winterthur.)

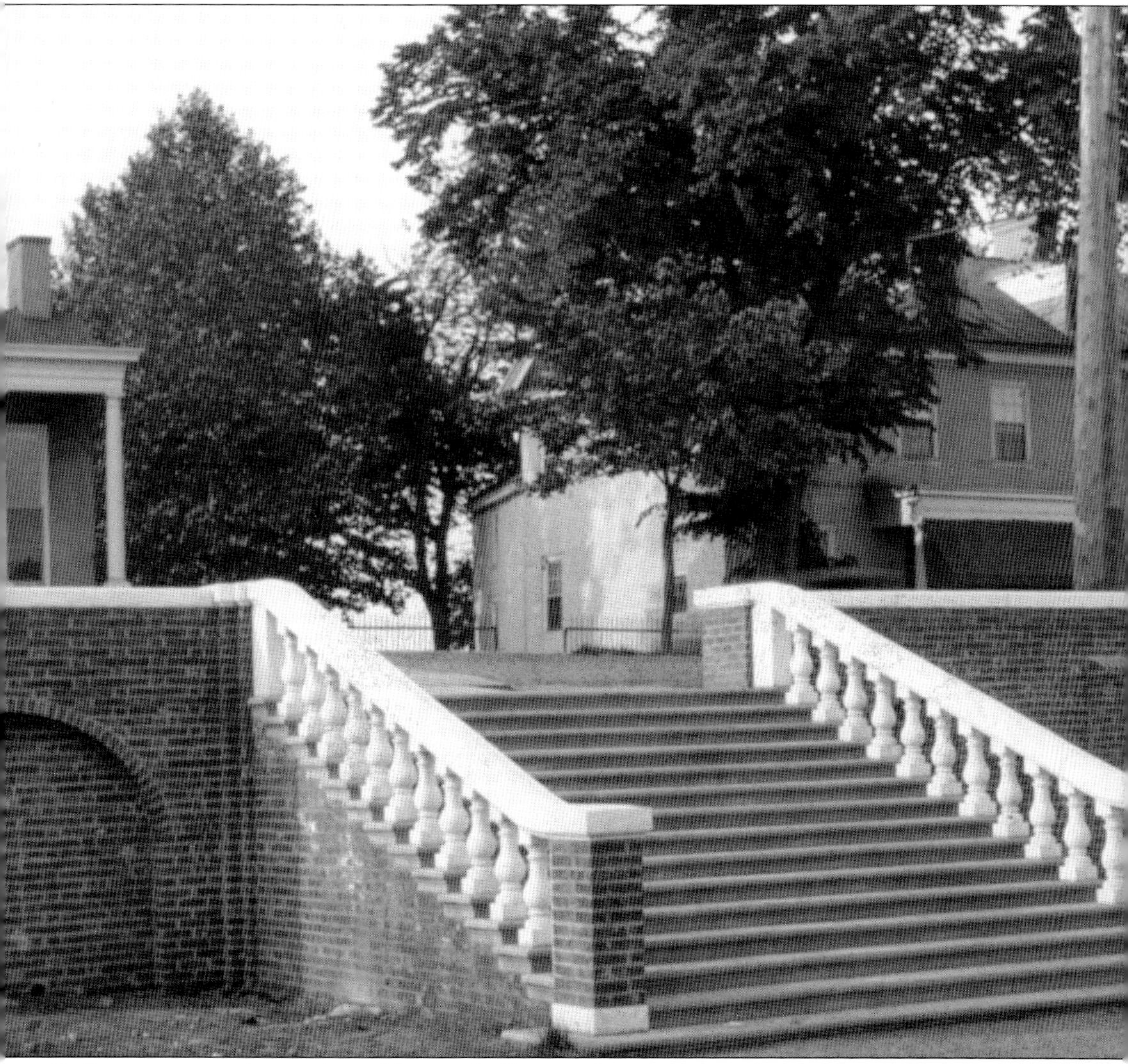

Coffin encountered a number of design challenges when designing the University of Delaware campus, most prominently how to separate the university from the surrounding community of Newark. While the university's original campus lay north of the town's primary thoroughfare on Main Street, the women's college and newly acquired land were located to the south. Due to the street's prominence, it could not be removed (as occurred farther south on campus). Instead, Coffin chose to excavate the Main Street intersection to separate the university from the town not by space, but by depth. Grand marble staircases were constructed from Main Street into the campus. A series of brick walls, mirroring the Colonial style of the campus and gesturing back to the Classical construction motif of relieving arches, accommodate the severe grade change. In this image, the stairs are seen shortly after their construction, as evidenced by the empty planting beds. Later, the beds were filled with low-maintenance evergreens, like English ivy and boxwoods. (Hagley.)

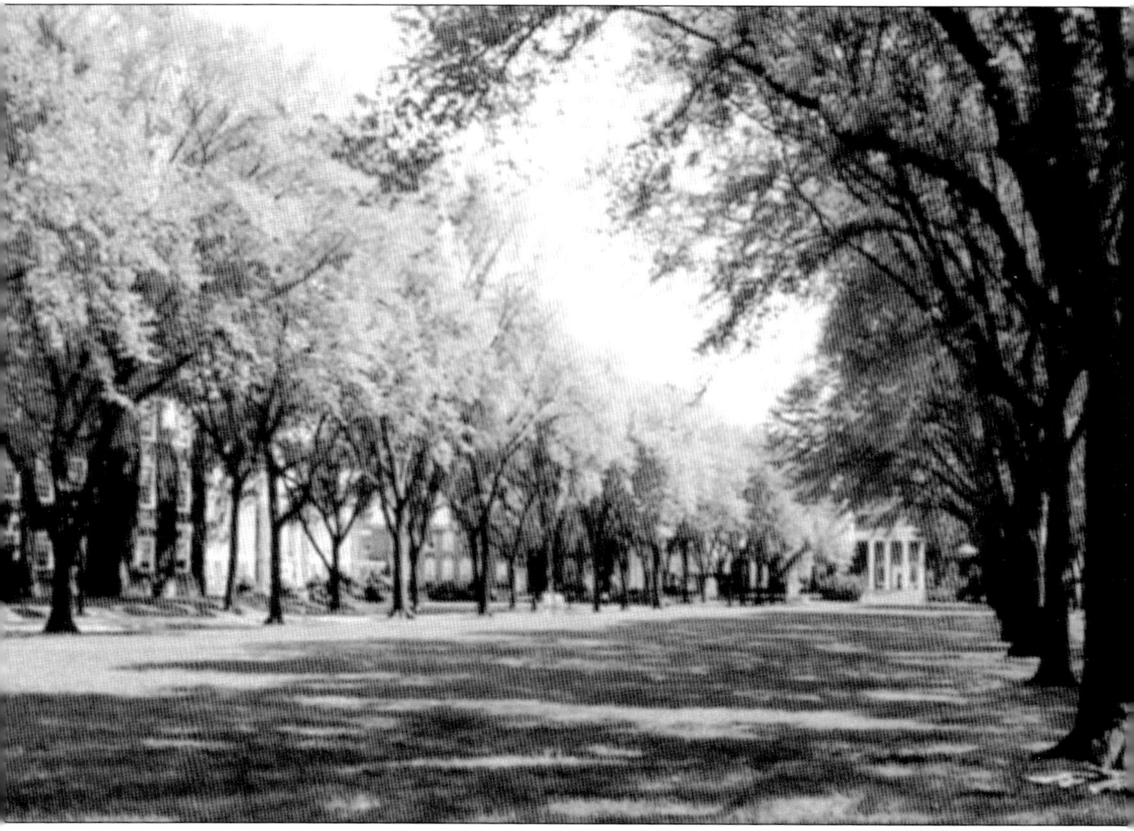

Perhaps the most iconic element of Coffin's design at the University of Delaware was her choice of tree canopy. North of Memorial Hall (at the time, the men's campus), she chose to line the pathways with American elms (*Ulnus americana*), while below Memorial on the women's campus, she chose honeylocust (*Gleditsia triacanthos var. inermis*). The choice was deliberate, as the strong coarse-textured elms to Coffin better represented the masculine, while the more delicate honeylocust, the feminine. These trees provided shading to cool the central green spaces while creating a cloistered environment in keeping with the educational atmosphere. While the campus was at one point home to more than 160 *Ulnus americana*, most of which were planted around 1917, only two of these originals remain. Most of the elms died off from a pathogen (*Ophiostoma novo-ulmi*) during the Dutch elm disease epidemic, which ravaged the country in the mid- to late 20th century. Japanese zelcova (*Zelkova serrata*) were first used to replace the elms. However, today, new disease-resistant elms are being planted on campus thanks to the efforts of graduate researchers, professors, and campus facilities staff. (Delaware Public Archives.)

Five

Gibraltar after 1968

Gibraltar mansion and estate passed from Sharp to his son Hugh Rodney Sharp Jr. after his death in 1968. At this time, the mansion was vacant, perpetuating a rapid decline in the building and gardens. The mid-1990s marked a turning point for Gibraltar as the Sharp grandchildren and a local preservation group began to collaborate to save the deteriorating property. Work was completed to deed the entire property to a preservation group called Preservation Delaware (now PDI). PDI is a statewide nonprofit organization dedicated to the preservation of Delaware's architectural heritage and historic settings through education, public policy initiatives, and technical assistance. Starting in the late 1990s, several redevelopment plans were explored to save the mansion by finding appropriate adaptive reuse. Meanwhile, the garden underwent a $1 million renovation in 1999–2000. In 2004, after a partial roof collapse, PDI paid for a temporary roof replacement over the mansion's solarium, and after determining the cost for a new slate roof was approximately $500,000, PDI realized the maintenance of the estate was too much for the small organization to carry. In 2008, PDI divested its share of the mansion and buildings to private developers while retaining ownership of the gardens. The current owners continue to search for appropriate adaptive reuse projects to sustain the house in a historically appropriate manner. As proposals come to fruition, PDI continues to weigh in and offer support for appropriate plans, including the most recent 2021 proposal to develop the mansion into a boutique hotel. This plan is under consideration by the community.

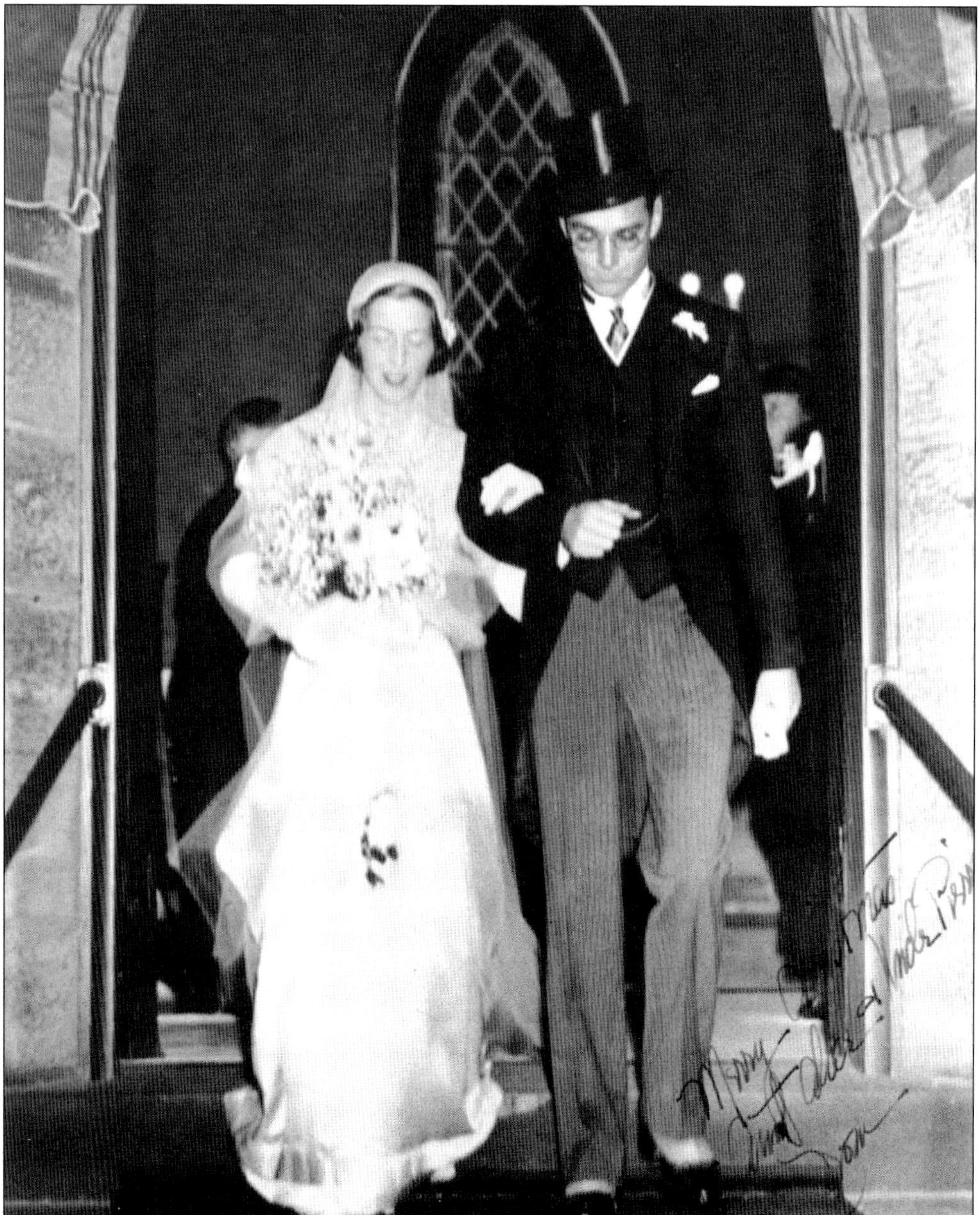

Sharp continued to reside at Gibraltar and remained a careful steward of the property until his death on August 8, 1968. Sharp's oldest son, Hugh R. Sharp Jr., shown here on his wedding day with his bride, Ada Barker Waldrop, inherited the estate. Sharp Jr., a World War II commander in the Delaware Civil Air Patrol, was a DuPont executive and also a University of Delaware trustee. He was influential in funding important projects for the University of Delaware's College of Earth Ocean and the Environment, but he did not share his father's passion for the estate gardens, and consequentially, the gardens and mansions declined into overgrown ruins. (Hagley.)

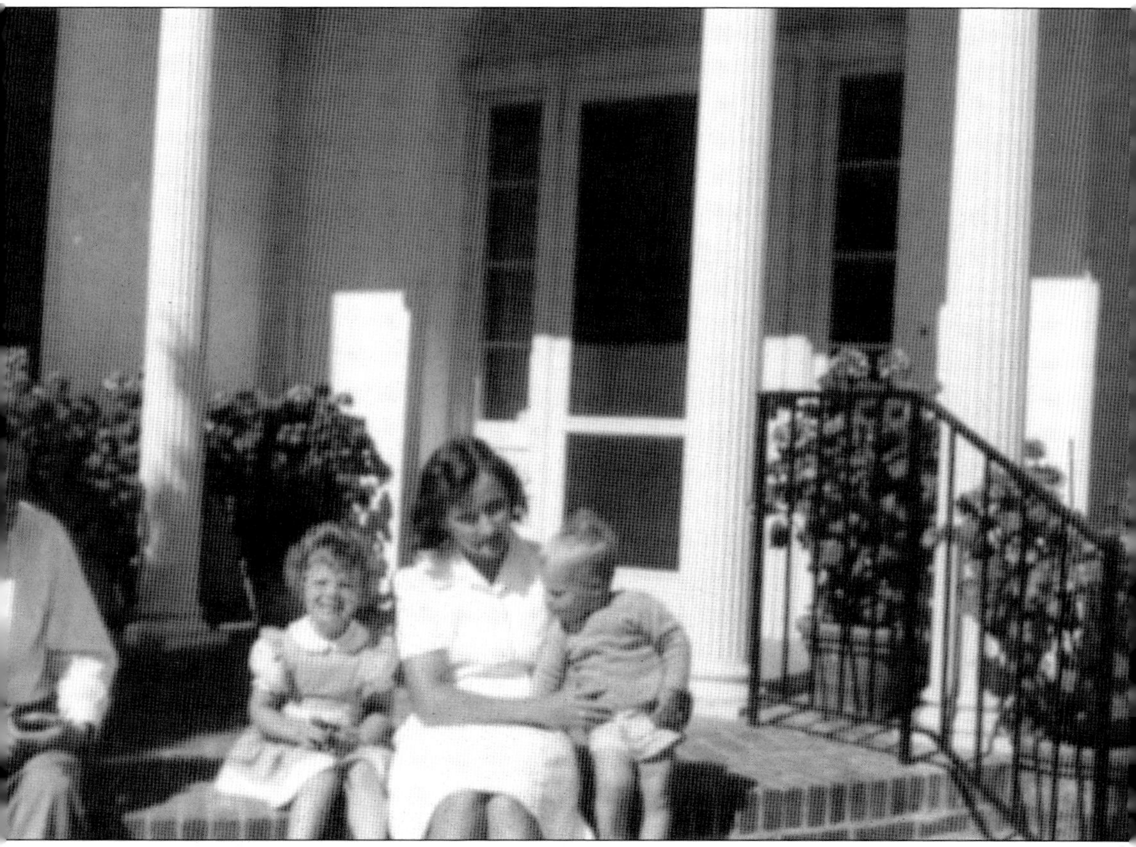

After Sharp Jr. died in 1990, the estate was then passed to the Sharp grandchildren, seen here, who considered a number of uses for the property. While the gardens were always, at least nominally, meant to be saved, the house had a less stable fate. Plans included keeping it as a residence or bulldozing it and replacing it with high-value condominiums, before the family settled on turning it into a small boutique hotel. With 10 bedrooms, each with its own bath, and numerous entertaining spaces, this seemed like the perfect second life for the home, but it fell through due to community protesting. (Hagley.)

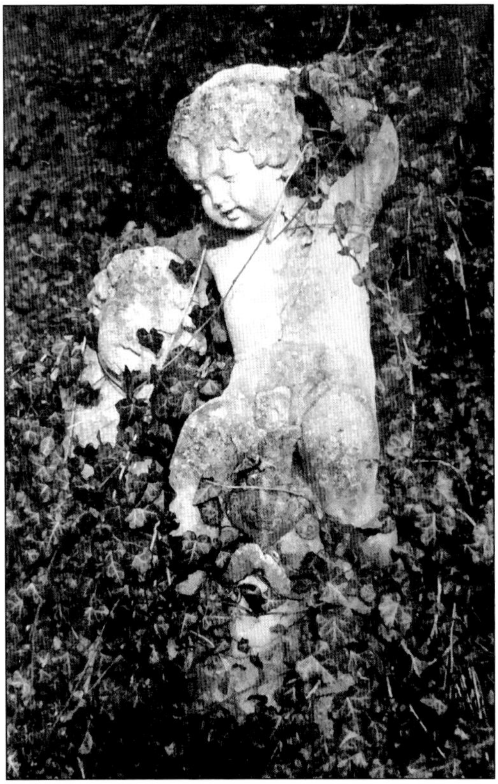

From 1968 to 1990, there is no record of the garden being presented on garden tours, and it is believed the gardens were minimally maintained until Sharp Jr.'s death in 1990. In the 1970s, the swimming pool was filled with soil and replaced with lawn. The concrete coping surrounding the pool and the cherub and dolphin statue on the pool's north side remained in place and visible, as seen in this photograph. Later, English ivy and other weeds overtook the statue. In Iris Gestram's 1997 thesis, she reported that both the coping and the ornament were in "fair condition." (Both, PDI.)

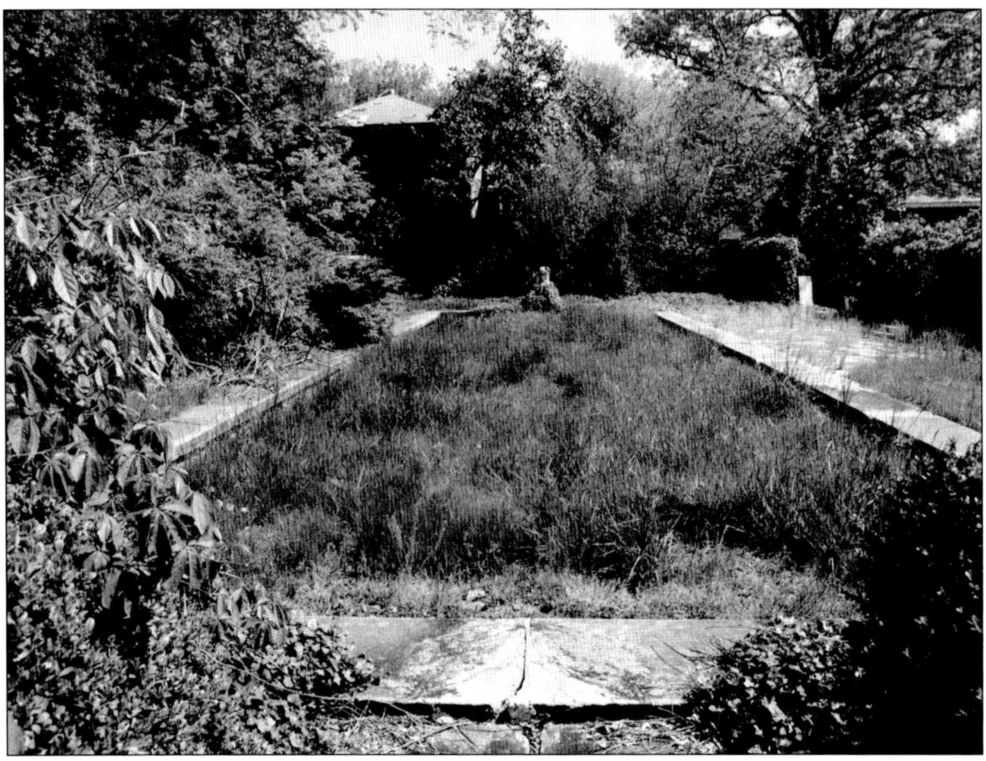

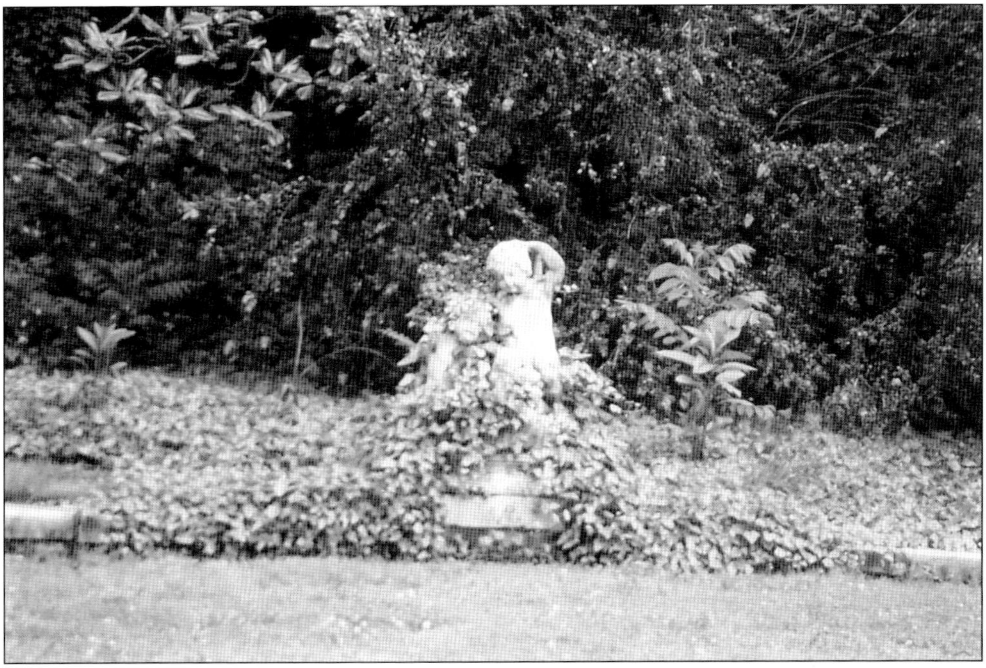

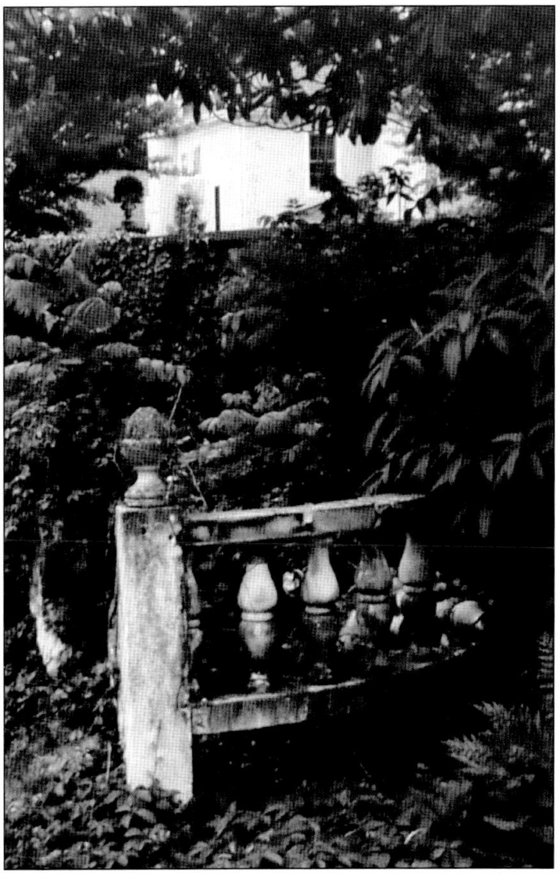

By the mid-1990s, discussions were taking place among interested parties about what to do with the property. An early proposal to raze the mansion and develop an upscale residential community catalyzed different interest groups around preservation efforts. During this time, the mansion was vacant, and vandalism at both the house and gardens was rampant. As seen in these photographs, vandals were not the only problem in the garden. Invasive plants and vines climbed over garden elements, including walls, benches, and statues, threatening their survival. While the gardens were overgrown and in disrepair, a shell of their former glory, the strong "bones" of the garden remained as a testament to the carefully planned Coffin design. (Both, PDI.)

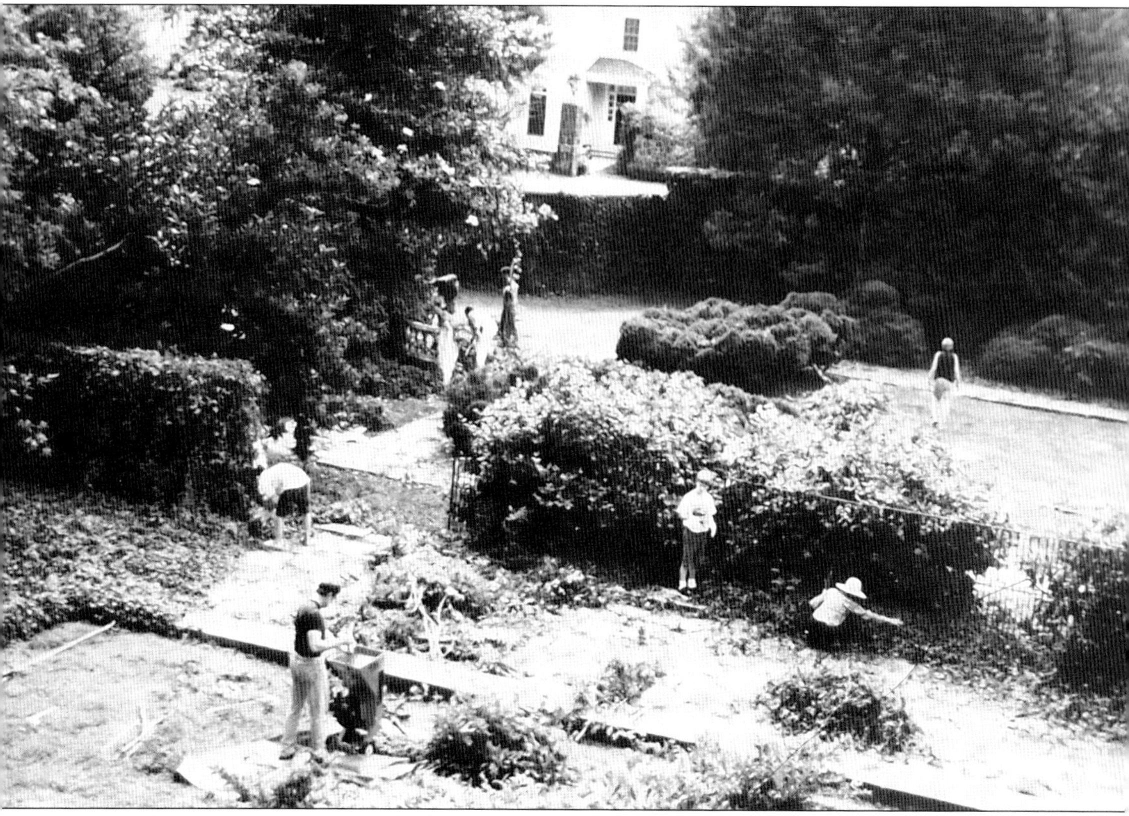

In 1995, the National Trust for Historic Preservation contacted Preservation Delaware, Inc., to persuade the group to help with the efforts to save Gibraltar. The Sharp family, the State of Delaware, and PDI collaborated to find self-sustaining economic reuse for the building and grounds. The group developed a proposal to convert the mansion into a small inn. PDI was awarded several grants through the state's bond bill process, and in March 1997, the State of Delaware's Open Space Council purchased the development rights to Gibraltar for $1 million. Those development rights were then transferred to PDI. In June 1997, the Sharp family deeded the estate to PDI for $750,000, and a conservation easement was placed on the property allowing for adaptive reuse as a hotel. With renewed interest in the mansion and gardens, volunteer groups cleaned up vines and debris, as seen in this photograph. (PDI.)

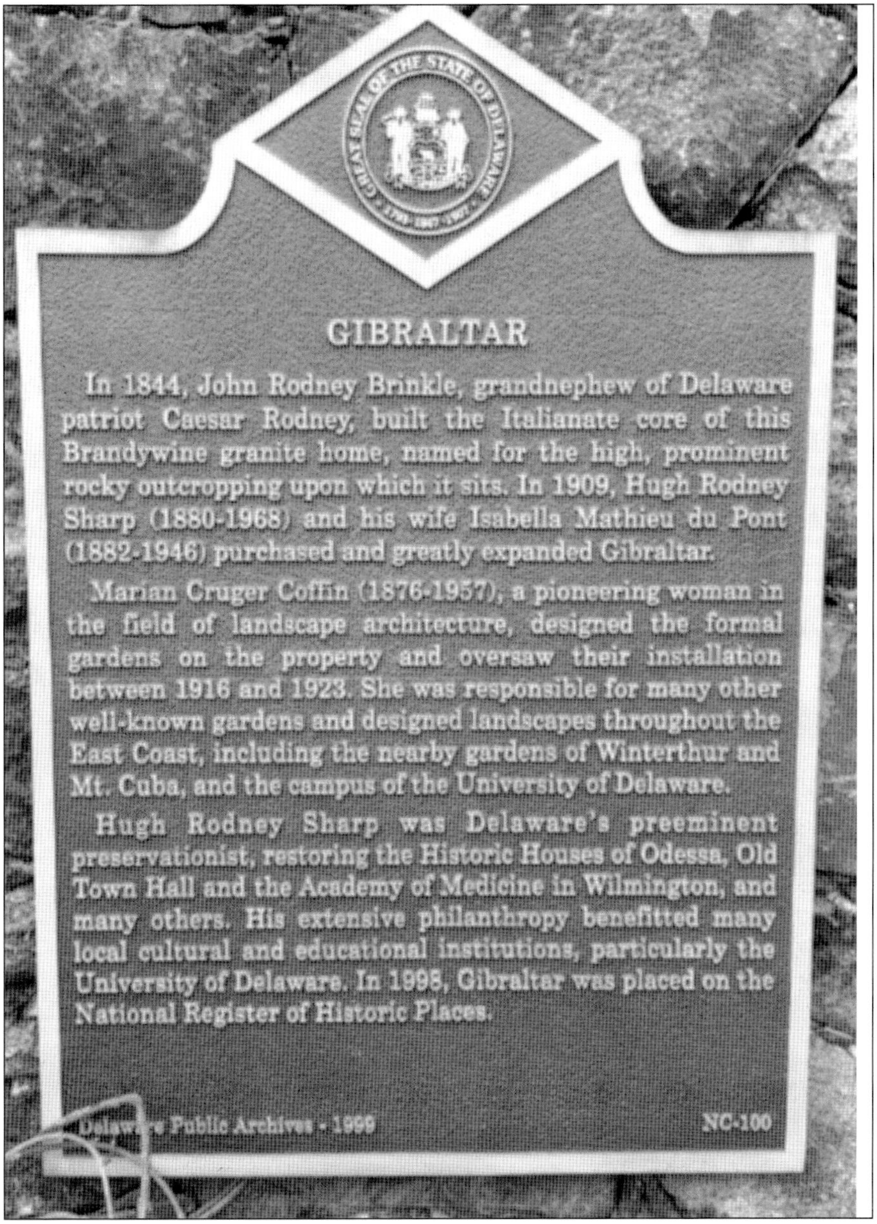

In September 1998, the mansion and gardens were entered into the National Register of Historic Places, and the plaque, pictured in the photograph, was installed at the property in 1999. The application, prepared by Mary Anna Ralph, who worked for the Wilmington Planning Department as the historic preservation planner, noted two specific criteria. First, the "property is associated with the lives of persons significant in our past," as it was the "residence of Hugh Rodney Sharp, one of Delaware's preeminent preservationists and philanthropists associated with the early twentieth century growth of the duPont Company." Secondly, the "property embodies the distinctive characteristics of a type, period, or method of construction or represents the work of a master, or possesses high artistic values, or represents a significant and distinguishable entity whose components lack individual distinction," for Coffin's contribution and representation of the "American Country Place era of landscape design." (Delaware Public Archives.)

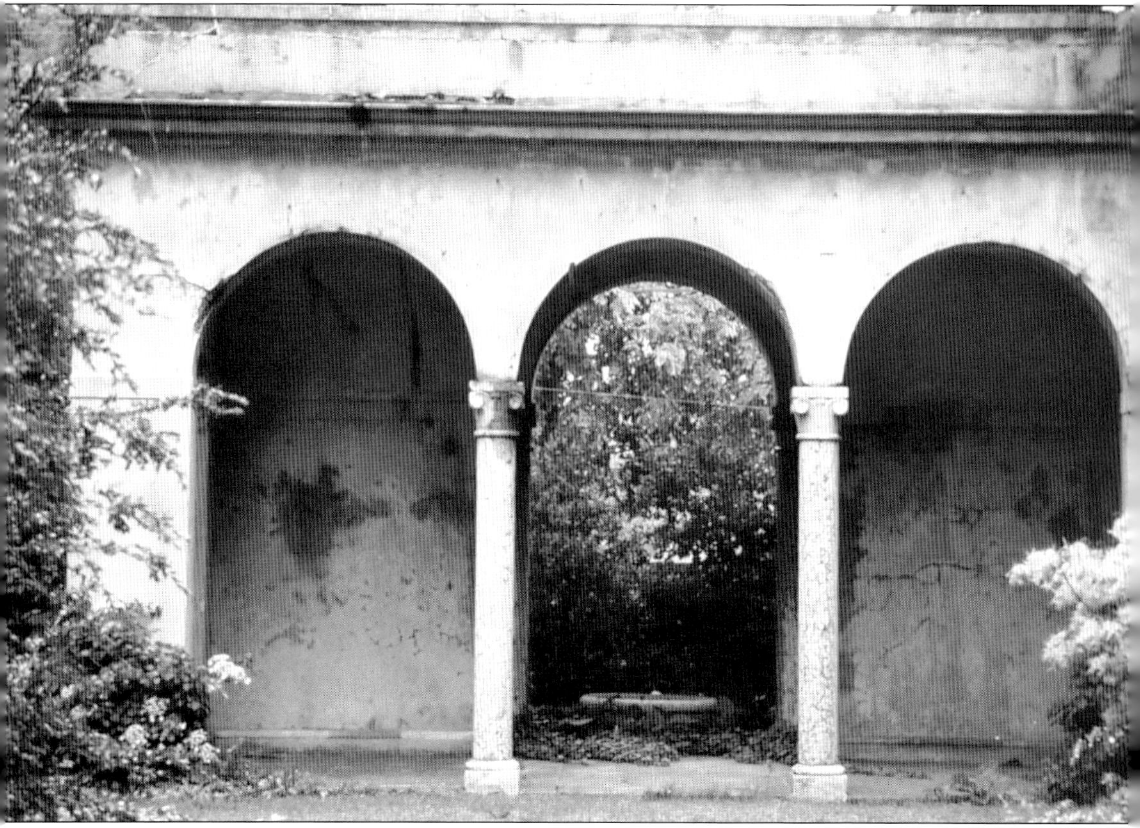

In October 1998, PDI entered into an agreement with a developer that permitted the conversion of the house to an "elegant country inn" with 30 rooms, meeting spaces, and a restaurant in the former greenhouses. The 1998 agreement spurred on community interest and was the catalyst for the fundraising that occurred to restore the gardens. Unfortunately, the agreement was terminated in May 2002 after the developer could not secure the financing. PDI and Gibraltar House Associates signed a new agreement for a similar project in 2002; however, that project also subsequently fell through. (PDI.)

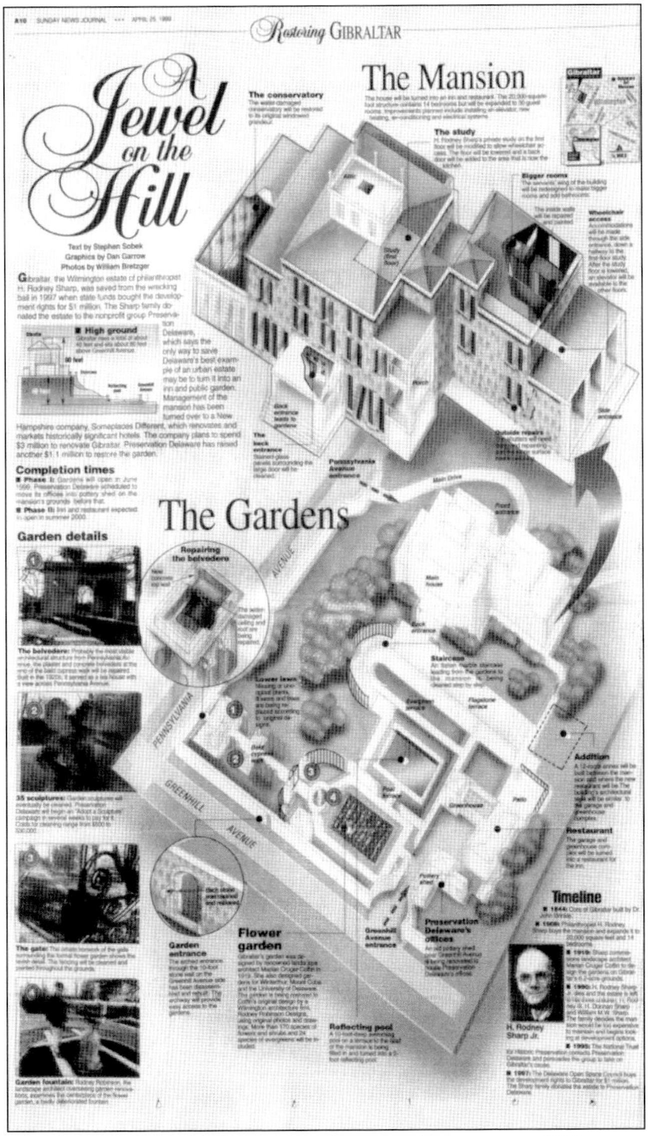

Restoring GIBRALTAR

A Jewel on the Hill

The Mansion

The Gardens

Completion times

Garden details

Timeline

The potential mansion and gardens restoration became big news in Wilmington, and on April 25, 1999, a full-page spread in Wilmington's *Sunday News Journal* highlighted the details. The captions describe how the redevelopment will turn the house into an inn and restaurant expected to open in summer 2000, when the "20,0000-square-foot structure," containing 14 bedrooms, "will be expanded to 30 guest rooms." The graphic also highlights the 1998 "Adopt a Sculpture" campaign launched after Preservation Delaware secured funding from a national Save Outdoor Sculpture! (SOS!) Conservation Assessment award and a Delaware Division of the Arts Project Support grant to fund a conservator to survey the sculpture collection and provide a report. The program's ultimate goal was to repair and clean 35 sculptures—work estimated at $500 to $30,000 per statue. Additionally, the graphic highlights the future garden restoration, a commission awarded to the Wilmington landscape architectural firm Rodney Robinson Landscape Architects (now Robinson Anderson Summers, Inc.). Overall, the image highlights the vast scale of the garden restoration that would include "more than 170 species of flowers and shrubs and 24 species of evergreens." (News Journal.)

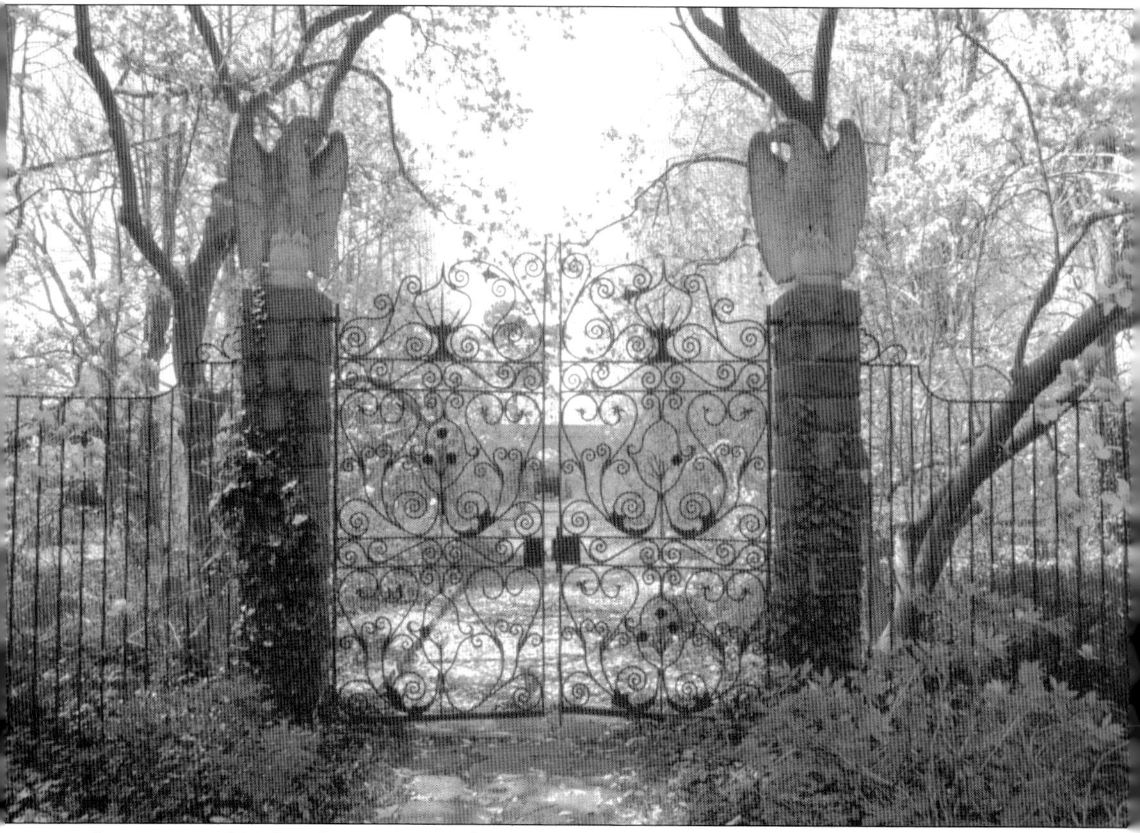

In summer 1997, Iris Gestram, a graduate student at the University of Delaware, completed her graduate thesis under a distinguished graduate committee led by James E. Swasey, a University of Delaware professor in plant and soil sciences. *The Historic Landscape at Gibraltar: A Proposal for its Preservation* is ambitious and provides thorough documentation of the garden's decline. In her acknowledgments, she credits the Sharp family for supporting her research and providing access to original documents, including the original Coffin landscape plans. Unfortunately, copies of these plans were shared with PDI and, later, lost in a 2012 flood and the original plans were thought to be lost as well. Gestram's thesis provides a detailed inventory of the background information and the evolution of Gibraltar from the early 1800s to 1996. It includes a plant list for the formal flower garden and a map and inventory of the garden ornaments and ironwork. The thesis concludes by describing a detailed recommended preservation process, including a list of the sculptures such as the eagles seen here on top of the stone pillars entering the allée. (PDI.)

The Four Seasons sculptures were installed in the garden in 1923 as an essential part of Coffin's plan for the bald cypress allée. According to the 1998 Gibraltar Adopt-A-Sculpture booklet, Coffin described the allée as a "path . . . accentuated by a break in the center and by four large Smoketrees and, still more importantly, by nearly life-size stone statues that once graced a pleasure house on the Brenta" in her 1940 book. As mentioned previously, the Sharps purchased the Four Seasons during their 1922 trip to Italy. At the time of the Adopt-A-Sculpture campaign, the condition of the Four Seasons sculptures was stable except for Autumn, described as "very unstable with all surfaces eroded and soiled with algae growing in many areas." The conservation recommendations provided an adoption cost for Autumn of $15,500 in 1998 dollars. (Both, PDI.)

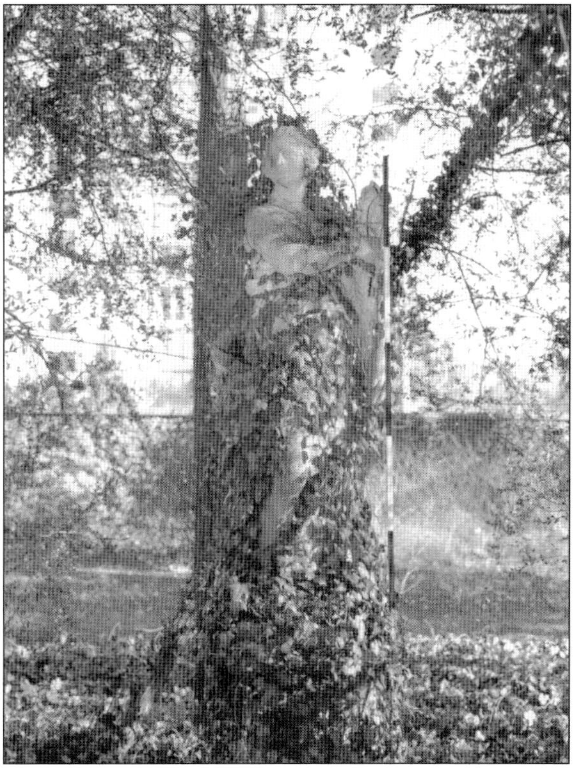

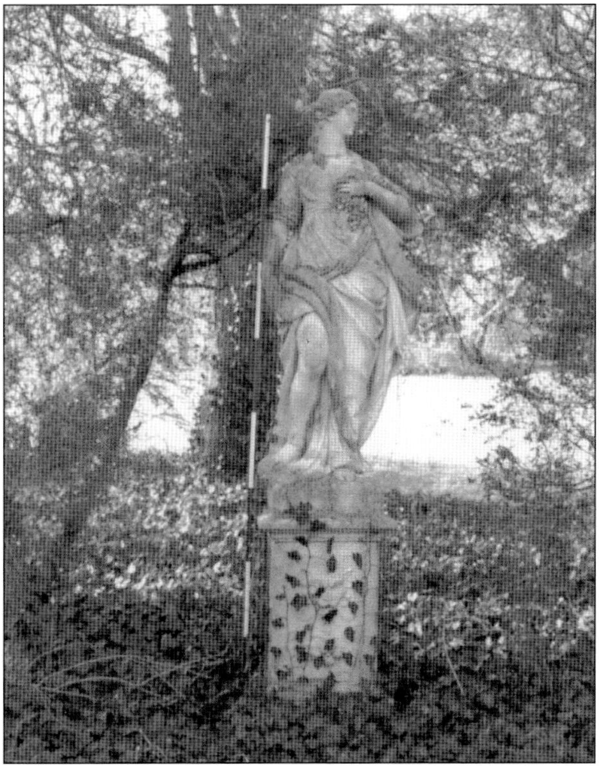

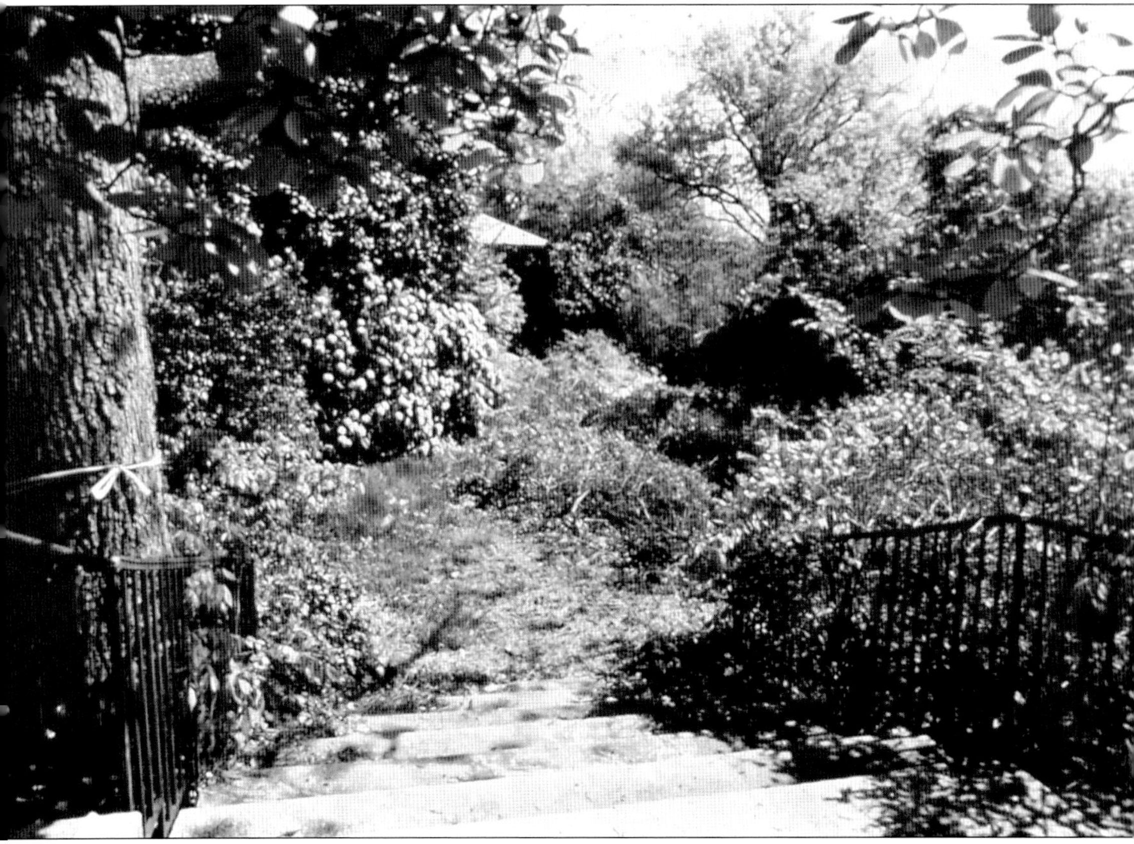

In 1998, Mary Jane Elliot became the head of the Gibraltar Gardens Capital Campaign Committee. This group raised $2.1 million for a garden renovation and garden maintenance endowment and selected Rodney Robinson Landscape Architects (RRLA) to complete the $1 million garden renovation. Gestram's thesis, Coffin's original plans, and historical photographs guided RRLA's work as they developed detailed renovation plans that included restoring the horticulture, sculpture, ironwork, hardscaping, and lighting. According to Robinson, the garden was completely overgrown and covered with English ivy, Virginia creeper (*Parthenocissus quinquefolia*), honeysuckle (*Lonicera sp.*), and other kinds of vines. However, he recalled the vines turned out to be a "blessing in disguise" because over time, as the garden was abandoned for decades, the vines hid many sculptures, which would have been vandalized or carried off. When volunteers cleared the vines, they found the many original sculptures still present and intact. (PDI.)

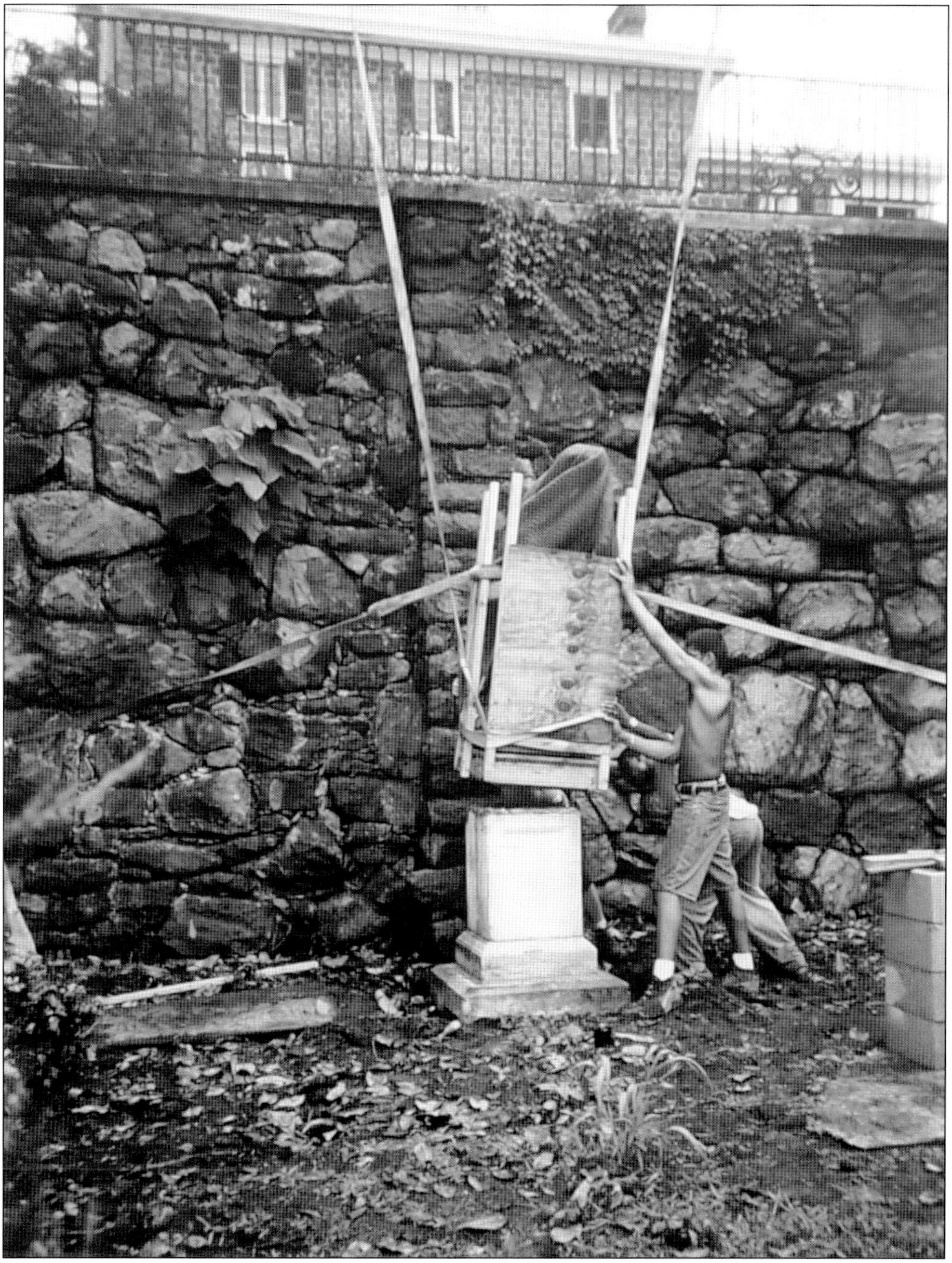

RRLA began the restoration by evaluating the safety of the garden. First, his team assessed and subsequently removed elements that could injure the public, like unhealthy trees and large tree limbs. Next, the walls, fences, paving, and sculptures were evaluated and stabilized before determining which specialists were required. For example, Robinson asked Lynn R. Batdorf, a boxwood expert from the US Arboretum, to evaluate the many old boxwood specimens. Batdorf recommended to keep the boxwood in the allée, because they were old plants and quite rare. He also to adjusting the soil pH for the boxwood plants that prefer a more basic soil since years of neglect allowed leaf litter to accumulate and lower the soil pH. (PDI.)

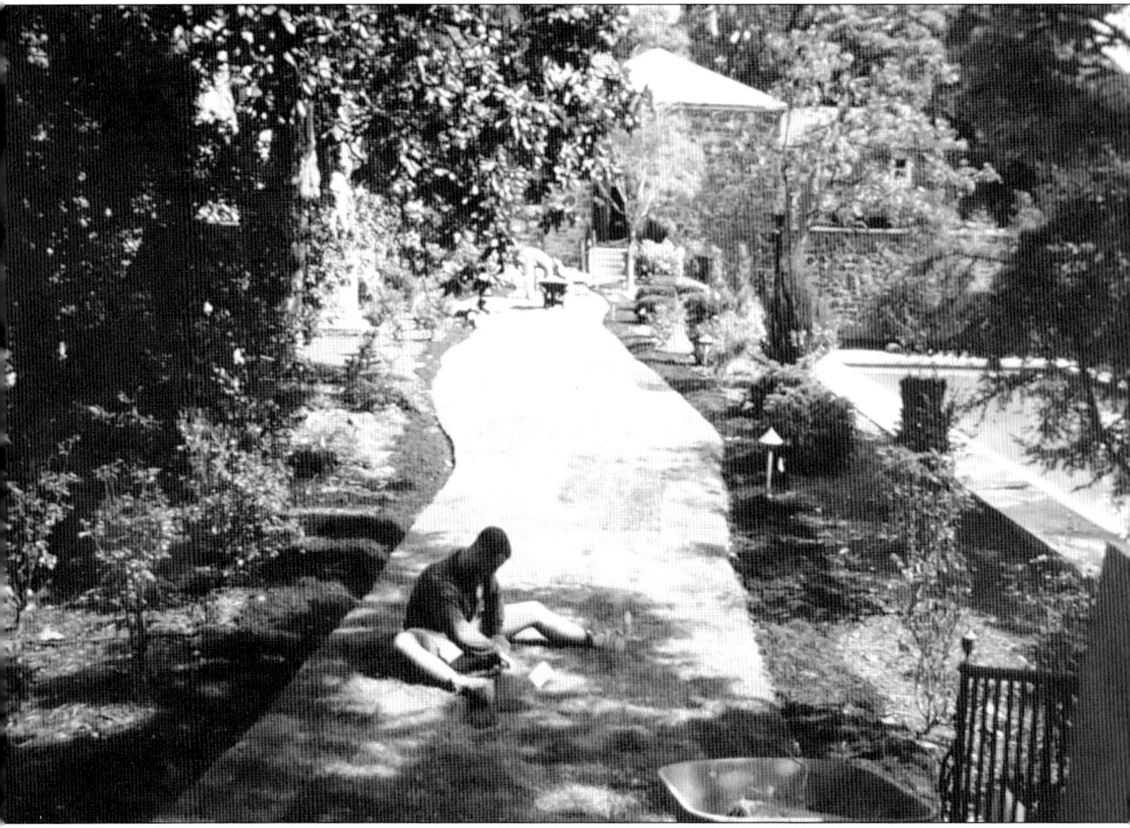

After RRLA completed a plan to replant the four major garden rooms at Gibraltar, it came time to install. Here, we can see a group of workers putting the finishing touches on a newly-restored evergreen terrace. The plantings in all garden rooms were extremely accurate to Coffin's original plans, making the garden rooms close to how the Sharps would have seen them in 1916. However, without the dedicated maintenance staff of the original estate, many of these plantings became unmanageable over time and during the years ahead, as development plans for the mansion—which, at the time of the design, were intended to fund the garden's maintenance—fell through. (PDI.).

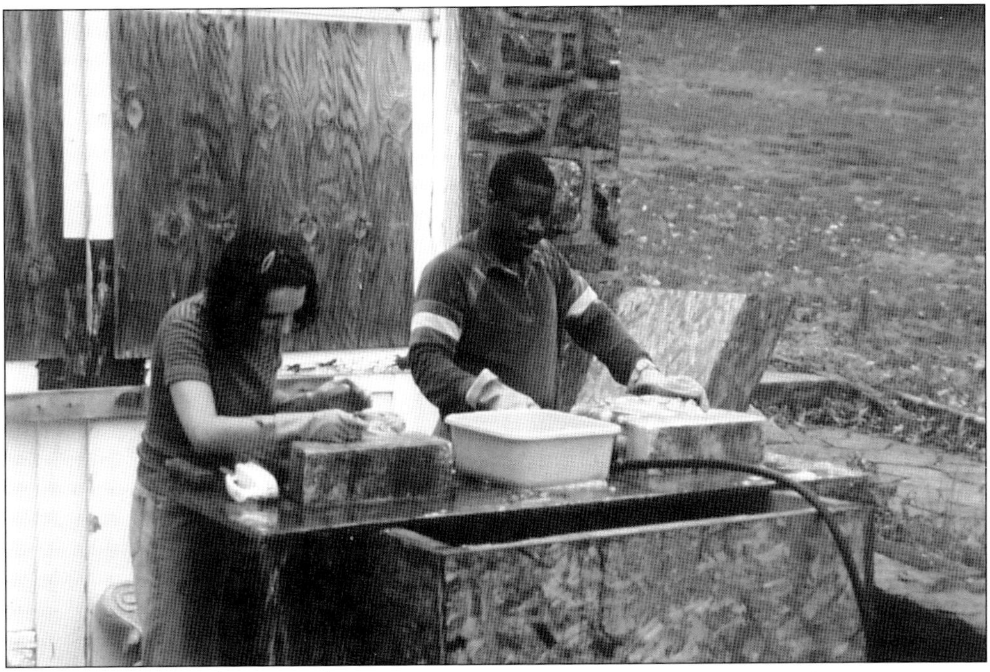

Nedda Moqtaderi, who majored in art conservation at the University of Delaware, evaluated all the statues before restoration. This painstaking process required care, as seen in the photograph from December 1999, as two artists labored to clean the basis of one garden bench. There was a great deal of complexity during the operation to remove the sculptures from their bases and place them in a safe area for cleaning. Notes from a 1998 meeting between active parties included discussions about moving sculpture pieces during construction and highlighting the conservator's need to direct the undertaking. The meeting notes also indicate the pool fountain cherubs and the flower garden fountain were a "restoration priority." (Both, PDI.)

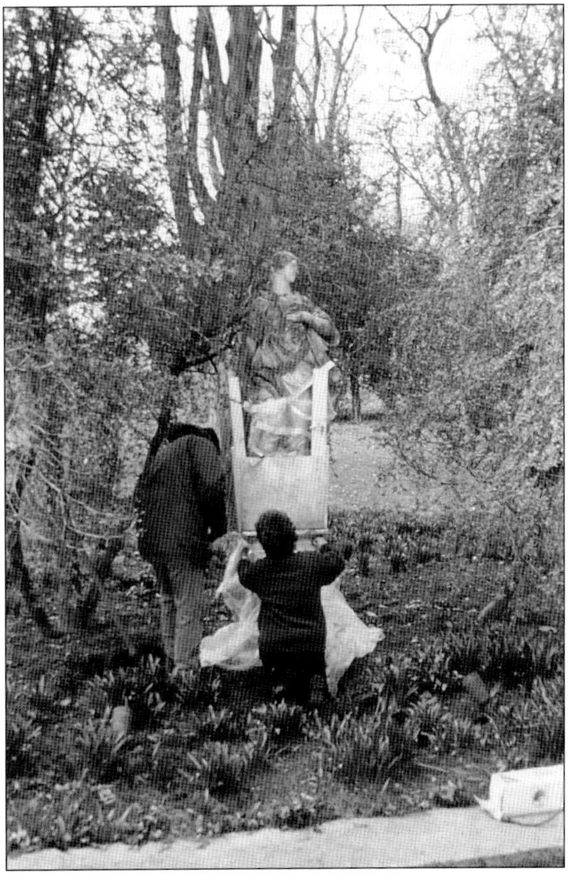

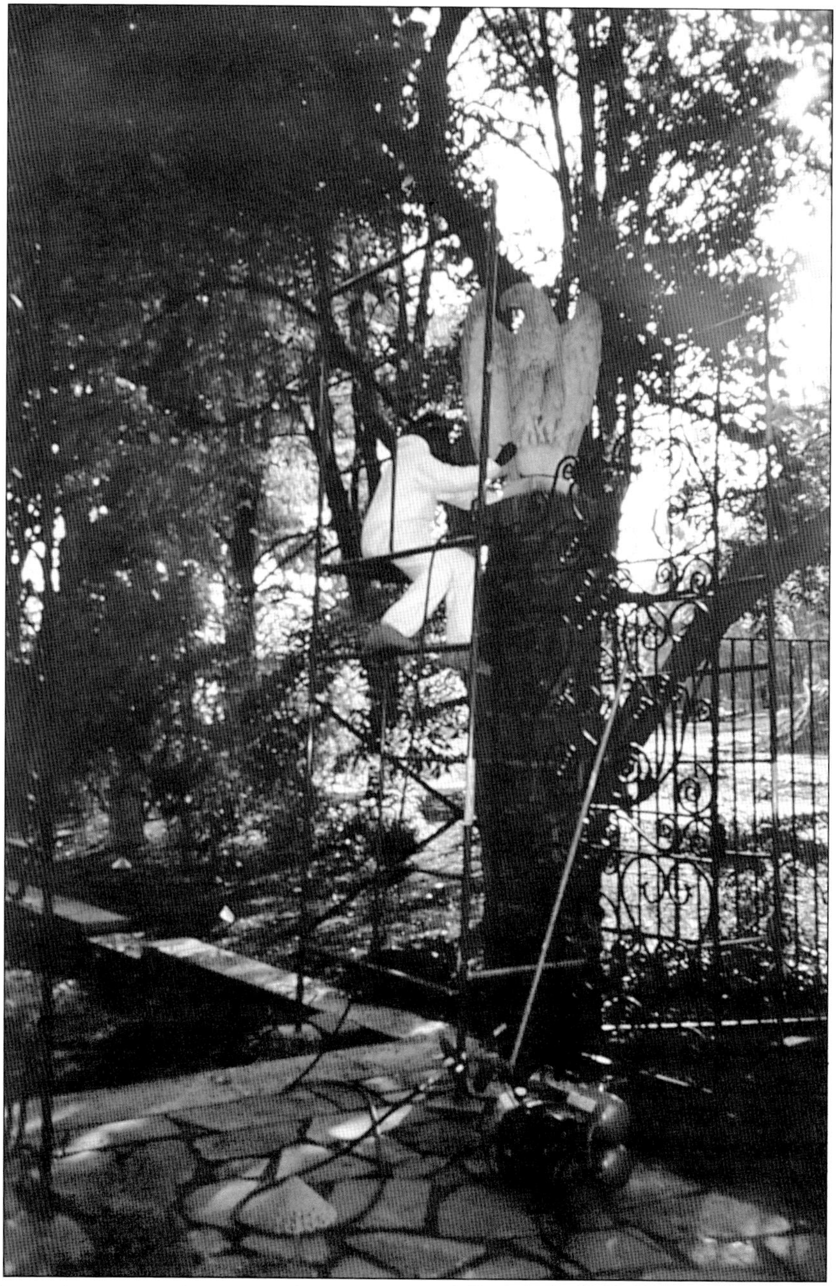

Once the garden renovation was underway, experts fully refurbished all of the statues and garden elements. This photograph shows a scaffold system erected around one of the entrance columns to the allée and an unknown artist working to restore one pair of eagles that sits atop one of the stone pillars. To clean the stone sculpture, the conservation team used a misting system. After draping hoses with small nozzles around each sculpture, they let the water mist the stone for several days to soften before delicately scrubbing with a soft brush. Importantly, no harsh chemicals were used in the restoration of the statuary. Also visible in this photograph is the marble paving stone pathway. Each stone was painstakingly lifted during the renovation, numbered, cleaned, and restored, and then returned to the exact spot to complete the renovation. (PDI.)

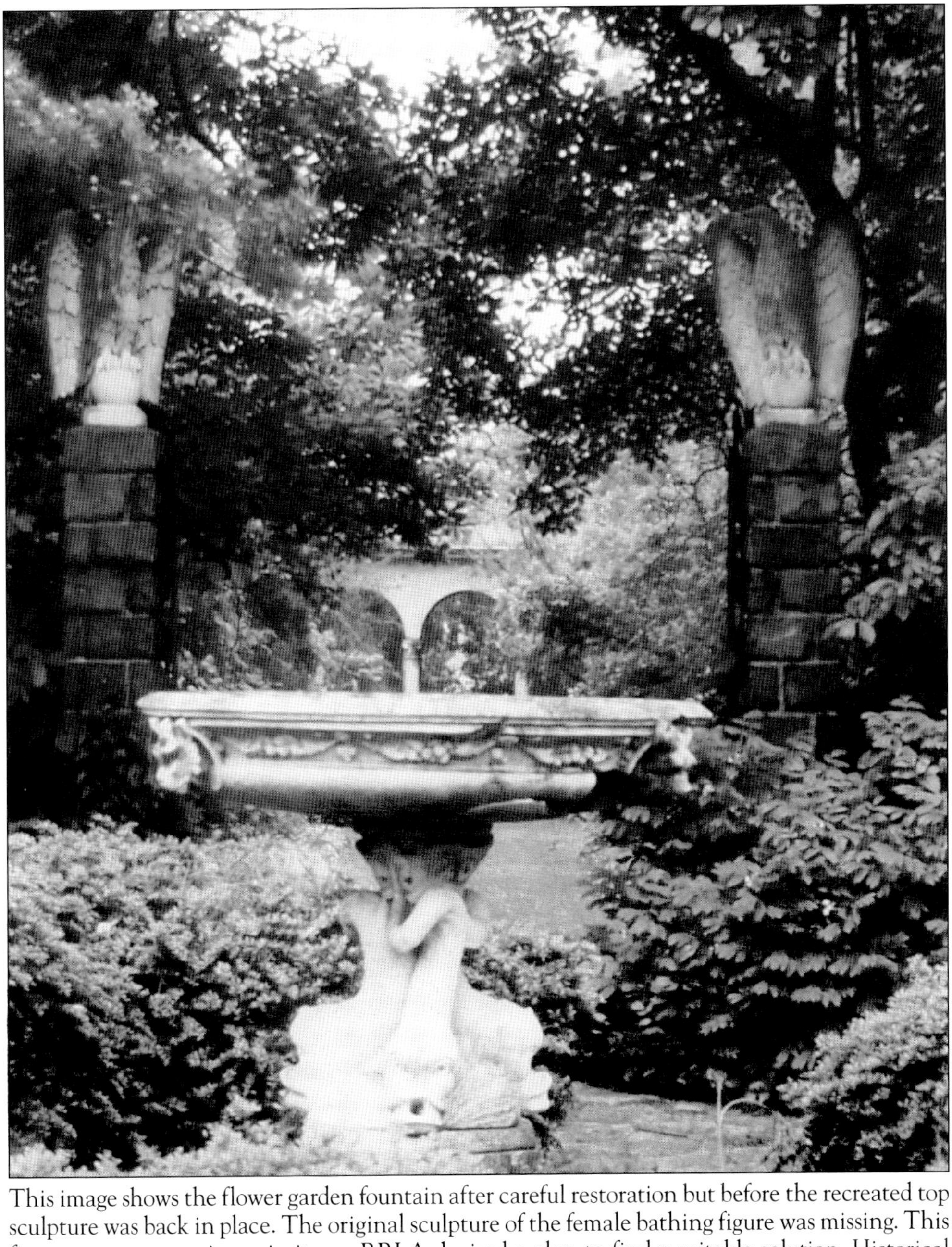

This image shows the flower garden fountain after careful restoration but before the recreated top sculpture was back in place. The original sculpture of the female bathing figure was missing. This figure was a restoration priority, so RRLA devised a plan to find a suitable solution. Historical photographs provided the only evidence of the statue. Armed with those images, Robinson visited a Quakertown, Pennsylvania, company called Campania International. He met with the proprietor, who shared all their catalogs. Fortunately, they found an available cast-stone replica in one of the catalogs. Using photographs, they determined the approximate size of the statue, and they ordered it from the source in Italy. When it arrived, Robinson was not pleased with some details, so he hired a Germantown artist to redo parts of the sculpture and complete additional work, including making a mold of the base that the female figure sat upon from broken pieces found on site. From those pieces, the artist was able to recast the basin. (PDI.)

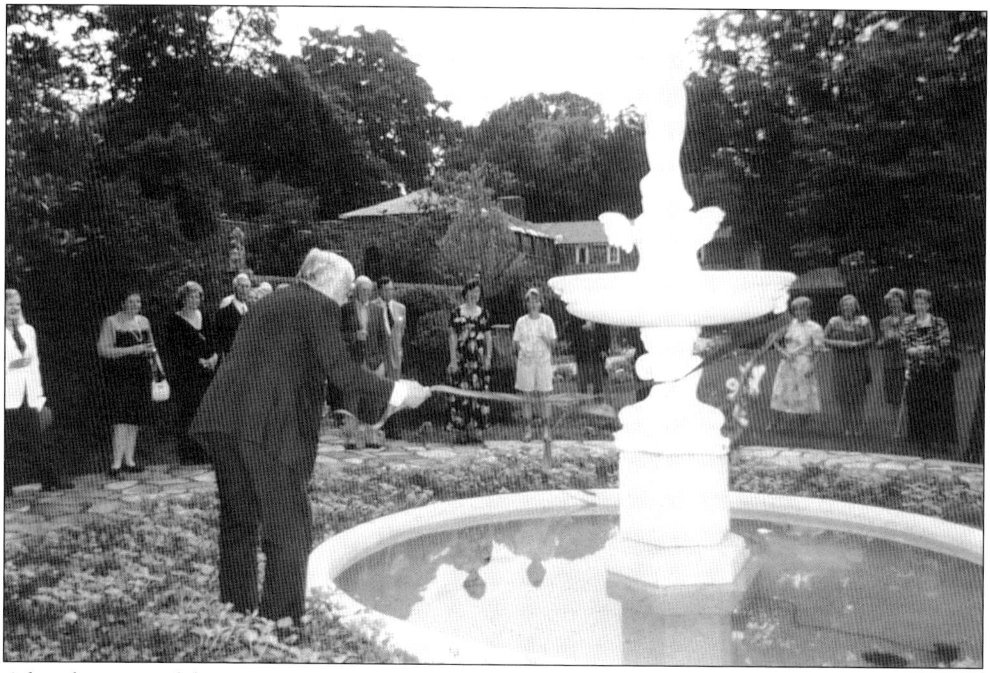

After the successful 1998–1999 renovation, PDI opened the gardens to the public. A ribbon-cutting commemorated the event; those pictured are unidentified. The first image shows the repaired, recast, and cleaned fountain basin and vaguely captures the new female bathing figure and recast base. The fountain was restored to its full function and to this day requires annual maintenance to keep it running for the public who are allowed to use the garden daily from dawn to dusk. The image below shows a beautiful winter photograph of the main fountain with the restored iron gates, bald cypress allée, and teahouse in the background. This image graced the front of a blank notecard produced by PDI. (Above, PDI; below, photographer Jonathan Blair.)

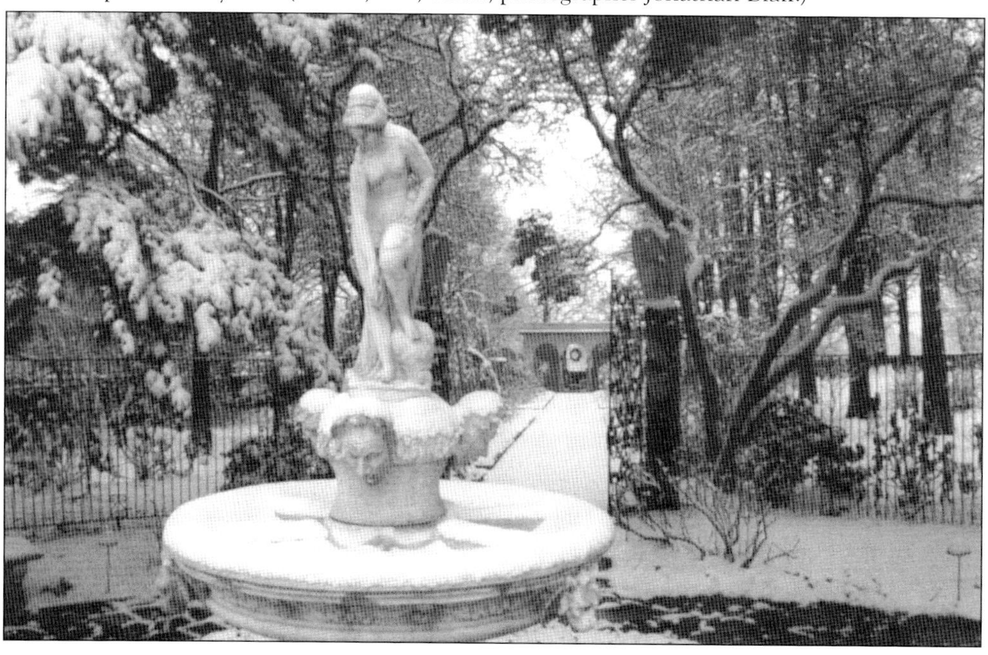

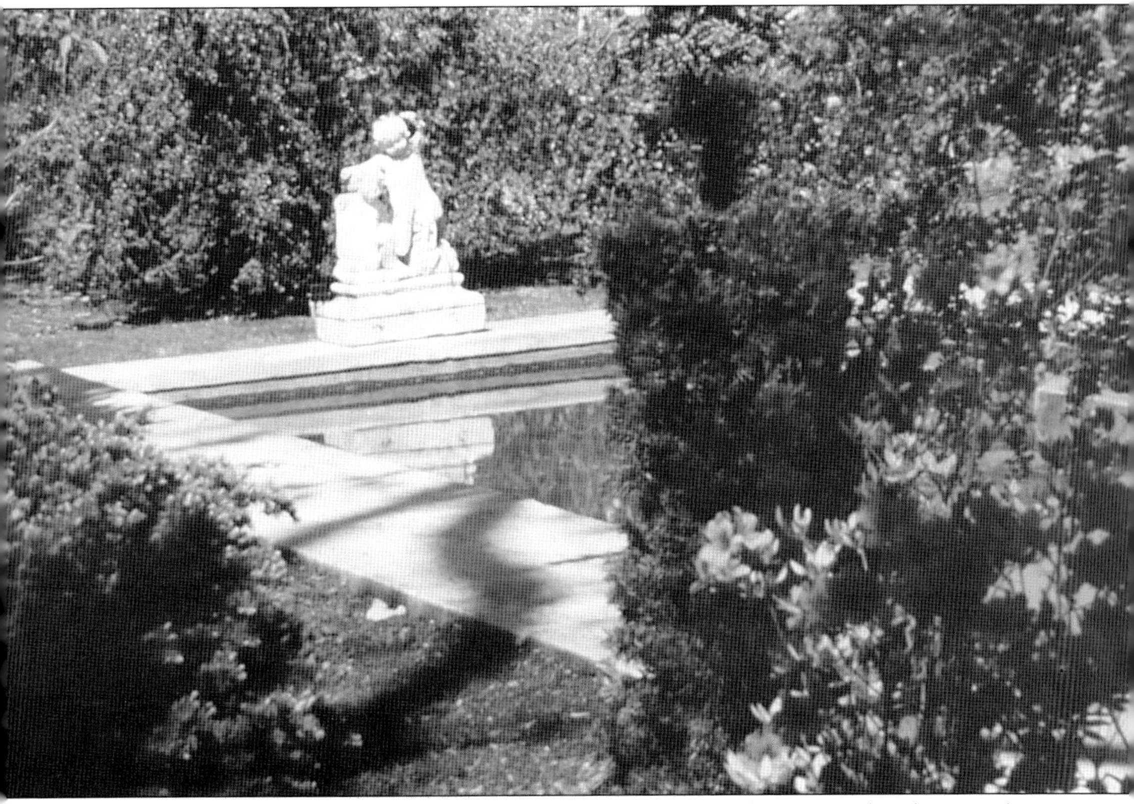

Here we see the restored cherub and dolphin sculpture at the reflecting pool's edge, another restoration priority, as well as renewed pool coping and a flowering azalea in the foreground. During the 1999 renovation, the 10-foot-deep family swimming pool was reconstructed into a two-foot reflecting pool, so legally, the garden could be open to the public without protective fencing around the pool. While a Friends of Gibraltar group, which formed during the renovation, hoped to take ownership of the gardens, negotiations with PDI fell through, and the Friends group disbanded. There is not much documentation of this time frame available, perhaps because of a 2012 flood in the PDI offices located in the property's potting shed. PDI took over the annual care of the garden; however, the garden never became financially self-sufficient. Instead, PDI relies on endowment funds and donations to continue yearly garden maintenance. (PDI.)

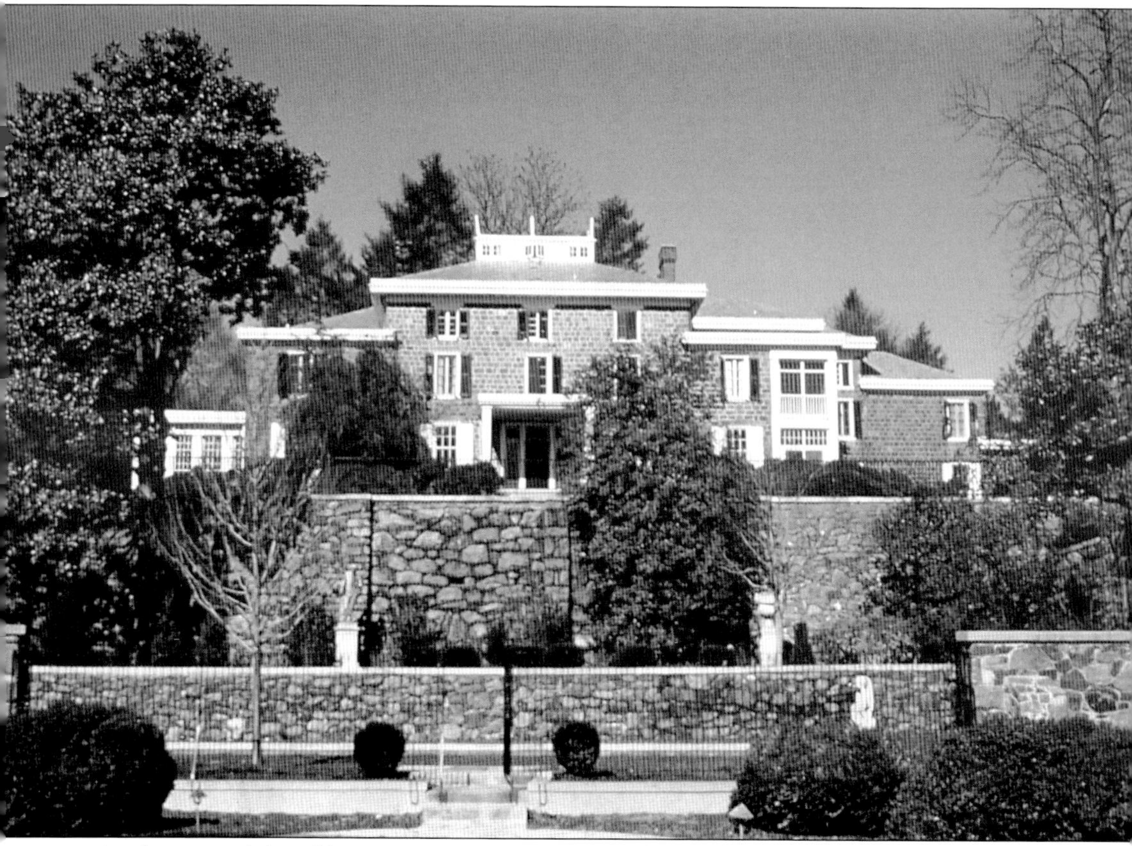

At the time of the ribbon-cutting commemorating the garden renovation, the house was still maintained by PDI. This image shows a view across the flower garden to the mansion in 2000, right after the renovation. In fall 2004, PDI paid a reduced cost of $30,000 for the temporary replacement of the roof over the mansion's solarium after its partial collapse. At that time, estimates for replacing the entire slate roof of the property were approximately $500,000. By 2008, unable to maintain the annual costs to maintain the property, PDI began to seek an opportunity to deed the mansion to a private redeveloper. Even after the mansion was deeded away, PDI maintained ownership of the garden. (PDI.)

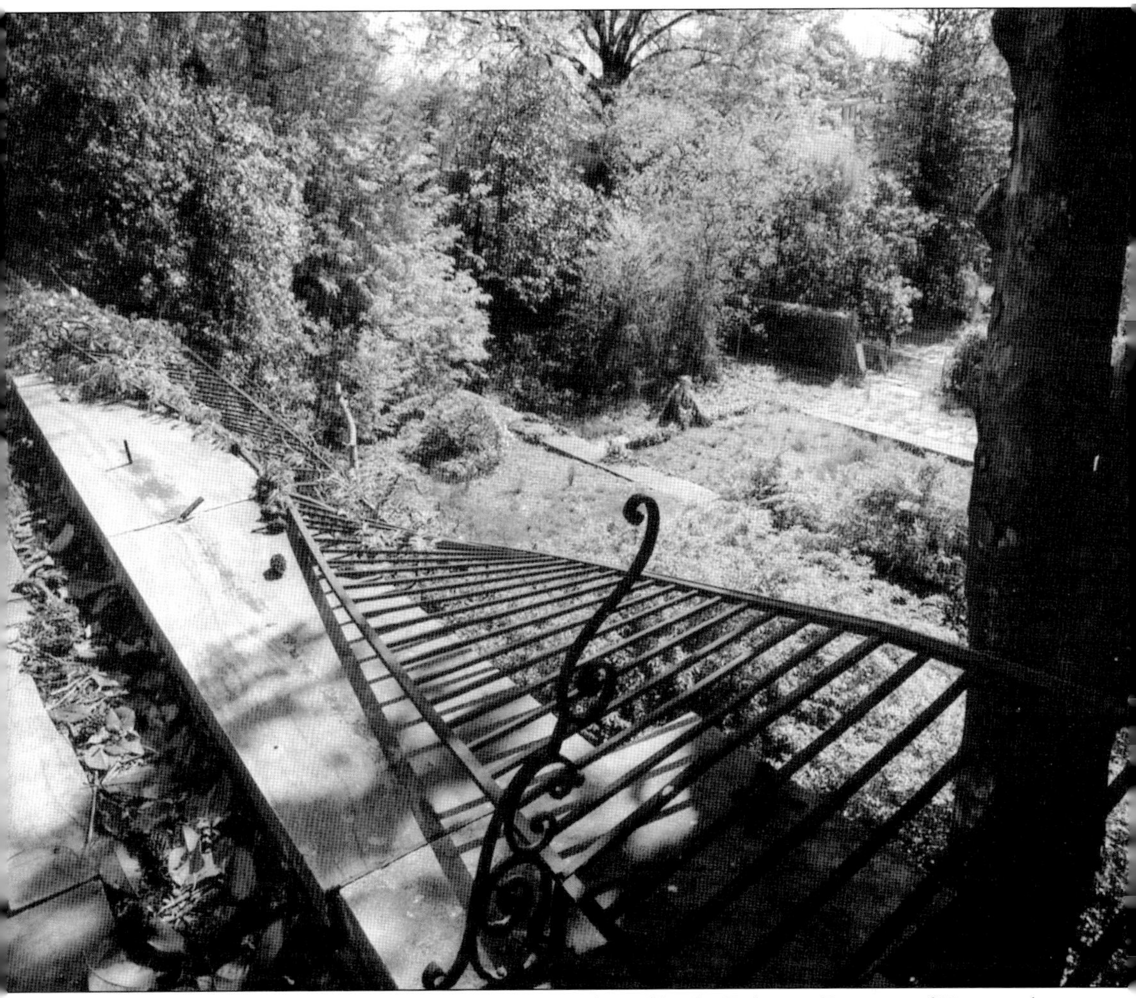

In 2008, an inspection of the property's buildings, conducted by the Delaware Division of Historical and Cultural Affairs, concluded the following: "The buildings . . . deteriorated and appear to be in physically worse condition" than when the state prepared the baseline documentation in 1999. Specifically, the report mentions broken window panes, deteriorating and falling off exterior shutters, failing flooring, and possible structural deficiency due to water penetration. With so much to maintain, the vegetation was allowed to grow up close to the exterior walls of the building, which both obscured visibility and potentially damaged the structure. While the house itself was reported in "deteriorated but sound condition," the report documented failing paint and plaster and evidence of debris and animal feces" in the rooms. The same year, PDI spent $68,000 on renovations to the potting shed, which would become the location of PDI's offices. (PDI.)

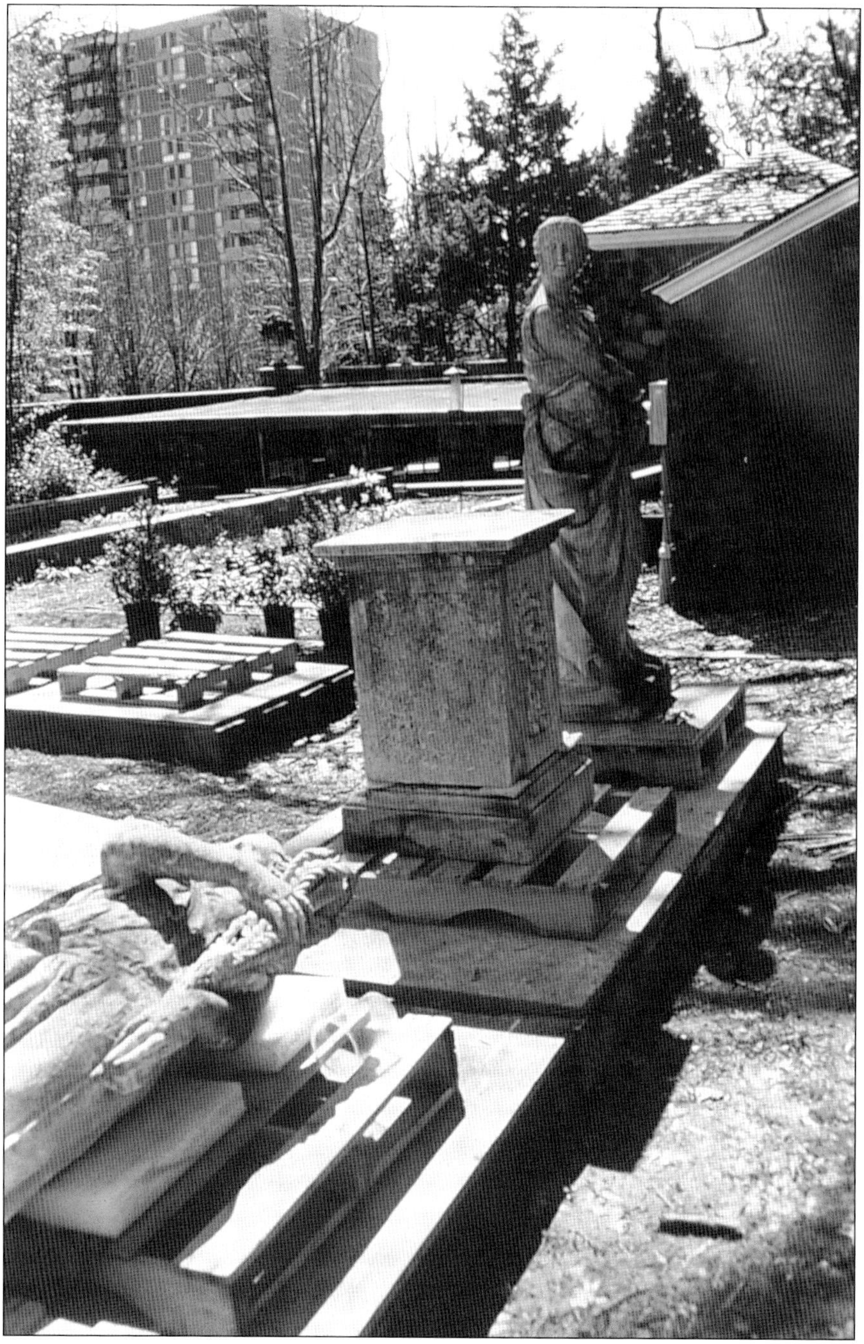

In summer 2009, David Scott, the executive director of PDI, responded to the 2008 state historic preservation officer's report of deteriorating conditions at the mansion. Scott noted that PDI was in the process of attempting to transfer the property to a private developer and included information about a potential developer's possible adaptive reuse project. While PDI shared the state's concerns about the mansion's condition, the organization lacked the means to undertake multiple tasks outlined in the state's report. The property was ultimately divided, and the mansion and buildings were deeded to a private developer in 2009, while PDI retained ownership of the gardens. (PDI.)

While PDI was struggling to maintain the house, the gardens were being tended by a well-qualified garden manager and a dedicated group of volunteers. Wendy Gentry was hired as the garden manager in 2006. She used her local horticultural connections to bring in talented volunteers, including Steve Lisic of Kennett Square, Pennsylvania, who had the idea to turn the reflecting pool into a water garden. Under Gentry's direction, the volunteer group transformed the shallow pool by filling it with 20 species of hardy and non-hardy flowering water lilies. Primarily tended by Lisic, the water garden became an instant draw for visitors who enjoyed the tranquility and came to watch the fish, frogs, and dragonflies in the newly created ecosystem. To this day, the self-sustaining "bog" is a favorite spot for garden visitors. (Right, *Delaware Today*; below, Erin Fogarty.)

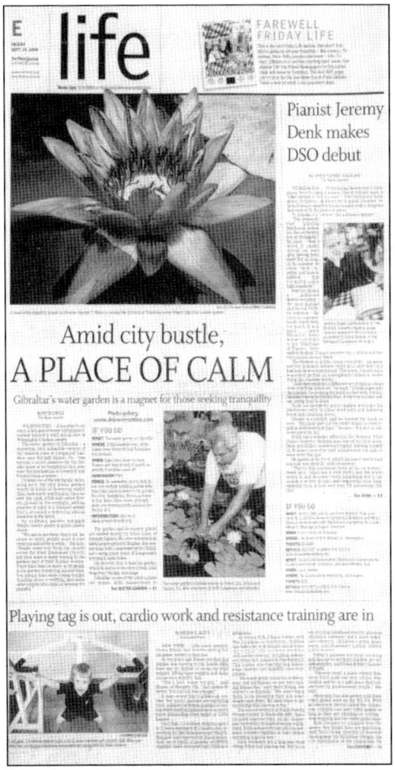

E

life

FAREWELL FRIDAY LIFE

Pianist Jeremy Denk makes DSO debut

Amid city bustle, A PLACE OF CALM

Gibraltar's water garden is a magnet for those seeking tranquility

Playing tag is out, cardio work and resistance training are in

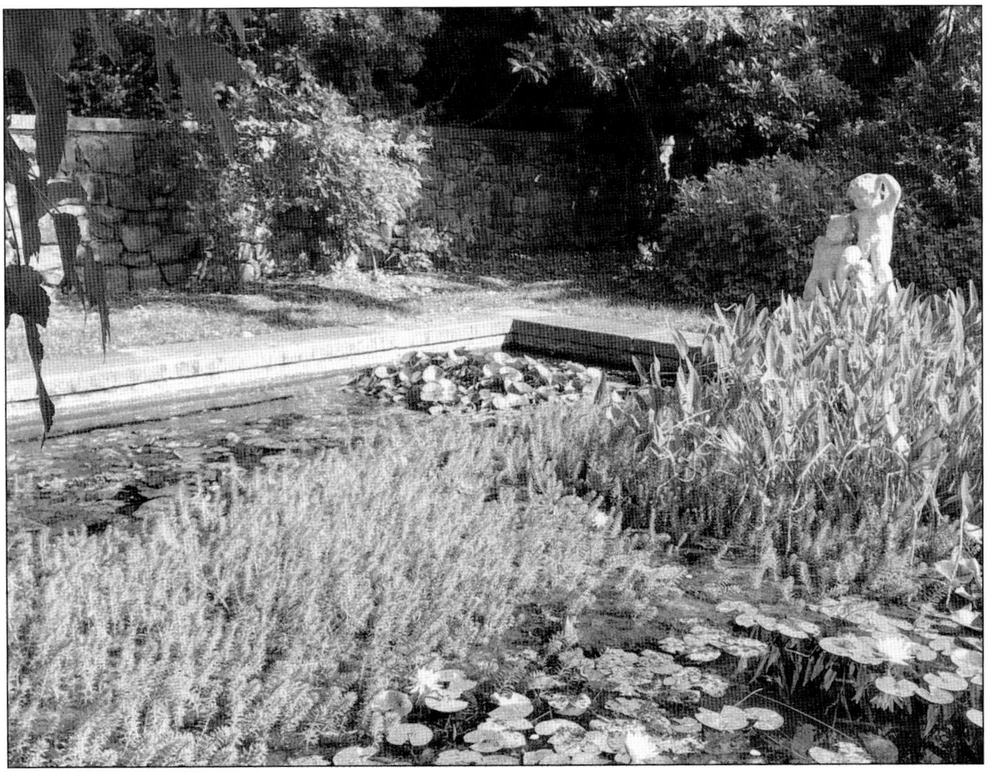

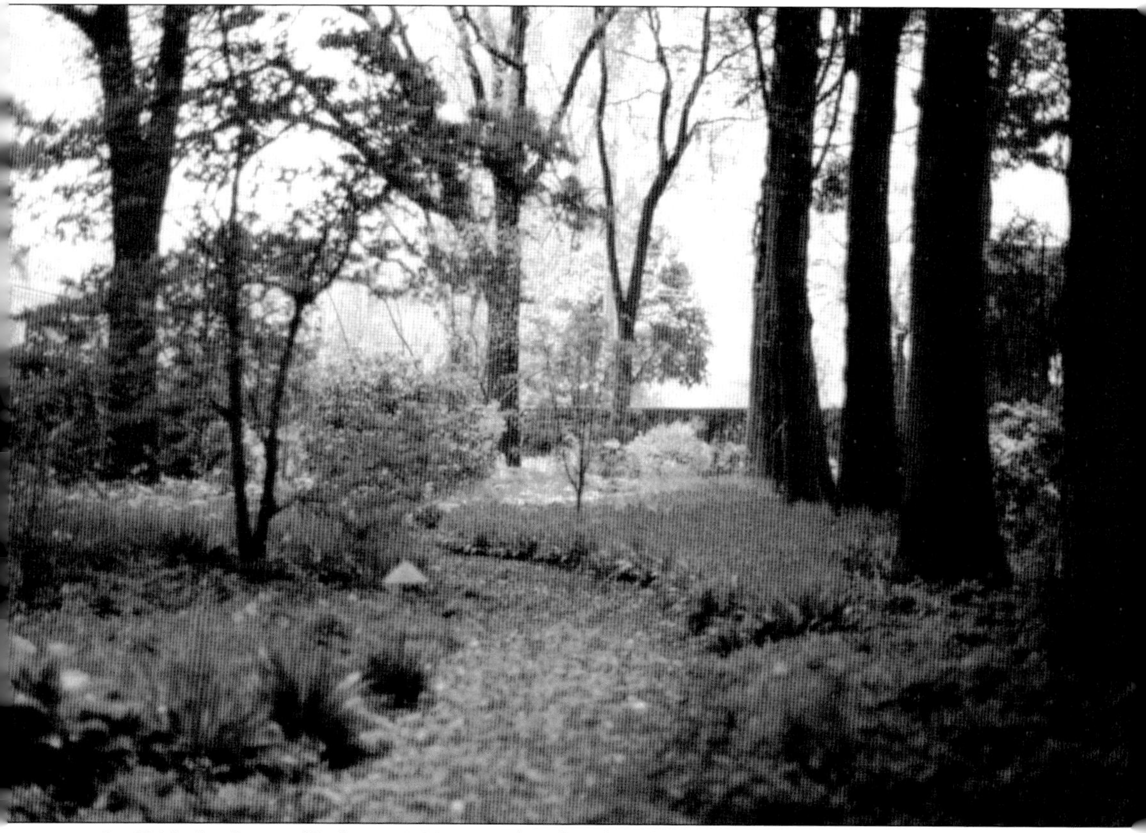

In 2012, the State of Delaware's Historical and Cultural Affairs group sent a letter to the developer who owned the mansion. Without a viable adaptive reuse project, maintenance was deferred, and the state suggested "protective and maintenance measures critical to stabilize and prevent further deterioration of the buildings." The landscape around the buildings was entirely overgrown with vines and vegetation; the gutters and roof were in poor condition in need of cleaning and repair; the windows were primarily broken or simply missing panes. Sadly, this same year, just three years after a renovation, the PDI offices located in the potting shed were flooded. A post-flood inventory of water-damaged boxes of institutional files belonging to PDI included Gibraltar redevelopment proposals, settlement contracts, the National Register application, copies of easements, and garden information contained in a box labeled "History." Also lost was a box of "various photos and slides." (PDI.)

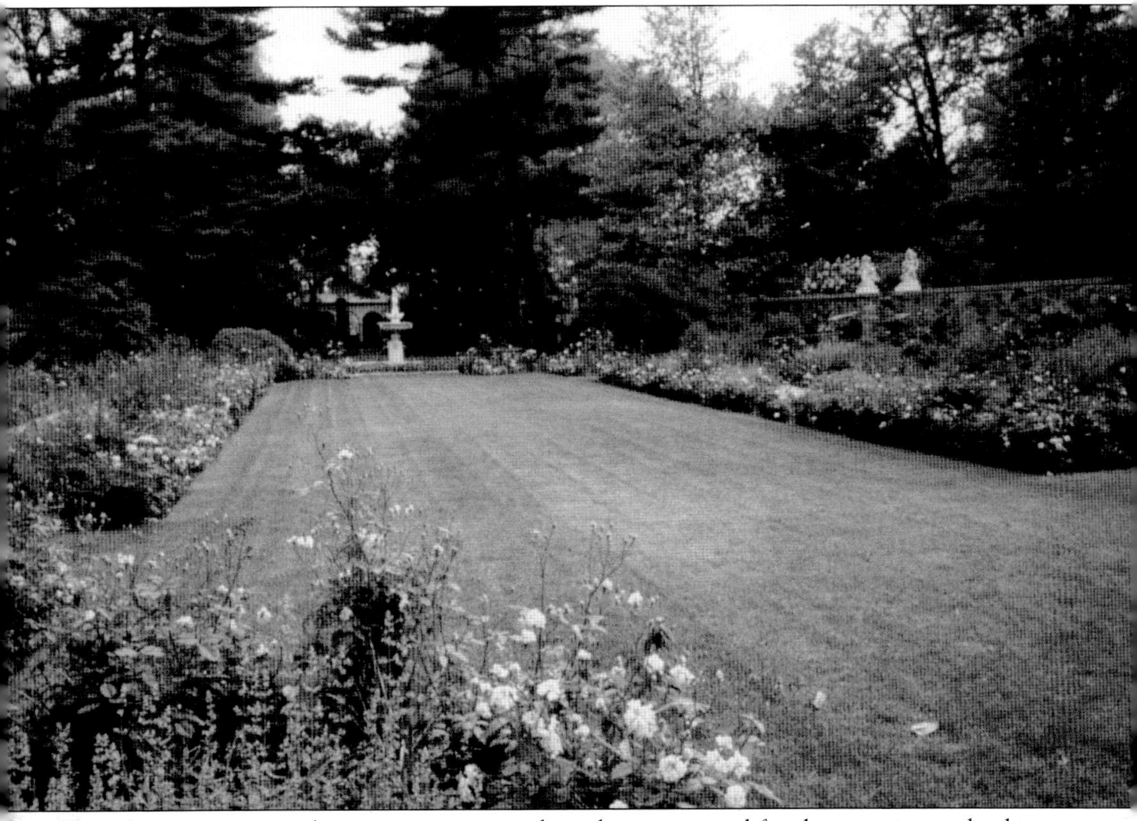

Over the years, many adaptive reuse projects have been proposed for the mansion and other buildings on the property, but none have come to fruition, so all of the buildings continue to decline. The garden has had a different fate. Since the $1 million garden renovation in 1999, there have been years of both good and poor maintenance. By the late 2010s, the garden was primarily maintained twice each year by landscape companies. Unattended for the rest of the year, it became weedy and overgrown which raised new concerns for public safety and the status of deteriorating garden elements. In 2019, twenty years after the $1 million renovation, Jules Bruck, professor and director of landscape architecture at UD, joined PDI as a board member and resumed responsibility for the garden. Jaime Manlove, a UD landscape architecture student, completed a capstone project in 2019 that included an Instagram analysis of the most photographed places within the garden. The iron gates, pool terrace, teahouse, flower garden, bald cypress allée, and grand staircase, in that order, are the most photographed and therefore the places where most volunteer maintenance time is focused. (PDI.)

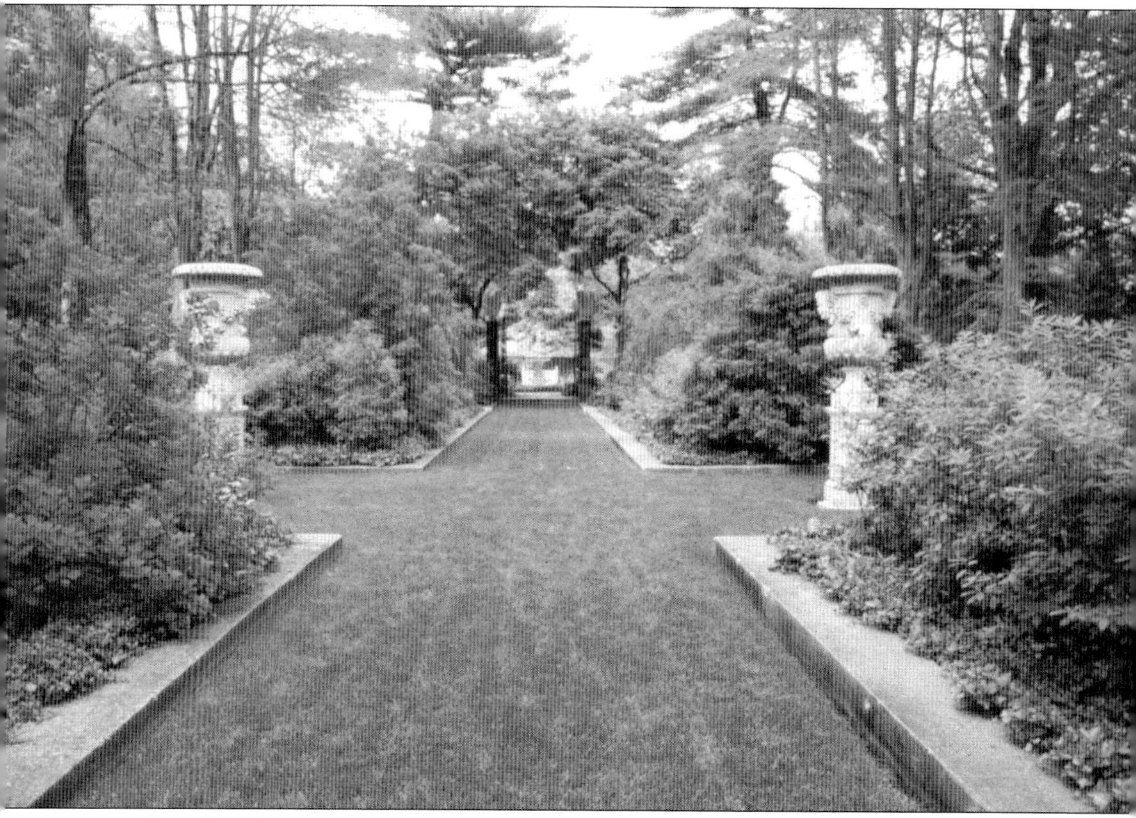

On the Atlas Obscura (AO) travel website, the Marian Coffin Gardens in Wilmington, Delaware, are listed as one of the "Top unusual attractions in Wilmington." As the "definitive guide to the world's hidden wonders," AO aptly describes the gardens to potential visitors as, "Practically hidden in plain sight behind an impressive stone wall, this derelict mansion towers above enchanting gardens. Though ivy climbs the mansion's stone walls and its shattered windows reveal a gloomy, deteriorated interior, the gardens are meticulously maintained and bursting with vibrant life." Indeed, the garden remains a popular place for photographs of weddings, prom-goers, and families. Perhaps visitors contemplate the former grandeur of the mansion and the lifestyle of its inhabitants. A first-time visit to the Marian Coffin Gardens at Gibraltar both surprises and enthralls, and regular visitors remain enchanted, regardless of the current state of garden maintenance, which is a testament to Coffin's enduring design. (PDI.)

BIBLIOGRAPHY

Garden Club of America Collection, Smithsonian Archive of American Gardens, Washington, DC.

Gestram, I. *The Historic Landscape at Gibraltar: A Proposal for Its Preservation.* The University of Delaware, 1996.

Lidz, M. *The Du Ponts: Houses and Gardens in the Brandywine, 1900–1951.* Acanthus Press, 2009.

Marian Coffin Collection, Winterthur Library Archives, Winterthur, DE. W.C. Spruance Lantern Slide Collection.

Varley, E. *The DuPont Family Legacy of Horticulture in the Brandywine.* The University of Delaware, 2009.

Hagley Museum Archives, Wilmington, DE.

SITES INDEX

About Preservation Delaware, Inc.

PDI, Inc., is the statewide nonprofit organization dedicated to the preservation of Delaware's architectural heritage and historic settings through education, public policy initiatives and technical assistance. They were founded in 1993 by a group of men and women dedicated to protecting the architectural and historical heritage of Delaware.

With an impassioned vision to restore and preserve local sites slated for demolition, the organization created a plan that included education programs, public outreach, and legislative advocacy. Primary to the founders' original vision was the establishment of a preservation revolving fund that would allow PDI to intervene to save threatened properties or to provide incentives for property owners to preserve them.

In the years since its founding, PDI has realized a number of accomplishments, which include sponsoring conferences and educational workshops, advocating to ensure the Historic Preservation Tax Credit program in 2001, and the reauthorization of the program for an additional ten years in 2010. Currently, PDI is developing a series of programs for members of historic preservation commissions, as well as launching hands-on workshops designed to teach participants the "how-to's" of rehabilitation and preservation projects such as weatherproofing, plumbing, and replacing and restoring windows.

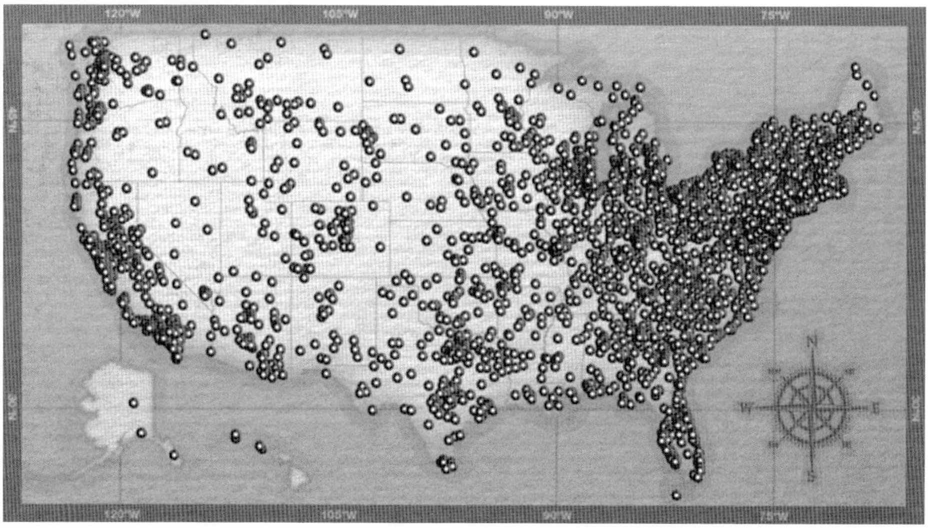